PEOPLE OF CHARACTER

Rosa Parks

A Life of Courage

Written by Tonya Leslie
Illustrated by Tina Walski

BLASTOFF!
4
READERS

BELLWETHER MEDIA • MINNEAPOLIS, MN

Note to Librarians, Teachers, and Parents:

Blastoff! Readers are carefully developed by literacy experts and combine standards-based content with developmentally-appropriate text.

Level 1 provides the most support through repetition of high-frequency words, light text, predictable sentence patterns, and strong visual support.

Level 2 offers early readers a bit more challenge through varied simple sentences, increased text load, and less repetition of high frequency words.

Level 3 advances early-fluent readers toward fluency through increased text and concept load, less reliance on visuals, longer sentences, and more literary language.

Level 4 builds reading stamina by providing more text per page, increased use of punctuation, greater variation in sentence patterns, and increasingly challenging vocabulary.

Level 5 encourages children to move from "learning to read" to "reading to learn" by providing even more text, varied writing styles, and less familiar topics.

Whichever book is right for your reader, Blastoff! Readers are the perfect books to build confidence and encourage a love of reading that will last a lifetime!

This edition first published in 2008 by Bellwether Media.

No part of this publication may be reproduced in whole or in part without written permission of the publisher. For information regarding permission, write to Bellwether Media Inc., Attention: Permissions Department, Post Office Box 1C, Minnetonka, MN 55345-9998.

Library of Congress Cataloging-in-Publication Data
Leslie, Tonya.
  Rosa Parks : a life of courage / by Tonya Leslie.
   p. cm. – (People of character) (Blastoff! readers)
Summary: "People of character explores important character traits through the lives of famous historical figures. Rosa Parks highlights how this great individual demonstrated courage during her life. Intended for grades three through six"–Provided by publisher.
  Includes bibliographical references and index.
  ISBN-13: 978-1-60014-088-4 (hardcover : alk. paper)
  ISBN-10: 1-60014-088-2 (hardcover : alk. paper)
  1. Parks, Rosa, 1913-2005–Juvenile literature. 2. Courage–United States–Juvenile literature. 3. African American women–Alabama–Montgomery–Biography–Juvenile literature. 4. African Americans–Alabama–Montgomery–Biography–Juvenile literature. 5. Civil rights workers–Alabama–Montgomery–Biography–Juvenile literature. 6. African Americans–Civil rights–Alabama–Montgomery–History–20th century–Juvenile literature. 7. Segregation in transportation–Alabama–Montgomery–History–20th century–Juvenile literature. 8. Montgomery (Ala.)–Race relations–Juvenile literature. 9. Montgomery (Ala.)–Biography–Juvenile literature. I. Title.

  F334.M753P385525 2008
  323.092–dc22
  [B]   2007015013

Contents

Meet Rosa Parks   4

A Life of Segregation   6

Taking a Stand   12

A Courageous Act   16

The Mother of the Movement   21

Glossary   22

To Learn More   23

Index   24

What does it mean to have **courage**? Could you be brave in the face of danger? Would you stand up for something that was right?

Rosa Parks did. She showed the world how to be courageous and she did it by sitting down.

Rosa Parks was born in Tuskegee, Alabama in 1913. As a child, Rosa couldn't go to certain schools. She could not shop in some stores. She couldn't eat in certain restaurants. She couldn't do these things because of the color of her skin. Rosa Parks was black.

In 1913, African-American people didn't have the same rights as white people. If you were African-American, you had to ride in a different train car. You had to use a different bathroom. You couldn't even drink from the same water fountain as a white person. Things were separate and definitely not equal. This was called **segregation** and it was the law in some states.

9

Rosa grew up and became a
seamstress in Montgomery, Alabama.
In her free time, she tried to change
things in her community.

She volunteered and worked with young people. She taught them about equal **rights**. Her work made a difference, but Rosa didn't think things were changing fast enough.

One day, Rosa got on the bus after work. The first four rows of seats were only for white people so Rosa sat behind them. However, she knew that if a white person wanted her seat, she would have to give it up. If she did not, she would be breaking the law.

The bus went from stop to stop. Rosa was tired. She was tired of not having equal rights. She was tired of being **discriminated** against because of the color of her skin. Then a white man got on the bus.

The driver asked Rosa to give her seat to the man. Rosa thought about what she should do. She could rise and give up her seat like she had so many times before. Or she could be courageous.

Rosa decided to take a stand. She told the driver she would not give up her seat. The police came. They told Rosa she was breaking the law. She was arrested. Soon, other people heard about Rosa's act. They thought she was brave. By sitting down, she showed the world that she wasn't going to stand segregation any longer.

Black people began a **boycott**. No one would ride the bus in Montgomery until the discriminating bus laws were changed. It took 381 days to change the laws.

African-Americans around the country heard about Rosa. They decided to stand up against discrimination. Some white people helped too. People marched in **protest**. This was called the **Civil Rights Movement**.

It was a serious time. People fought and struggled to get **equality** for everyone. Rosa got out of jail and continued to protest discrimination. Eventually the laws were changed to give all people equal rights.

After many years, the Civil Rights Movement was a success. Today, people call Rosa the mother of the Civil Rights Movement. She sat down to show the world how to stand up.

Glossary

boycott—when people refuse to buy goods or a service to force a change

Civil Rights Movement—a national effort led by African-American people in the United States in the 1950s and 1960s to establish equal rights

courage—the strength of mind to face danger and difficulties

discrimination—to treat someone differently because of their race, class, or gender

equality—having the same measure or status

protest—to express disapproval

rights—something a person deserves to have

segregation—the forced separation of groups of people according to their race, class, or gender

To Learn More

AT THE LIBRARY
Edwards, Pamela Duncan. *The Bus Ride That Changed History*. Boston, Mass.: Houghton Mifflin, 2005.

Giovanni, Nikki. *Rosa*. New York: Henry Holt & Co, 2005.

Haskins, Jim and Rosa Parks. *I Am Rosa Parks*. New York: Dial Books, 1997.

Ringgold, Faith. *If a Bus Could Talk: The Story of Rosa Parks*. New York: Simon and Schuster, 1999.

ON THE WEB
Learning more about Rosa Parks is as easy as 1, 2, 3.

1. Go to www.factsurfer.com

2. Enter "Rosa Parks" into search box.

3. Click the "Surf" button and you will see a list of related web sites.

With factsurfer.com, finding more information is just a click away.

Index

1913, 6, 8

African-Americans, 8, 19

boycott, 18

bus, 12, 14, 18

Civil Rights Movement, 19, 21

community, 10

courage, 4, 5, 15

discrimination, 14, 18, 19, 20

equal rights, 8, 11, 14, 20

Montgomery, Alabama, 10, 18

protest, 19, 20

segregation, 8, 12, 16

skin color, 6, 14

Tuskegee, Alabama, 6

ROME
TOTAL WAR
PRIMA OFFICIAL GAME GUIDE

Stephen and Bryan Stratton

PRIMA GAMES
A Division of Random House, Inc.
3000 Lava Ridge Court
Roseville, CA 95661
1-800-733-3000
www.primagames.com

Product Manager: Damien Waples

Editors: Alaina Yee, Brooke N. Hall

Design & Layout: Scott Watanabe

ISBN: 0-7615-4781-9

Library of Congress Catalog Card Number: 2004108580

Printed in the United States of America

04 05 06 07 AA 10 9 8 7 6 5 4 3 2 1

TABLE OF CONTENTS

CHAPTER 1: Welcome to *Rome—Total War* 2

How *Rome* Works 2

How to Use This Book 2

The Main Menu 3

    Single Player Menu 3

    Multiplayer 4

    Load Game 4

    Options 5

CHAPTER 2: Factions 6

Unit Stats 6

Unit Abilities 7

Building Classes 9

Roman Military Units 10

Roman Naval Units 15

Roman Buildings 15

Armenian Military Units .28

Armenian Naval Units 29

British Military Units 30

British Naval Units 32

British Buildings 32

Carthaginian Military Units 36

Carthaginian Naval Units .39

Carthaginian Buildings 39

Dacian Military Units 46

Dacian Naval Units 48

Egyptian Military Units 49

Egyptian Naval Units 51

Egyptian Buildings 52

Gaulish Military Units 59

Gaulish Naval Units 60

Gaulish Buildings 61

German Military Units 66

German Naval Units 68

German Buildings 68

Greek Military Units 73

Greek Naval Units 75

Greek Buildings 75

Macedonian Military Units 82

Macedonian Naval Units .84

Mercenary Units 85

Numidian Military Units .88

Numidian Naval Units 89

Parthian Military Units 90

Parthian Naval Units 92

Parthian Buildings 97

Pontic Military Units 98

Pontic Naval Units 101

Scythian Military Units 101

Scythian Naval Units 103

Seleucid Military Units 104

Seleucid Naval Units 107

Seleucid Buildings 107

Spanish Military Units 116

Spanish Naval Units 118

Thracian Military Units 118

Thracian Naval Units 120

CHAPTER 3: Total War: Fighting (and Winning) Battles .121

Picking a Fight 121

    Battle Deployment Scroll .121

    Sieges 121

    Reinforcements 121

    Terrain and Weather 121

Before the Battle 122

    General's Speech 122

    Deploying the Troops 122

    Military Advisor 123

Viewing the Battlefield 123

Battlefield Control Panel .123

Managing Your Troops 124

    Selecting Units 124

    Issuing Commands 124

    Grouping Units 124

    Importance of the General 125

Moving and Attacking 125

    Setting Waypoints 125

    Charging 125

    Alternate Attack Modes 125

    Group Formations 125

    Unit Facing 127

    Unit vs. Unit Strengths and Weaknesses 127

    Withdraw 128

    Halt 129

    Morale 129

    Fatigue 129

Siege Warfare 129

    Capturing Walls 130

    Siege Defense 130

    Conditions for Victory 130

Reinforcements 130

    Friendly vs. Allied 130

Chapter 4: Imperial Campaign 131

   Beginning an Imperial Campaign 133

      Campaign Setup Options 133

      The Campaign Map 134

      The Control Panel 134

      Viewing the Campaign Map 140

      Victoria, the Campaign Advisor 141

      Messages and Notifications 142

      Named Characters 142

      Captains 144

      Dealing with the Senate 144

      Settlements 145

      Armies 152

      Agents 160

      Naval Vessels and Fleets 162

CHAPTER 5: Historic Battles 165

   The Battle of Lake Trasimene—217 BC 165

      Battle Overview 165

      Strategy 166

   The Battle of Raphia—217 BC 167

      Battle Overview 167

      Strategy 168

   The Battle of Telamon—225 BC 169

      Battle Overview 169

Strategy 170

The Siege of Gergovia—53 BC 171

      Battle Overview 171

      Strategy 172

The Battle of the River Trebia—218 BC 173

      Battle Overview 173

      Strategy 174

The Battle of Asculum—279 BC 175

      Battle Overview 175

      Strategy 176

The Battle of Carrhae—55 BC 177

      Battle Overview 177

      Strategy 178

The Battle of Cynoscephalae—197 BC 180

      Battle Overview 180

      Strategy 181

The Battle of Teutoburg Forest—9 AD 182

      Battle Overview 182

      Roman Strategy 183

      German Strategy 184

The Siege of Sparta—272 BC 185

      Battle Overview 185

      Strategy 186

WELCOME TO ROME: TOTAL WAR

Ever wanted to conquer the world for the glory of the Roman Empire? Now's your chance! *Rome: Total War* is a game of real-time warfare and grand-scale empire building, spanning more than 100 years of history.

From 270 BC to around 14 AD, the Romans rose to power, conquering the Mediterranean world and much of Europe, and establishing an empire that would remain for centuries. *Rome: Total War* is set in this time period, where opportunities await you around every corner. It's a game filled with politics, treachery, and conflict, where the strong become heroes and emperors, and the weak are crushed beneath their heel.

The third installment in the *Total War* series, *Rome: Total War* raises the bar and sets a whole new standard for other warfare games to live up to. It presents you with a rich, stimulating world that's filled with real-time combat and political intrigue. Only those who have the power to conquer shall survive, and as knowledge is power, the key to survival now rests in your hands!

How *Rome* Works

Rome: Total War can be thought of as two games in one. On the one hand, you have the awesome real-time battles that occur in all modes of play. This is where you command your troops on the **battlefield**, and where the courageous actions of regular men can transform them into renowned heroes of legend.

On the other hand, you have the turn-based **Campaign Map**, where you manage your settlements, deal in politics, make war with rival factions, and conquer their lands to expand your glorious empire. The Campaign Map is only used in the **Imperial Campaign** mode—all other modes of play consist of nothing but pure, real-time battle.

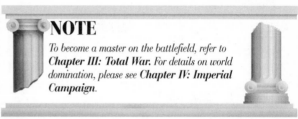

NOTE

*To become a master on the battlefield, refer to **Chapter III: Total War**. For details on world domination, please see **Chapter IV: Imperial Campaign**.*

How to Use This Book

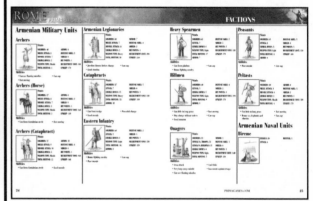

The **Factions** chapter of this guide gives details on each of the military units for all 20 factions featured in *Rome: Total War*. Turn to this chapter to discover the statistical information and special abilities of every unit in the game.

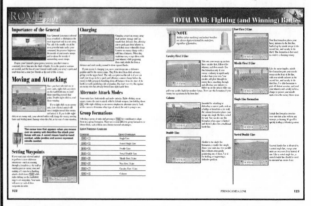

When battle erupts (and trust us, it does!), you need to be able to react quickly to any situation. Fortunately, the **Total War** chapter contains everything you need to know about waging war on the battlefield.

Controlling your troops, issuing commands, using your Generals and reinforcements, details on the various terrain and weather effects, winning battle tactics, and much more are all conveniently located in this chapter. This information can be applied to any battle in the game—even the multiplayer battles you wage online!

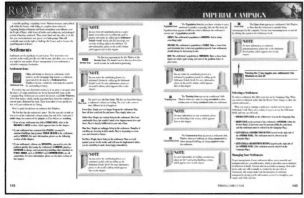

This chapter deals with the main single-player mode featured in *Rome: Total War*—the epic Imperial Campaign. From settlement management to the use of agents, such as spies and diplomats, every detail of the Imperial Campaign is revealed here. The gigantic Campaign Map is exposed at the very end of the chapter, where each territory and every settlement is labeled to assist you in your quest to become the Imperator.

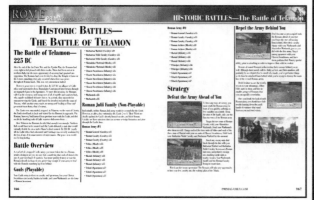

Rome: Total War rips 11 battles from the pages of history, and we give you winning strategies for each one in the **Historical Battles** chapter of this guide. Flip to this chapter when you're ready for an exciting history lesson! The information we provide also gives you an edge over your opponents in the multiplayer versions of the Historical Battles.

The Main Menu

After the opening cinema plays, you're taken to the game's **Main Menu**. Here, you're presented with the following options:

- **SINGLE PLAYER:** Choose to play a new single-player game.

- **CONTINUE CAMPAIGN:** Continue the IMPERIAL CAMPAIGN from the most-recent saved game.

- **MULTIPLAYER:** Choose to play a multiplayer CUSTOM BATTLE or HISTORICAL BATTLE.

- **LOAD GAME:** Load a game (or a Battle Replay) you've previously saved.

- **OPTIONS:** View and adjust various gameplay options and settings.

- **QUIT:** Exits and closes *Rome: Total War*.

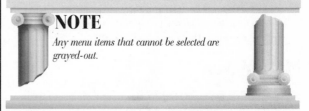

NOTE
Any menu items that cannot be selected are grayed-out.

Single Player Menu

Click **Single Player** from the Main Menu to visit the **Single Player Menu**. Here, you're presented with the following single-player game modes:

PROLOGUE: Play an in-depth tutorial of Rome: Total War. This introduces you to the basics of battle and teaches you how to manage your empire using the various functions of the CAMPAIGN MAP. Helpful advisors are there to guide you every step of the way. This is highly recommended for first-timers!

IMPERIAL CAMPAIGN: Begin a new IMPERIAL CAMPAIGN. This is the main single-player mode—the only mode that features the use of the CAMPAIGN MAP (other than the short Prologue). We provide extensive information and loads of tips for the Imperial Campaign in CHAPTER IV of this guide.

HISTORICAL BATTLE: Play battles that have been taken from the pages of history and recreated in Rome: Total War. There are 11 Historical Battles to choose from, and we provide winning strategies for each one in CHAPTER V of this guide.

CUSTOM BATTLE: Create your own battle, down to the very last detail. You have total control over the battle's victory conditions, the computer's level of AI difficulty, the battlefield terrain, the time of day, the weather conditions, the number of armies, the units that make up each army, and more. This is a great way to hone your battlefield skills, or to prepare for war against rival factions you face in the IMPERIAL CAMPAIGN. To ensure you're never at a loss for knowledge, we cover everything you need to know about battlefield warfare in CHAPTER III of this guide.

QUICK BATTLE: Enter the battlefield immediately by fighting a randomly-generated CUSTOM BATTLE. There are no options to adjust, and you never know who you'll control, where you'll fight, or who you'll be up against when you play a Quick Battle.

Multiplayer

Rome: Total War allows you to play both **Custom Battles** and **Historical Battles** online, or over a Local Area Network (LAN) between two or more computers. Click **Multiplayer** from the Main Menu to visit the **Multiplayer Menu**, where you're presented with the following options:

ONLINE BATTLES: Either host multiplayer battles of your own design, or choose to view and join online battles hosted through GameSpy™. This style of multiplayer action requires an active broadband Internet connection, and the proper configuration of any firewall software you may be running on your PC.

LAN BATTLES: Choose to either host or join multiplayer battles across your LAN. These battles are fought on local machines that have been networked together, so an active Internet connection isn't required. The process for setting up LAN Battles is the same as Online Battles.

CHANGE CD KEY: If you're sharing your PC with a friend who has their own copy of Rome: Total War, you may want to change the CD key before beginning multiplayer battles. This conveniently allows you to keep separate online records of your victories and defeats.

NOTE

While this guide doesn't feature a specific chapter for multiplayer battles, you can learn everything you need to know about waging online war in both Custom Battles and Historical Battles by reading Chapter III: Total War, and also Chapter V: Historical Battles.

Load Game

Choose **Load Game** from the Main Menu to visit the **Load Game Menu**. Here, you're presented with the following options:

LOAD CAMPAIGN GAME: This allows you to load up any previously-saved IMPERIAL CAMPAIGN games.

LOAD CUSTOM BATTLE: This lets you load up any previously-saved Custom Battle. You can load Custom Battles you saved in mid-battle, or ones that you saved just after setting all options to your liking.

LOAD BATTLE REPLAY: Click this option to load any of your previously-saved Battle Replays. You're given the option to save a Battle Replay at the end of each battle. Battle Replays let you relive the action from any angle!

Options

Click **Options** from the Main Menu to visit the **Options Menu**. Here, you're presented with the following adjustable options:

VIDEO SETTINGS: Increase the various video settings to improve the game's graphical appearance, or lower the settings to maximize performance.

AUDIO OPTIONS: Adjust an assortment of audio settings to get the game sounding just right.

CONTROL SETTINGS: Modify the game's controls to your liking. You also have the option to save and load Control Settings you've created, or to restore the default controls.

CAMERA SETTINGS: Fine-tune the camera rotation speed, movement speed, and other such camera-specific options. You can also choose between the classic Total War camera, or the new RTS camera.

VIEW THE CREDITS: Rome certainly wasn't built in a day! View the list of hardworking men, women, and slaves who helped make this ambitious title what it is.

FACTIONS

This chapter of the guide focuses on the 18 separate factions featured in *Rome: Total War*. Each faction's military units are listed, and their individual statistics and abilities are presented in list form. Buildings for factions that can be controlled in the Imperial Campaign mode are detailed as well. In short, everything you need to know about each faction is found in this chapter. Use this information to your advantage as you play through the game.

Unit Classes

Each military unit in *Rome: Total War* belongs to a certain class. Knowing the differences between the various unit classes helps you determine how to best command your units on the battlefield. For easy reference, each faction's military units have been grouped together according to their classes in the individual faction sections that appear later in this chapter.

The following list details the differences between the unit classes, and also provides some general tips on how to use them effectively against one another:

ANIMALS (LIGHT): Animal units belonging to this class are lightly armored and won't last very long in direct combat. Incendiary Pigs and Wardogs are examples of light animal units.

ANIMALS (HEAVY): Animal units belonging to this class are better able to defend themselves and can withstand more punishment than those belonging to the light animal unit class. Warhounds are the most common unit in this class.

ARTILLERY: Units belonging to this class are powerful destructive forces, but cannot withstand a direct attack for very long. Ballistae and Onagers are examples of artillery units.

CAVALRY (LIGHT): Units belonging to this class are mounted atop a horse or other steed. (Some chariots are considered to be light cavalry units as well.) These units are at their best when used to flank and charge light infantry units, or to harass missile units. They're also effective at chasing down fleeing troops.

CAVALRY (HEAVY): Units belonging to this class are mounted atop a horse, camel, or elephant. (Some chariots are considered to be heavy cavalry units as well.) These units are at their best when used to flank and charge infantry units, or to harass infantry missile units.

CAVALRY (MISSILE): Units belonging to this class are mounted atop a horse or camel. (Some chariots are considered to be missile cavalry units as well.) These units are at their best when used to harass enemy infantry units.

INFANTRY (LIGHT): Units belonging to this class are lightly-armored foot soldiers. While infantry units are very versatile, they're often best used to "soften up" the enemy in the early stages of battle before the real carnage begins. These are your "expendable" units—use them to hold a line while you move your cavalry around to flank the enemy, or to defend your vulnerable missile units.

INFANTRY (HEAVY): Units belonging to this class are heavily-armored, well-trained foot soldiers. They're quite versatile and are at their best when used to hold the enemy lines while your missile units punish them and your cavalry moves to flank. If possible, try to use your light infantry units to wear down the opposing army before sending in your heavy infantry units.

INFANTRY (MISSILE): Units belonging to this class are lightly-armored foot soldiers that attack from range with missile weapons, such as bows, slings, or javelins. They're at their best when used against enemy cavalry units, particularly slow moving or stationary ones, as a mounted soldier is a larger target then a soldier traveling on foot. Make sure you protect your missile infantry units with a strong line of light or heavy infantry—missile units are highly vulnerable to direct combat, especially from a cavalry charge.

SPEARMEN: Units belonging to this class usually carry large shields, wield long spears or pikes, and are well-armored. These units are the bane of cavalry units—their spears are lethal when used to defend against a cavalry charge. As such, these units are at their best when used to protect your infantry units from the enemy's cavalry. However, try to keep your spearmen from engaging infantry units in direct combat, as a sword is much easier to wield in close quarters than a spear or pike.

NOTE

A small "tool tip" appears when you move the mouse cursor over a unit on the battlefield. The unit's class is displayed within the tool tip, along with its name and current battle status.

Unit Stats

Each unit in *Rome: Total War* has its own unique statistics. These "stats" give you an idea of the strength and value of each unit when they're fighting on the battlefield. Descriptions for each statistical category are provided in the following list:

SOLDIERS: The number of individual soldiers who make up the unit.

ATTACK: The unit's soldiers' attack value when they're attacking normally. This can be a MELEE or MISSILE attack, or an ATTACK VS. TROOPS/BUILDINGS.

CHARGE BONUS: The "initial shock" bonus that's applied to the unit's soldiers' attack value when they charge in to attack.

WEAPON TYPE: The class of weapon the unit's soldiers use in combat. It also determines the type of upgrade the unit can receive. Weapon types are classified as one of the following: LIGHT, HEAVY, MISSILE, or CANNOT BE UPGRADED.

TOTAL DEFENSE: The total of the unit's soldiers' **ARMOR, DEFENSE SKILL,** and **SHIELD** values. This total represents each soldier's overall defensive capability.

ARMOR: A number that represents the amount and quality of armor the unit's soldiers wear.

DEFENSE SKILL: A number that represents the unit's soldiers' skill in defending themselves against incoming attacks.

SHIELD: A number that represents the quality and effectiveness of the unit's soldiers' brand of shields. Be aware that shields only provide defense to the front, regardless of their type.

HIT POINTS: The number of hits the unit's soldiers can withstand before falling in combat. Such hits must first penetrate their defenses.

RECRUITMENT COST: The cost of training and recruiting the unit's soldiers at a settlement.

UPKEEP: The cost of maintaining the unit over each turn during the Imperial Campaign mode. This fee is automatically subtracted from your cash reserves at the start of each new turn.

THE MARIAN REFORM: The "Marian Reform" was the reorganization of the Roman military by Senator Gaius Marius. Marius made it legal for ordinary (poor) Romans to join his army. In return for years of military service, soldiers received land. This reform passed in the People's Assembly without the Senate's approval. Thus began the first professional-standing Roman Legionary army, which is still recognized today.

In this game, Roman troops produced after this point are much improved. This event occurs the first time you build a top-level barracks-class building (The fifth-tier **URBAN BARRACKS**).

Unit Abilities

There are many different units in *Rome: Total War*, and each one features its own special abilities. Becoming familiar with the different types of unit abilities allows you to use your troops more effectively on the battlefield. Some abilities are good, and others are bad. We detail the effects of each one in the following list:

ANIMALS MAY RUN AMOK: Units with this drawback-ability feature animals that are liable to run about the battlefield indiscriminately, causing chaos to any troops that get in their path. This drawback-ability is primarily found in elephant and Incendiary Pig units.

AREA ATTACK: Units with this ability damage a wide region when they attack and are capable of wiping out several troops with one shot. This ability is primarily found in Onagers.

BONUS FIGHTING CAVALRY: Units with this ability deal extra damage against cavalry units. This ability is commonly found in Spearmen and Pikemen.

BONUS VS. ELEPHANTS AND CHARIOTS: Units with this ability deal extra damage against elephant and chariot units. This ability is mainly found in units that throw javelins, such as Velites, Skirmishers, and Peltasts.

CAN FORM CANTABRIAN CIRCLE: The Cavalry circles in close proximity to enemy and concentrates fire while maintaining its distance if the enemy approaches.

CAN FORM PHALANX: Units with this ability can group themselves together in a tight formation, using their shields to defend against incoming missile fire. This ability is mainly found in Spearmen and Pikemen. While in this formation, the unit's spears are pointed forward so as to inflict heavy casualties on any charging cavalry units.

CAN FORM TESTUDO: Units with this ability can group themselves together in a tight formation, using their shields to defend against incoming missile fire, especially from above. This is also known as the "turtle" formation and can be very useful when it comes to attacking a settlement's defenses. This ability is found in highly disciplined Roman Legionary units.

CAN FORM WEDGE: Units with this ability can group themselves together in a triangular formation. This ability is mainly found in melee-attack cavalry units. When such units charge and use their wedge formation against a line of enemy infantry, for example, the impact often splits the line into two smaller, vulnerable groups.

CAN HIDE ANYWHERE: Units with this ability become invisible to the enemy when they remain motionless anywhere on the battlefield. This ability is found only in extremely stealthy infantry units.

CAN HIDE IN LONG GRASS: Units with this ability become invisible to the enemy when they remain motionless in a patch of tall grass on the battlefield. This ability is sometimes found in light infantry units.

CAN SAP: Units with this ability can be ordered to tunnel under a settlement's walls and use saps to weaken the foundation of the wall, causing a segment to collapse. This ability is found in many infantry units.

CAN USE FLAMING MISSILES: Units with this ability can ignite their missile weapons before they fire them at the enemy. This often reduces accuracy and casualties, but can cause the enemy to lose morale and flee in terror. This ability is commonly found in archer units.

CAN'T HIDE: Units with this drawback-ability cannot hide in any area of the battlefield and are always visible to the enemy. This drawback-ability is mainly found in large units such as elephants and Onagers.

CHANTING INSPIRES NEARBY TROOPS: Units with this ability chant holy incantations, filling their troops with a sense of cause and duty and raising their morale. This ability is primarily found in Druid units.

COMBAT BONUS IN DESERTS: Units with this ability fare better at combat when they're fighting in a desert. This ability is commonly found in units belonging to factions that come from hot, arid regions of the world.

COMBAT BONUS IN SNOW: Units with this ability fare better at combat when they're fighting in snow. This ability is mainly found in barbarian units belonging to factions that must endure cold, harsh winters each year.

COMBAT BONUS IN WOODS: Units with this ability fare better at combat when they're fighting in forests. This ability is commonly found in archer and infantry units, but rarely in cavalry units.

COMBAT BONUS IN WOODS OR SNOW: Units with this ability fare better at combat when they're fighting in forests or snow. This ability is mainly found in barbarian infantry units.

EAGLE INSPIRES NEARBY TROOPS: Units with this ability carry a sacred emblem of an eagle on their unit's banner. This symbol represents the good and noble cause of the Roman Empire and inspires all nearby troops with a cause and need to win the battle at hand, raising their morale. This ability is primarily found in the Roman faction's very best units. Note that losing a unit that carries the eagle emblem is likely to be a severe negative factor against your army's morale.

EFFECTIVE AGAINST ARMOR: Units with this ability wield weapons that are capable of piercing the armor of an enemy unit. This ability is commonly found in units that wield axes as their primary weapons.

EXCELLENT MORALE: Units with this ability are naturally resistant to the horrors of war. They're extremely unlikely to tuck tail and run, even when death is apparently imminent. This ability is mainly found in well-trained, disciplined units.

EXPERT AT HIDING IN WOODS: Units with this ability are in their element in woods on the battlefield. When they are hiding, the range at which the enemy detects them is less than if they were not hiding and exposed. This ability is found in barbarian infantry units.

FAST MOVING: Units with this ability move faster than normal. This ability is found in many different types of lightly armored units.

FRIGHTEN ELEPHANTS: Units with this ability are capable of scaring formidable elephant units, causing them to run away, possibly trampling troops behind them. This ability is primarily found in Incendiary Pig units.

FRIGHTEN NEARBY ENEMY: Units with this ability are capable of causing any type of enemy unit to lose morale and run for their lives. This ability is mainly found in elephant units.

FRIGHTEN NEARBY ENEMY INFANTRY: Units with this ability are capable of causing enemy infantry units to lose morale and run for their lives. This ability is mainly found in chariot units.

GOOD MORALE: Units with this ability are naturally resistant to the horrors of war. They're unlikely to tuck tail and run unless faced with the most hopeless of odds. This ability is mainly found in well-trained, disciplined units.

GOOD STAMINA: Units with this ability are able to run for long periods of time without tiring. This ability is mainly found in well-trained, disciplined units.

INACCURATE AGAINST TROOPS: Units with this drawback-ability are less likely to score a direct hit against a unit of moving troops. This drawback-ability is mainly found in Onagers, which are intended for use against walls and buildings.

INEFFECTIVE AGAINST WALLS AND BUILDINGS: Units with this drawback-ability cannot damage a wall, building, or other such structure. This drawback-ability is mainly found in Ballistae, which are intended for use against units of troops.

JAVELINS THROWN BEFORE CHARGE: Units with this ability will throw one or two pilum (plural: pila) at the enemy before charging in to attack with their primary melee weaponry. The pila are quite effective, and often thin the ranks of the enemy line before the main assault begins. This ability is mainly found in versatile infantry units.

LONG RANGE MISSILES: Units with this ability can accurately fire their missiles over longer distances than normal. This ability is mainly found in well-trained archer units.

MAY CHARGE WITHOUT ORDERS: Units with this drawback-ability are undisciplined and may decide to charge into battle before the order is given by their commander. This drawback-ability is mainly found in headstrong barbarian units.

MISSILES CAN IMPALE SEVERAL MEN: Units with this ability can wipe out a number of soldiers with a single missile attack. This ability is primarily found in Ballistae.

POOR MORALE: Units with this drawback-ability are not true warriors and don't enjoy being on the battlefield. They are likely to run at the first sign of danger. This drawback-ability is mainly found in untrained, undisciplined units, such as Peasants.

POWERFUL CHARGE: Units with this ability have a high charge value and inflict heavy casualties when they first charge in to attack. This ability is mainly found in melee-cavalry units.

RALLY: Units with this ability are able call out a rally cry that raises the morale of fleeing troops. This unique ability is only available to Generals.

SCARE HORSES: Units with this ability are capable of frightening enemy cavalry units when in their presence. The enemy cavalry unit's horses may run away from the fight, and if so, they won't respond to their riders' orders. This ability is mainly found in units that ride mounted on camels.

SCREECHING DISMAYS ENEMY: Units with this ability can let out a bloodcurdling screech that confuses the enemy and lowers their morale. This ability is primarily found in Screeching Women units.

SPECIAL ATTACK: Units with this ability are capable of trampling the enemy, inflicting massive casualties. This ability is primarily found in elephant units.

VERY GOOD STAMINA: Units with this ability are in perfect shape and are able to run for very long periods of time before they become winded. This ability is only found in the most highly trained units.

VERY LONG RANGE MISSILES: Units with this ability can accurately fire their missiles over extremely long distances. This ability is mainly found in highly trained archer units and is also found in Ballistas and Onagers.

VERY LONG SPEARS: Units with this ability wield spears that are over 18 feet in length. Such units are the bane of melee cavalry units, especially when they assume the phalanx formation. This ability is primarily found in Pikemen.

WARCRY IMPROVES ATTACK: Units with this ability can let out a battle cry that strengthens their resolve and increases their attack value. This ability is mainly found in barbarian infantry units.

Building Classes

There are several different classes of buildings in *Rome: Total War*, and each one offers its own special benefits to a settlement after construction. We provide descriptions for each building class in the following list:

NOTE

*In each of the following faction sections, buildings are listed in the order they appear in the faction's unique **technology tree**. A faction's technology tree can be viewed by calling up the **Building Browser Scroll**. For more information on the use of this scroll, please see its section in **Chapter IV: Imperial Campaign**.*

ACADEMY-CLASS BUILDINGS: Buildings belonging to this class improve upon a settlement's leadership figures, offering them places to learn and develop their governing skills.

AMPHITHEATER-CLASS BUILDINGS: Buildings belonging to this class improve a settlement's Public Order percentage by keeping its citizens entertained and happy. They also allow the training of Gladiator units.

BARRACK-CLASS BUILDINGS: Buildings belonging to this class allow you to train and recruit infantry units within the settlement.

CARAVAN-CLASS BUILDINGS: Buildings belonging to this class increase the amount of taxable income a settlement generates through land trade.

FARM-CLASS BUILDINGS: Buildings belonging to this class improve a settlement's food supply. This extends the number of turns a settlement can withstand a siege and also adds to a settlement's rate of Population Growth.

GOVERNMENT-CLASS BUILDINGS: These important buildings enable settlement growth, allowing you to construct more-advanced versions of other building classes. They also allow the training of Agents such as spies, diplomats, and assassins.

LAW ENFORCEMENT-CLASS BUILDINGS: Buildings belonging to this class improve a settlement's Public Order percentage due to law.

MINES: Mines allow workers in a settlement to "harvest" precious metals from the surrounding territory. Only settlements whose surrounding lands are rich in such metals are able to construct mines.

PORT-CLASS BUILDINGS: Buildings belonging to this class enable you to train and recruit naval units within the settlement. They also allow the settlement to generate taxable income through sea trade.

RANGE-CLASS BUILDINGS: Buildings belonging to this class allow you to train missile-armed units within the settlement.

ROADS: Roads allow for faster movement of armies within the territory, and also increase the amount of taxable income the settlement generates through land trade.

SMITH-CLASS BUILDINGS: Buildings belonging to this class improve the quality of your units' weapons and armor. These upgrades happen automatically for newly recruited units within the settlement, while preexisting units must be retrained at the settlement to receive the upgrades.

STABLE-CLASS BUILDINGS: Buildings belonging to this class allow you to train and recruit cavalry units within the settlement.

TAVERN-CLASS BUILDINGS: Buildings belonging to this class improve a settlement's Public Order percentage due to citizen happiness.

TEMPLE-CLASS BUILDINGS: Buildings belonging to this class offer a variety of benefits to a settlement, depending on the god or goddess to which the temple is dedicated.

THEATER-CLASS BUILDINGS: Buildings belonging to this class improve a settlement's Public Order percentage by keeping its citizens entertained and happy. (These are similar to Amphitheater-Class buildings.)

TRADER-CLASS BUILDINGS: Buildings belonging to this class allow a settlement to generate taxable income through trade.

WALL-CLASS BUILDINGS: Buildings belonging to this class improve the defenses of a settlement.

WATER SUPPLY-CLASS BUILDINGS: Buildings belonging to this class improve the settlement's state of public health, which increases its Public Order and Population Growth values.

Roman Military Units
Animal Units (Light)

Incendiary Pigs

STATS	
SOLDIERS: 12	DEFENSE SKILL: 1
ATTACK: 7	SHIELD: 0
CHARGE BONUS: 2	HIT POINTS: 1
WEAPON TYPE: Light	RECRUITMENT COST: 260
TOTAL DEFENSE: 4	UPKEEP: 50
ARMOR: 3	

Incendiary Pigs are 'one shot' weapons intended to spread panic and terror amongst enemies, particularly elephants.

ABILITIES
- Frighten elephants
- Fast moving

Wardogs

STATS	
SOLDIERS: 12	DEFENSE SKILL: 1
ATTACK: 12	SHIELD: 0
CHARGE BONUS: 2	HIT POINTS: 1
WEAPON TYPE: Light	RECRUITMENT COST: 630
TOTAL DEFENSE: 3	UPKEEP: 50
ARMOR: 2	

Wardogs are bred for a savage nature and great size, but then hunting men is only a little more dangerous than hunting wild boar!

ABILITIES
- Frighten nearby enemy
- Fast moving

Artillery Units
Ballistae

STATS	
SOLDIERS: 25	ARMOR: 7
ATTACK VS. TROOPS: 53	DEFENSE SKILL: 3
ATTACK VS. BUILDINGS: 12	SHIELD: 0
CHARGE BONUS: 0	HIT POINTS: 1
WEAPON TYPE: Light	RECRUITMENT COST: 540
TOTAL DEFENSE: 10	UPKEEP: 160

A Ballista is a sinew-powered weapon that looks like an enormous crossbow. It has tremendous range and can skewer files of men with a single bolt!

ABILITIES
- Missiles can impale several men
- Long range missiles
- Can use flaming missiles
- Can't hide

Heavy Onagers

STATS	
SOLDIERS: 32	ARMOR: 7
ATTACK VS. TROOPS: 63	DEFENSE SKILL: 3
ATTACK VS. BUILDINGS: 55	SHIELD: 0
CHARGE BONUS: 0	HIT POINTS: 1
WEAPON TYPE: Light	RECRUITMENT COST: 1980
TOTAL DEFENSE: 10	UPKEEP: 190

The Heavy Onager is a siege engine capable of reducing even stone ramparts to rubble, but can be vulnerable to enemy catapults.

ABILITIES
- Area attack
- Very long range missiles
- Can use flaming missiles
- Can't hide
- Inaccurate against troops

Onagers

STATS	
SOLDIERS: 32	ARMOR: 7
ATTACK VS. TROOPS: 53	DEFENSE SKILL: 3
ATTACK VS. BUILDINGS: 35	SHIELD: 0
CHARGE BONUS: 0	HIT POINTS: 1
WEAPON TYPE: Light	RECRUITMENT COST: 1550
TOTAL DEFENSE: 10	UPKEEP: 190

The Onager is a versatile catapult that can launch boulders or incendiary firepots at enemy troops and fortifications.

ABILITIES
- Area attack
- Very long range missiles
- Can use flaming missiles
- Can't hide
- Inaccurate against troops

Repeating Ballistae

STATS

SOLDIERS: 24	ARMOR: 7
ATTACK VS. TROOPS: 33	DEFENSE SKILL: 3
ATTACK VS. BUILDINGS: 0	SHIELD: 0
CHARGE BONUS: 0	HIT POINTS: 1
WEAPON TYPE: Light	RECRUITMENT COST: 690
TOTAL DEFENSE: 10	UPKEEP: 160

The Repeating Ballista is a semi-automatic artillery weapon. As long as it is loaded with bolts and cranked it will keep firing.

ABILITIES

- Missiles can impale several men
- Can't hide
- Ineffective against walls and buildings

Scorpions

STATS

SOLDIERS: 24	ARMOR: 7
ATTACK VS. TROOPS: 43	DEFENSE SKILL: 3
ATTACK VS. BUILDINGS: 0	SHIELD: 0
CHARGE BONUS: 0	HIT POINTS: 1
WEAPON TYPE: Light	RECRUITMENT COST: 650
TOTAL DEFENSE: 10	UPKEEP: 160

A Roman Scorpion is a sinew-powered weapon that looks like a large bow laid sideways on a frame. It has tremendous range and can skewer a man with a single shot!

ABILITIES

- Missiles can impale several men
- Very long range missiles
- Can use flaming missiles
- Can't hide
- Ineffective against walls and buildings

Cavalry Units (Light)

Equites

STATS

SOLDIERS: 27	DEFENSE SKILL: 5
ATTACK: 7	SHIELD: 4
CHARGE BONUS: 7	HIT POINTS: 1
WEAPON TYPE: Light	RECRUITMENT COST: 360
TOTAL DEFENSE: 12	UPKEEP: 110
ARMOR: 3	

Equites are light cavalrymen armed with spears. In the Roman system of war, they are intended to drive off skirmishers and pursue fleeing enemies.

ABILITIES

- Can form wedge
- Good stamina

Cavalry Units (Heavy)

Legionary Cavalry (Post Marian Reform)

STATS

SOLDIERS: 27	DEFENSE SKILL: 6
ATTACK: 9	SHIELD: 4
CHARGE BONUS: 9	HIT POINTS: 1
WEAPON TYPE: Light	RECRUITMENT COST: 730
TOTAL DEFENSE: 22	UPKEEP: 140
ARMOR: 12	

Legionary Cavalry are a heavy force of spear-armed cavalry who charge home using shock and mass to achieve victory.

ABILITIES

- Can form wedge
- Good morale
- Powerful charge
- Good stamina

Praetorian Cavalry (Post Marian Reform)

STATS

SOLDIERS: 27	DEFENSE SKILL: 7
ATTACK: 12	SHIELD: 4
CHARGE BONUS: 9	HIT POINTS: 1
WEAPON TYPE: Light	RECRUITMENT COST: 750
TOTAL DEFENSE: 22	UPKEEP: 240
ARMOR: 11	

Praetorian Cavalry are an elite within the elite: dedicated bodyguards who serve as heavy cavalry.

ABILITIES

- Can form wedge
- Good morale
- Powerful charge
- Good stamina

Roman Cavalry (Post Marian Reform)

STATS

SOLDIERS: 27	DEFENSE SKILL: 5
ATTACK: 7	SHIELD: 4
CHARGE BONUS: 7	HIT POINTS: 1
WEAPON TYPE: Light	RECRUITMENT COST: 470
TOTAL DEFENSE: 15	UPKEEP: 110
ARMOR: 6	

Roman Cavalry are auxiliary spear-armed cavalry who have a screening role in a Roman army.

ABILITIES

- Can form wedge
- Good stamina

Cavalry Units (Missile)

Cavalry Auxilia

STATS

SOLDIERS: 27	ARMOR: 2
MELEE ATTACK: 7	DEFENSE SKILL: 3
MISSILE ATTACK: 7	SHIELD: 4
CHARGE BONUS: 2	HIT POINTS: 1
WEAPON TYPE: Missile	RECRUITMENT COST: 430
TOTAL DEFENSE: 9	UPKEEP: 110

Cavalry Auxilia are javelin-armed mounted skirmishers who strike quickly and retire with equal (and prudent) haste.

ABILITIES

- Can form Cantabrian circle
- Fast moving

Infantry Units (Light)

Auxilia (Post Marian Reform)

STATS

SOLDIERS: 41	DEFENSE SKILL: 4
ATTACK: 5	SHIELD: 5
CHARGE BONUS: 5	HIT POINTS: 1
WEAPON TYPE: Light	RECRUITMENT COST: 420
TOTAL DEFENSE: 16	UPKEEP: 170
ARMOR: 7	

Auxilia are highly disciplined and tough spearmen who provide support to Roman legionaries in battle.

ABILITIES

- Bonus fighting cavalry
- Good stamina
- Combat bonus in woods
- Can sap

Hastati

STATS

SOLDIERS: 40	ARMOR: 5
MELEE ATTACK: 7	DEFENSE SKILL: 4
MISSILE ATTACK: 11	SHIELD: 5
CHARGE BONUS: 2	HIT POINTS: 1
WEAPON TYPE: Heavy	RECRUITMENT COST: 420
TOTAL DEFENSE: 14	UPKEEP: 170

Hastati fight as the leading edge of a Legion, wearing the enemy down for the next wave of attackers.

ABILITIES

- Javelins thrown before charge
- Can sap

Peasants

STATS

SOLDIERS: 61	DEFENSE SKILL: 1
ATTACK: 1	SHIELD: 0
CHARGE BONUS: 1	HIT POINTS: 1
WEAPON TYPE: Light	RECRUITMENT COST: 60
TOTAL DEFENSE: 1	UPKEEP: 100
ARMOR: 0	

Peasants are reluctant warriors, at best. Going to war is just one more burden of a hard life.

ABILITIES

- Poor morale
- Can sap

Town Watch

STATS

SOLDIERS: 40	DEFENSE SKILL: 2
ATTACK: 3	SHIELD: 5
CHARGE BONUS: 4	HIT POINTS: 1
WEAPON TYPE: Light	RECRUITMENT COST: 150
TOTAL DEFENSE: 7	UPKEEP: 100
ARMOR: 0	

The Town Watch are local workers and peasants given enough training to defend their homes and keep order in the streets.

ABILITIES

- Poor moral
- Can sap

Infantry Units (Heavy)

Arcani

STATS

SOLDIERS: 16	DEFENSE SKILL: 6
ATTACK: 12	SHIELD: 2
CHARGE BONUS: 4	HIT POINTS: 2
WEAPON TYPE: Light	RECRUITMENT COST: 850
TOTAL DEFENSE: 15	UPKEEP: 160
ARMOR: 7	

Arcani are small units of elite stealth troops well suited for laying ambushes for enemy skirmishers and missile troops.

ABILITIES

- Can hide anywhere
- Very good stamina
- Good morale
- Fast moving

Early Legionary Cohort (Post Marian Reform)

STATS

SOLDIERS: 41	ARMOR: 7
MELEE ATTACK: 9	DEFENSE SKILL: 5
MISSILE ATTACK: 13	SHIELD: 5
CHARGE BONUS: 4	HIT POINTS: 1
WEAPON TYPE: Heavy	RECRUITMENT COST: 590
TOTAL DEFENSE: 17	UPKEEP: 210

Well-armed and armored infantrymen, who go into combat flinging heavy javelins (Pila) that are followed up with hand-to-hand attacks.

ABILITIES

- Can form testudo
- Javelins thrown before charge
- Good morale
- Good stamina
- Can sap

Early Legionary First Cohort (Post Marian Reform)

STATS

SOLDIERS: 62	ARMOR: 7
MELEE ATTACK: 9	DEFENSE SKILL: 5
MISSILE ATTACK: 13	SHIELD: 5
CHARGE BONUS: 4	HIT POINTS: 1
WEAPON TYPE: Heavy	RECRUITMENT COST: 970
TOTAL DEFENSE: 17	UPKEEP: 310

The first cohort consists of well-armed and armored infantrymen, who go into combat carrying a Legionary Eagle, an inspirational symbol for the other Roman troops.

ABILITIES

- Eagle inspires nearby troops
- Can form testudo
- Javelins thrown before charge
- Good morale
- Good stamina
- Can sap

Legionary Cohort (Post Marian Reform)

STATS

SOLDIERS: 41	ARMOR: 12
MELEE ATTACK: 9	DEFENSE SKILL: 5
MISSILE ATTACK: 13	SHIELD: 5
CHARGE BONUS: 4	HIT POINTS: 1
WEAPON TYPE: Heavy	RECRUITMENT COST: 720
TOTAL DEFENSE: 22	UPKEEP: 210

Well-armed and armored infantrymen, who go into combat flinging heavy spears that are followed up with hand-to-hand attacks.

ABILITIES

- Can form testudo
- Javelins thrown before charge
- Good morale
- Good stamina
- Can sap

Legionary First Cohort (Post Marian Reform)

STATS

SOLDIERS: 62	ARMOR: 12
MELEE ATTACK: 9	DEFENSE SKILL: 5
MISSILE ATTACK: 13	SHIELD: 5
CHARGE BONUS: 4	HIT POINTS: 1
WEAPON TYPE: Heavy	RECRUITMENT COST: 1170
TOTAL DEFENSE: 22	UPKEEP: 310

The first cohort consists of well-armed and armored infantrymen, who go into combat carrying a Legionary Eagle, an inspirational symbol for the other Roman troops.

ABILITIES

- Eagle inspires nearby troops
- Can form testudo
- Javelins thrown before charge
- Good morale
- Good stamina
- Can sap

Praetorian Cohort (Post Marian Reform)

STATS

SOLDIERS: 41	ARMOR: 12
MELEE ATTACK: 12	DEFENSE SKILL: 6
MISSILE ATTACK: 16	SHIELD: 5
CHARGE BONUS: 4	HIT POINTS: 1
WEAPON TYPE: Heavy	RECRUITMENT COST: 770
TOTAL DEFENSE: 23	UPKEEP: 320

A Praetorian Cohort is made up of elite legionaries, recruited because of their superb soldiering skills and political loyalties.

ABILITIES

- Can form testudo
- Javelins thrown before charge
- Good morale
- Good stamina
- Can sap

Principes

STATS

SOLDIERS: 41	ARMOR: 7
MELEE ATTACK: 7	DEFENSE SKILL: 4
MISSILE ATTACK: 11	SHIELD: 5
CHARGE BONUS: 2	HIT POINTS: 1
WEAPON TYPE: Heavy	RECRUITMENT COST: 460
TOTAL DEFENSE: 16	UPKEEP: 170

Principes are older, more reliable soldiers who have seen some service. They fight as heavy infantry in the second line of battle.

ABILITIES

- Javelins thrown before charge
- Can sap

Samnite Gladiators

STATS

SOLDIERS: 20	DEFENSE SKILL: 7
ATTACK: 14	SHIELD: 0
CHARGE BONUS: 4	HIT POINTS: 2
WEAPON TYPE: Light	RECRUITMENT COST: 670
TOTAL DEFENSE: 14	UPKEEP: 260
ARMOR: 7	

Samnite Gladiators are more than mere soldiers—they are superb individual fighters, unmatched by ordinary warriors.

ABILITIES

- Excellent morale
- May charge without orders
- Very good stamina
- Can sap

Urban Cohort (Post Marian Reform)

STATS

SOLDIERS: 42	ARMOR: 12
MELEE ATTACK: 14	DEFENSE SKILL: 7
MISSILE ATTACK: 18	SHIELD: 5
CHARGE BONUS: 4	HIT POINTS: 1
WEAPON TYPE: Heavy	RECRUITMENT COST: 820
TOTAL DEFENSE: 24	UPKEEP: 320

The Urban Cohorts are an elite within the Praetorian Guard, dedicated to the defense of Rome and its cities.

ABILITIES

- Can form testudo
- Javelins thrown before charge
- Excellent morale
- Very good stamina
- Can sap

Infantry Units (Missile)

Archer Auxilia (Post Marian Reform)

STATS

SOLDIERS: 42	ARMOR: 3
MELEE ATTACK: 4	DEFENSE SKILL: 4
MISSILE ATTACK: 9	SHIELD: 0
CHARGE BONUS: 2	HIT POINTS: 1
WEAPON TYPE: Missile	RECRUITMENT COST: 370
TOTAL DEFENSE: 7	UPKEEP: 170

Archer Auxilia are supporting troops for the heavier legionary infantry, an important secondary role in Roman warfare.

ABILITIES

- Combat bonus in woods
- Long range missiles
- Can use flaming missiles
- Good stamina
- Fast moving
- Can sap

Light Auxilia (Post Marian Reform)

STATS

SOLDIERS: 41	ARMOR: 2
MELEE ATTACK: 5	DEFENSE SKILL: 3
MISSILE ATTACK: 7	SHIELD: 2
CHARGE BONUS: 2	HIT POINTS: 1
WEAPON TYPE: Missile	RECRUITMENT COST: 280
TOTAL DEFENSE: 7	UPKEEP: 170

Light Auxilia are skirmishers who act as a screening force for heavier troops. They also attack enemies with showers of javelins.

ABILITIES

- Can hide in long grass
- Bonus vs. elephants and chariots
- Combat bonus in woods
- Good stamina
- Fast moving
- Can sap

Roman Archers

STATS

SOLDIERS: 40	ARMOR: 0
MELEE ATTACK: 3	DEFENSE SKILL: 2
MISSILE ATTACK: 7	SHIELD: 0
CHARGE BONUS: 2	HIT POINTS: 1
WEAPON TYPE: Missile	RECRUITMENT COST: 180
TOTAL DEFENSE: 2	UPKEEP: 170

Roman Archers are supporting troops for heavier infantry, very much a secondary role in Roman warfare.

ABILITIES

- Combat bonus in woods
- Can use flaming missiles
- Fast moving
- Can sap

Velites

STATS

SOLDIERS: 40	ARMOR: 2
MELEE ATTACK: 5	DEFENSE SKILL: 3
MISSILE ATTACK: 7	SHIELD: 2
CHARGE BONUS: 2	HIT POINTS: 1
WEAPON TYPE: Missile	RECRUITMENT COST: 270
TOTAL DEFENSE: 7	UPKEEP: 170

Velites are light skirmishing troops who screen the main battle line of an early-pattern Legion as it advances.

ABILITIES

- Can hide in long grass
- Bonus vs. elephants and chariots
- Combat bonus in woods
- Fast moving
- Can sap

Spearmen

Triarii

STATS

SOLDIERS: 42	DEFENSE SKILL: 5
ATTACK: 7	SHIELD: 5
CHARGE BONUS: 7	HIT POINTS: 1
WEAPON TYPE: Light	RECRUITMENT COST: 490
TOTAL DEFENSE: 17	UPKEEP: 210
ARMOR: 7	

Triarii are tough, experienced spearmen who are the senior element—the backbone—of an early Roman Legion. They can be a decisive force in battle.

ABILITIES
- Bonus fighting cavalry
- Can sap
- Good morale

Roman Naval Units

Bireme

VESSELS: 20   DEFENSE: 2
ATTACK: 6

Trireme

VESSELS: 30   DEFENSE: 3
ATTACK: 8

Quinquireme

VESSELS: 50   DEFENSE: 5
ATTACK: 10

Corvus Quinquireme

VESSELS: 50   DEFENSE: 4
ATTACK: 14

Decere

VESSELS: 60   DEFENSE: 8
ATTACK: 16

Roman Buildings

Government-Class Buildings

Governor's House

- Enables training of Peasants
- Enables construction of "First Tier" buildings

Governor's Villa

- Enables training of Peasants
- Enables recruitment of diplomats
- Enables construction of "Second Tier" buildings

Governor's Palace

- Enables training of Peasants
- Enables recruitment of diplomats
- Enables construction of "Third Tier" buildings

Pro-Consul's Palace

- Enables training of Peasants
- Enables recruitment of diplomats
- Enables construction of "Fourth Tier" buildings

Imperial Palace

- Improved Generals' bodyguards
- Enables training of Peasants
- Enables training of Praetorian Cohort
- Enables recruitment of diplomats
- Enables construction of "Fifth Tier" buildings

Wall-Class Buildings

Wooden Palisade (First Tier)

- Extra wall defenses

Wooden Wall (Second Tier)

- Extra wall defenses
- Reinforced gates

Stone Wall (Third Tier)

- Extra wall defenses
- Reinforced gates
- Boiling oil

Large Stone Wall (Fourth Tier)

- Extra wall defenses
- Boiling oil
- Iron gates

Epic Stone Wall (Fifth Tier)

- Extra wall defenses
- Boiling oil
- Iron gates

Barrack-Class Buildings

Barracks (First Tier)

- Enables training of Town Watch

Militia Barracks (Second Tier)

- Enables training of Town Watch
- Enables training of Hastati

Legion Barracks (Third Tier)

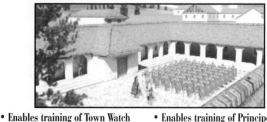

- Enables training of Town Watch
- Enables training of Hastati
- Enables training of Principes

Army Barracks (Fourth Tier)

- Enables training of Town Watch
- Enables training of Hastati
- Enables training of Principes
- Enables training of Triarii

Urban Barracks (Fifth Tier)

- Enables training of Town Watch
- Enables training of Hastati
- Enables training of Principes
- Enables training of Triarii
- Enables training of Urban Cohort

Stable-Class Buildings

Stables (Second Tier)

- Enables training of Equites
- Enables training of Wardogs

Cavalry Stables (Third Tier)

- Enables training of Equites
- Enables training of Wardogs
- Enables training of Cavalry Auxilia

Hippodrome (Fourth Tier)

- Enables training of Equites
- Enables training of Wardogs
- Enables training of Cavalry Auxilia
- Enables training of Legionary Cavalry
- Enables training of Incendiary Pigs
- Allows races to be held

Circus Maximus (Fifth Tier)

- Enables training of Equites
- Enables training of Wardogs
- Enables training of Cavalry Auxilia
- Enables training of Legionary Cavalry
- Enables training of Incendiary Pigs
- Allows races to be held
- Enables training of Praetorian Cavalry

Range-Class Buildings

Practice Range (Second Tier)

- Enables training of Velites

Archery Range (Third Tier)

- Enables training of Velites
- Enables training of Roman Archers
- Enables training of Ballistae

Catapult Range (Fourth Tier)

- Enables training of Velites
- Enables training of Roman Archers
- Enables training of Ballistae
- Enables training of Scorpions
- Enables training of Onagers

Siege Engineer (Fifth Tier)

- Enables training of Velites
- Enables training of Roman Archers
- Enables training of Ballistae
- Enables training of Scorpions
- Enables training of Onagers
- Enables training of Heavy Onagers
- Enables training of Repeating Ballistae

Trader-Class Buildings

Trader (First Tier)

- Increase in tradable goods
- Population Growth bonus: 0.5%

Market (Second Tier)

- Increase in tradable goods
- Population Growth bonus: 0.5%
- Enables recruitment of spies

Forum (Third Tier)

- Increase in tradable goods
- Population Growth bonus: 0.5%
- Enables recruitment of spies
- Enables recruitment of assassins

Great Forum (Fourth Tier)

- Increase in tradable goods
- Population Growth bonus: 1%
- Enables recruitment of spies
- Enables recruitment of assassins

Curia (Fifth Tier)

- Increase in tradable goods
- Population Growth bonus: 1%
- Enables recruitment of spies
- Enables recruitment of assassins
- Public Order bonus due to happiness: 10%

Smith-Class Buildings

Blacksmith (Second Tier)

- SPECIAL REQUIREMENT: Trader Building
- Upgrades light weapons +1
- Upgrades heavy weapons +1

Armourer (Third Tier)

- SPECIAL REQUIREMENT: Market Building
- Upgrades light weapons +1
- Upgrades heavy weapons +1
- Upgrades missile weapons +1
- Upgrades armor +1

Foundry (Fifth Tier)

- SPECIAL REQUIREMENT: Great Forum Building
- Upgrades light weapons +2
- Upgrades heavy weapons +2
- Upgrades missile weapons +2
- Upgrades armor +2

Port-Class Buildings

Port (Second Tier)

- Grants one sea-trade fleet for extra income
- Enables training of Biremes

Shipwright (Third Tier)

- Grants two sea-trade fleets for extra income
- Enables training of Biremes
- Enables training of Triremes

Dockyard (Fourth Tier)

- Grants three sea-trade fleets for extra income
- Enables training of Biremes
- Enables training of Triremes
- Enables training of Quinquiremes

Water Supply-Class Buildings

Sewers (Second Tier)

- SPECIAL REQUIREMENT: Trader Building
- Public health bonus: 5%

Public Baths (Third Tier)

- SPECIAL REQUIREMENT: Market Building
- Public health bonus: 10%

Aqueduct (Fourth Tier)

- SPECIAL REQUIREMENT: Forum Building
- Public health bonus: 15%

City Plumbing (Fifth Tier)

- SPECIAL REQUIREMENT: Great Forum Building
- Public health bonus: 20%

Farm-Class Buildings

Land Clearance (First Tier)

- Improved farms and food production: +1

Communal Farming (Second Tier)

- Improved farms and food production: +2

Crop Rotation (Third Tier)

- Improved farms and food production: +3

Irrigation (Fourth Tier)

- Improved farms and food production: +4

Latifundia (Fifth Tier)

- Improved farms and food production: +5

Roads

Roads (First Tier)

- Improved roads and trade

Paved Roads (Second Tier)

- Improved roads and trade

Highways (Third Tier)

- Improved roads and trade

Academy-Class Buildings

Academy (Third Tier)

- SPECIAL REQUIREMENT: Market Building
- Governors gain skills and knowledge

Scriptorium (Fourth Tier)

- SPECIAL REQUIREMENT: Forum Building
- Governors gain skills and knowledge

Ludus Magna (Fifth Tier)

- SPECIAL REQUIREMENT: Great Forum Building
- Governors gain skills and knowledge

Amphitheater-Class Buildings

Arena (Third Tier)

- SPECIAL REQUIREMENT: Market Building
- Allows Gladiatorial games to be held
- Public Order bonus due to happiness: 5%

Amphitheater (Fourth Tier)

- SPECIAL REQUIREMENT: Forum Building
- Allows Gladiatorial games to be held
- Public Order bonus due to happiness: 10%
- Enables training of Samnite Gladiators

Coliseum (Fifth Tier)

- SPECIAL REQUIREMENT: Great Forum Building
- Allows Gladiatorial games to be held
- Public Order bonus due to happiness: 15%
- Enables training of Samnite Gladiators

Temple-Class Buildings (Julii Family)

Shrine to Ceres (First Tier)

- Public Order bonus due to happiness: 5%
- Population Growth bonus: 0.5%

Temple of Ceres (Second Tier)

- Public Order bonus due to happiness: 10%
- Population Growth bonus: 1%

Large Temple of Ceres (Third Tier)

- Public Order bonus due to happiness: 15%
- Population Growth bonus: 1.5%

Awesome Temple of Ceres (Fourth Tier)

- Public Order bonus due to happiness: 20%
- Population Growth bonus: 2%

Pantheon (Ceres, Fifth Tier)

- Public Order bonus due to happiness: 35%
- Public Order bonus due to law: 10%
- Population Growth bonus: 2.5%

Shrine to Bacchus (First Tier)

- Public Order bonus due to happiness: 10%

Temple of Bacchus (Second Tier)

- Public Order bonus due to happiness: 20%

Large Temple of Bacchus (Third Tier)

- Public Order bonus due to happiness: 30%

Awesome Temple of Bacchus (Fourth Tier)

- Public Order bonus due to happiness: 40%

Pantheon (Bacchus, Fifth Tier)

- Public Order bonus due to happiness: 50%
- Population Growth bonus: 1%
- Public Order bonus due to law: 10%

Shrine to Jupiter (First Tier)

- Public Order bonus due to happiness: 5%
- Public Order bonus due to law: 5%

Temple of Jupiter (Second Tier)

- Public Order bonus due to happiness: 10%
- Public Order bonus due to law: 10%

Large Temple of Jupiter (Third Tier)

- Public Order bonus due to happiness: 15%
- Public Order bonus due to law: 15%

Awesome Temple of Jupiter (Fourth Tier)

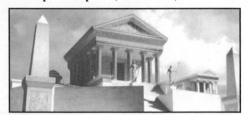

- Public Order bonus due to happiness: 20%
- Public Order bonus due to law: 20%
- Enables training of Arcani

Pantheon (Jupiter, Fifth Tier)

- Public Order bonus due to happiness: 35%
- Public Order bonus due to law: 10%
- Enables training of Arcani

Temple-Class Buildings (Brutii Family)

Shrine to Juno (First Tier)

- Public Order bonus due to happiness: 5%
- Public health bonus: 5%

Temple of Juno (Second Tier)

- Public Order bonus due to happiness: 10%
- Public health bonus: 10%

Large Temple of Juno (Third Tier)

- Public Order bonus due to happiness: 15%
- Public health bonus: 15%

Awesome Temple of Juno (Fourth Tier)

- Public Order bonus due to happiness: 20%
- Public health bonus: 20%

Pantheon (Juno, Fifth Tier)

- Public Order bonus due to happiness: 25%
- Public health bonus: 25%
- Increase in tradable goods
- Experience bonus to troops trained here: +2

Shrine to Mercury (First Tier)

- Public Order bonus due to happiness: 5%
- Increase in tradable goods

Temple of Mercury (Second Tier)

- Public Order bonus due to happiness: 10%
- Increase in tradable goods

Large Temple of Mercury (Third Tier)

- Public Order bonus due to happiness: 15%
- Increase in tradable goods

Awesome Temple of Mercury (Fourth Tier)

- Public Order bonus due to happiness: 20%
- Increase in tradable goods

Pantheon (Mercury, Fifth Tier)

- Public Order bonus due to happiness: 25%
- Increase in tradable goods
- Public health bonus: 10%
- Experience bonus to troops trained here: +1

Shrine to Mars (First Tier)

- Public Order bonus due to happiness: 5%

Temple of Mars (Second Tier)

- Public Order bonus due to happiness: 10%
- Experience bonus to troops trained here: +1

Large Temple of Mars (Third Tier)

- Public Order bonus due to happiness: 15%
- Experience bonus to troops trained here: +2

Awesome Temple of Mars (Fourth Tier)

- Public Order bonus due to happiness: 20%
- Experience bonus to troops trained here: +3
- Enables training of Arcani

Pantheon (Mars, Fifth Tier)

- Public Order bonus due to happiness: 25%
- Experience bonus to troops trained here: +3
- Morale bonus to troops trained here: +1
- Increase in tradable goods
- Public health bonus: 10%

Temple-Class Buildings (Scipii Family)

Shrine to Vulcan (First Tier)

- Public Order bonus due to happiness: 5%
- Upgrades light weapons: +1

Temple of Vulcan (Second Tier)

- Public Order bonus due to happiness: 10%
- Upgrades light weapons: +1
- Upgrades heavy weapons: +1

Large Temple of Vulcan (Third Tier)

- Public Order bonus due to happiness: 15%
- Upgrades light weapons: +1
- Upgrades heavy weapons: +1
- Upgrades Armor: +1

Awesome Temple of Vulcan (Fourth Tier)

- Public Order bonus due to happiness: 20%
- Upgrades light weapons: +1
- Upgrades heavy weapons: +1
- Upgrades Armor: +1
- Experience bonus to troops trained here: +1

Pantheon (Vulcan, Fifth Tier)

- Public Order bonus due to happiness: 25%
- Upgrades light weapons: +1
- Upgrades heavy weapons: +1
- Upgrades Armor: +1
- Experience bonus to troops trained here: +2
- Public Order bonus due to law: 10%

Shrine to Saturn (First Tier)

- Public Order bonus due to happiness: 5%
- Public Order bonus due to law: 5%

Temple of Saturn (Second Tier)

- Public Order bonus due to happiness: 10%
- Public Order bonus due to law: 10%

Large Temple of Saturn (Third Tier)

- Public Order bonus due to happiness: 15%
- Public Order bonus due to law: 15%

Awesome Temple of Saturn (Fourth Tier)

- Public Order bonus due to happiness: 20%
- Public Order bonus due to law: 20%
- Enables training of Arcani

Pantheon (Saturn, Fifth Tier)

- Public Order bonus due to happiness: 25%
- Public Order bonus due to law: 25%
- Upgrades light weapons: +1
- Upgrades heavy weapons: +1
- Upgrades Armor: +1
- Enables training of Arcani

Shrine to Neptune (First Tier)

- Public Order bonus due to happiness: 5%

Temple of Neptune (Second Tier)

- Public Order bonus due to happiness: 10%

Large Temple of Neptune (Third Tier)

- Public Order bonus due to happiness: 15%

Awesome Temple of Neptune (Fourth Tier)

- Public Order bonus due to happiness: 20%
- Enables training of Corvus Quinquireme

Pantheon (Neptune, Fifth Tier)

- Public Order bonus due to happiness: 25%
- Public Order bonus due to law: 10%
- Upgrades light weapons: +1
- Upgrades heavy weapons: +1
- Upgrades Armor: +1
- Enables training of Decere
- Enables training of Corvus Quinquireme

Armenian Military Units

Artillery Units

Onagers

STATS

SOLDIERS: 32	ARMOR: 2
ATTACK VS. TROOPS: 53	DEFENSE SKILL: 3
ATTACK VS. BUILDINGS: 35	SHIELD: 0
CHARGE BONUS: 0	HIT POINTS: 1
WEAPON TYPE: Light	RECRUITMENT COST: 1440
TOTAL DEFENSE: 5	UPKEEP: 180

The Onager is a versatile catapult that can launch boulders or incendiary firepots at enemy troops and fortifications.

ABILITIES

- Area attack
- Very long range missile
- Can use flaming missiles
- Can't hide
- Inaccurate against troops

Cavalry Units (Heavy)

Cataphracts

STATS

SOLDIERS: 27	DEFENSE SKILL: 5
ATTACK: 7	SHIELD: 0
CHARGE BONUS: 15	HIT POINTS: 1
WEAPON TYPE: Heavy	RECRUITMENT COST: 810
TOTAL DEFENSE: 23	UPKEEP: 140
ARMOR: 18	

Cataphracts are extremely heavily-armored shock cavalry who can turn a battle with one thunderous charge.

ABILITIES

- Can form wedge
- Good morale
- Powerful charge

Cavalry Units (Missile)

Cataphract Archers

STATS

SOLDIERS: 27	ARMOR: 18
MELEE ATTACK: 9	DEFENSE SKILL: 4
MISSILE ATTACK: 10	SHIELD: 0
CHARGE BONUS: 3	HIT POINTS: 1
WEAPON TYPE: Missile	RECRUITMENT COST: 910
TOTAL DEFENSE: 22	UPKEEP: 140

Cataphract Archers are very heavily armored, but slow, horse-archers that are almost impervious to attacks and can fight in close combat.

ABILITIES

- Can form Cantabrian circle
- Good morale

Horse Archers

STATS

SOLDIERS: 27	ARMOR: 0
MELEE ATTACK: 3	DEFENSE SKILL: 2
MISSILE ATTACK: 7	SHIELD: 0
CHARGE BONUS: 2	HIT POINTS: 1
WEAPON TYPE: Missile	RECRUITMENT COST: 260
TOTAL DEFENSE: 2	UPKEEP: 110

Horse Archers are a specialty of the East: swift horses and expert marksmen make a deadly combination.

ABILITIES

- Can form Cantabrian circle
- Fast moving

Infantry Units (Light)

Hillmen

STATS

SOLDIERS: 40	DEFENSE SKILL: 4
ATTACK: 5	SHIELD: 2
CHARGE BONUS: 5	HIT POINTS: 1
WEAPON TYPE: Light	RECRUITMENT COST: 290
TOTAL DEFENSE: 9	UPKEEP: 170
ARMOR: 3	

The Hillmen are a wild, savage people but they are skilled hunters, making them superb ambushers.

ABILITIES

- Can hide in long grass
- May charge without orders
- Good stamina
- Fast moving
- Can sap

Peasants

STATS

SOLDIERS: 61	DEFENSE SKILL: 3
ATTACK: 3	SHIELD: 0
CHARGE BONUS: 2	HIT POINTS: 1
WEAPON TYPE: Light	RECRUITMENT COST: 120
TOTAL DEFENSE: 3	UPKEEP: 100
ARMOR: 0	

Peasants are reluctant warriors, at best. Going to war is just one more burden of a hard life.

ABILITIES

- Poor morale
- Can sap

Infantry Units (Heavy)

Armenian Legionaries

STATS

SOLDIERS: 41	ARMOR: 7
MELEE ATTACK: 7	DEFENSE SKILL: 4
MISSILE ATTACK: 11	SHIELD: 5
CHARGE BONUS: 2	HIT POINTS: 1
WEAPON TYPE: Heavy	RECRUITMENT COST: 490
TOTAL DEFENSE: 16	UPKEEP: 220

Armenian Legionaries are an attempt to copy the fighting style and skills of the Roman Legions, and give other commanders the war-winning troops of Rome.

ABILITIES

- Javelins thrown before charge
- Good stamina
- Can sap

Infantry Units (Missile)

Archers

STATS

SOLDIERS: 40	ARMOR: 0
MELEE ATTACK: 3	DEFENSE SKILL: 2
MISSILE ATTACK: 7	SHIELD: 0
CHARGE BONUS: 2	HIT POINTS: 1
WEAPON TYPE: Missile	RECRUITMENT COST: 180
TOTAL DEFENSE: 2	UPKEEP: 170

Archers are rightly feared for the casualties they can inflict, but they are vulnerable in hand-to-hand combat.

ABILITIES

- Can use flaming missiles
- Fast moving
- Can sap

Peltasts

STATS

SOLDIERS: 40	ARMOR: 0
MELEE ATTACK: 3	DEFENSE SKILL: 2
MISSILE ATTACK: 6	SHIELD: 2
CHARGE BONUS: 2	HIT POINTS: 1
WEAPON TYPE: Missile	RECRUITMENT COST: 180
TOTAL DEFENSE: 4	UPKEEP: 170

Eastern Peltasts rush forward to pepper an enemy with javelins, and then withdraw in good order before a counter-attack can be organized.

ABILITIES

- Can hide in long grass
- Bonus vs. elephants and chariots
- Fast moving
- Can sap

Spearmen Units

Eastern Infantry

STATS

SOLDIERS: 60	DEFENSE SKILL: 2
ATTACK: 3	SHIELD: 5
CHARGE BONUS: 4	HIT POINTS: 1
WEAPON TYPE: Light	RECRUITMENT COST: 330
TOTAL DEFENSE: 10	UPKEEP: 150
ARMOR: 3	

Eastern Infantry are easily recruited militia-spearmen, who are good for defense against less able opponents.

ABILITIES

- Bonus fighting cavalry
- Poor morale
- Can sap

Heavy Spearmen

STATS

SOLDIERS: 41	DEFENSE SKILL: 5
ATTACK: 7	SHIELD: 5
CHARGE BONUS: 6	HIT POINTS: 1
WEAPON TYPE: Light	RECRUITMENT COST: 510
TOTAL DEFENSE: 17	UPKEEP: 170
ARMOR: 7	

Heavy Spearmen can be the backbone of an Eastern army and are well able to take on many opponents.

ABILITIES

- Can form phalanx
- Bonus fighting cavalry
- Can sap

Armenian Naval Units

Bireme

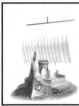

VESSELS: 20	DEFENSE: 2
ATTACK: 6	

Trireme

VESSELS: 30	DEFENSE: 3
ATTACK: 8	

Quinquireme

VESSELS: 50	DEFENSE: 5
ATTACK: 10	

NOTE

You cannot play as the Armenians in the Imperial Campaign mode, so their buildings are not listed in this guide.

British Military Units

Animal Units (Heavy)

Warhounds

STATS

SOLDIERS: 12	DEFENSE SKILL: 1
ATTACK: 14	SHIELD: 0
CHARGE BONUS: 4	HIT POINTS: 1
WEAPON TYPE: Light	RECRUITMENT COST: 570
TOTAL DEFENSE: 3	UPKEEP: 40
ARMOR: 2	

Warhounds are bred for a savage nature and great size, but then hunting men is only a little more dangerous than hunting wild boar!

ABILITIES

- Frighten nearby enemy
- Combat bonus in woods or snow
- Fast moving

Cavalry Units (Heavy)

British Heavy Chariots

STATS

SOLDIERS: 18	DEFENSE SKILL: 1
ATTACK: 13	SHIELD: 0
CHARGE BONUS: 8	HIT POINTS: 3
WEAPON TYPE: Light	RECRUITMENT COST: 560
TOTAL DEFENSE: 1	UPKEEP: 190
ARMOR: 0	

Heavy Chariots are ridden into battle by elite tribal nobles. They are shock troops, relying on speed and shock to break enemy formations.

ABILITIES

- Special attack
- Can form Cantabrian circle
- Combat bonus in snow
- Frighten nearby enemy infantry
- Excellent morale
- May charge without orders
- Fast moving

Cavalry Units (Missile)

British Chariots (Light)

STATS

SOLDIERS: 18	ARMOR: 0
MELEE ATTACK: 10	DEFENSE SKILL: 1
MISSILE ATTACK: 14	SHIELD: 0
CHARGE BONUS: 7	HIT POINTS: 2
WEAPON TYPE: Missile	RECRUITMENT COST: 350
TOTAL DEFENSE: 1	UPKEEP: 170

Light Chariots are very fast, very noisy, and combine the swiftness of cavalry with the 'staying power' of infantry.

ABILITIES

- Special attack
- Can form Cantabrian circle
- Combat bonus in snow
- Frighten nearby enemy infantry
- Excellent morale
- May charge without orders
- Fast moving

Infantry Units (Light)

Barbarian Peasants

STATS

SOLDIERS: 61	DEFENSE SKILL: 1
ATTACK: 1	SHIELD: 0
CHARGE BONUS: 1	HIT POINTS: 1
WEAPON TYPE: Light	RECRUITMENT COST: 150
TOTAL DEFENSE: 4	UPKEEP: 100
ARMOR: 3	

Peasants are reluctant warriors, but Barbarian Peasants are better fighters than most: hard lives produce hard men.

ABILITIES

- Warcry improves attack
- Expert at hiding in woods
- Combat bonus in woods or snow
- Poor morale

Druids

STATS

SOLDIERS: 16	DEFENSE SKILL: 5
ATTACK: 13	SHIELD: 2
CHARGE BONUS: 5	HIT POINTS: 1
WEAPON TYPE: Light	RECRUITMENT COST: 450
TOTAL DEFENSE: 14	UPKEEP: 90
ARMOR: 7	

Druids are spiritual leaders with practical fighting skills who instill confidence in nearby friendly warriors.

ABILITIES

- Chanting inspires nearby troops
- Expert at hiding in woods
- Combat bonus in woods or snow
- Excellent morale
- Very good stamina

Warband

STATS

SOLDIERS: 61	DEFENSE SKILL: 2
ATTACK: 7	SHIELD: 5
CHARGE BONUS: 7	HIT POINTS: 1
WEAPON TYPE: Light	RECRUITMENT COST: 420
TOTAL DEFENSE: 10	UPKEEP: 200
ARMOR: 3	

Warbands are bound to the service of a strongman or petty village head. They fight well as personal glory is the way to status, but are often difficult to control.

ABILITIES

- Warcry improves attack
- Expert at hiding in woods
- Combat bonus in woods or snow
- May charge without orders

Infantry Units (Heavy)

Chosen Swordsmen

STATS

SOLDIERS: 41	DEFENSE SKILL: 5
ATTACK: 13	SHIELD: 5
CHARGE BONUS: 5	HIT POINTS: 1
WEAPON TYPE: Light	RECRUITMENT COST: 640
TOTAL DEFENSE: 17	UPKEEP: 210
ARMOR: 7	

Chosen Swordsmen are the best fighting individuals in their tribe, and armed with the finest swords available.

ABILITIES

- Warcry improves attack
- Expert at hiding in woods
- Combat bonus in woods or snow
- Excellent morale
- May charge without orders
- Good stamina

Swordsmen

STATS

SOLDIERS: 41	DEFENSE SKILL: 4
ATTACK: 10	SHIELD: 5
CHARGE BONUS: 5	HIT POINTS: 1
WEAPON TYPE: Light	RECRUITMENT COST: 440
TOTAL DEFENSE: 12	UPKEEP: 170
ARMOR: 3	

Swordsmen are steadfast and aggressive warriors, the 'infantry of the line' for barbarian warlords.

ABILITIES

- Warcry improves attack
- Expert at hiding in woods
- Combat bonus in woods or snow
- May charge without orders
- Good morale

Woad Warriors

STATS

SOLDIERS: 41	DEFENSE SKILL: 2
ATTACK: 13	SHIELD: 2
CHARGE BONUS: 6	HIT POINTS: 1
WEAPON TYPE: Light	RECRUITMENT COST: 330
TOTAL DEFENSE: 4	UPKEEP: 130
ARMOR: 0	

Religion and magic are powerful reasons for bravery. Woad Warriors are brave fighters—and mad.

ABILITIES

- Warcry improves attack
- Expert at hiding in woods
- Combat bonus in woods or snow
- May charge without orders
- Good morale
- Good stamina
- Fast moving

Infantry Units (Missile)

Head Hurlers

STATS

SOLDIERS: 40	ARMOR: 0
MELEE ATTACK: 12	DEFENSE SKILL: 2
MISSILE ATTACK: 17	SHIELD: 0
CHARGE BONUS: 6	HIT POINTS: 1
WEAPON TYPE: Missile	RECRUITMENT COST: 370
TOTAL DEFENSE: 2	UPKEEP: 130

In battle, Head Hurlers throw the heads of fallen foes coated with quicklime. These missiles are both dangerous and loathsome.

ABILITIES

- Expert at hiding in woods
- Effective against armor
- Combat bonus in woods or snow
- May charge without orders
- Good morale
- Fast moving

Slingers

STATS

SOLDIERS: 40	ARMOR: 0
MELEE ATTACK: 3	DEFENSE SKILL: 2
MISSILE ATTACK: 3	SHIELD: 2
CHARGE BONUS: 2	HIT POINTS: 1
WEAPON TYPE: Missile	RECRUITMENT COST: 150
TOTAL DEFENSE: 4	UPKEEP: 170

A sling is a deceptively simple weapon: a Slinger can bring down the strongest man with a single shot.

ABILITIES

- Expert at hiding in woods
- Fast moving
- Combat bonus in woods or snow

British Naval Units

Boats

VESSELS: 15	DEFENSE: 1
ATTACK: 6	

Large Boats

VESSELS: 30	DEFENSE: 3
ATTACK: 8	

British Buildings
Government-Class Buildings

Warrior's Hold

- Enables training of Barbarian Peasants
- Enables construction of "First Tier" buildings

Warlord's Hold

- Enables training of Barbarian Peasants
- Enables recruitment of diplomats
- Enables construction of "Second Tier" buildings

High King's Hall

- Improved Generals' Bodyguards
- Enables training of Barbarian Peasants
- Enables recruitment of diplomats
- Enables construction of "Third Tier" buildings

Wall-Class Buildings

Wooden Palisade (First Tier)

- Extra wall defenses

Stockade (Second Tier)

- Extra wall defenses
- Reinforced gates

Barrack-Class Buildings

Muster Field (First Tier)

- Enables training of Warband

Meeting Hall (Second Tier)

- Enables training of Warband
- Enables training of Swordsmen

Hall of Heroes (Third Tier)

- Enables training of Warband
- Enables training of Swordsmen
- Enables training of Chosen Swordsmen

Stable-Class Buildings

Stables (Second Tier)

- Enables training of Warhounds

Range-Class Buildings

Practice Range (Second Tier)

- Enables training of Slingers

Trader-Class Buildings

Trader (First Tier)

- Increase in tradable goods
- Population Growth bonus: 0.5%

Market (Second Tier)

- Increase in tradable goods
- Population Growth bonus: 0.5%
- Enables recruitment of spies

Great Market (Third Tier)

- Increase in tradable goods
- Population Growth bonus: 0.5%
- Enables recruitment of spies
- Enables recruitment of assassins

Smith-Class Buildings

Blacksmith (Second Tier)

- SPECIAL REQUIREMENT: Trader Building
- Upgrades light weapons +1
- Upgrades heavy weapons +1
- Enables training of British Light Chariots

Weaponsmith (Third Tier)

- SPECIAL REQUIREMENT: Market Building
- Upgrades light weapons +1
- Upgrades heavy weapons +1
- Upgrades missile weapons +1
- Upgrades armor +1
- Enables training of British Light Chariots
- Enables training of British Heavy Chariots

Port-Class Buildings

Port (Second Tier)

- Grants one sea-trade fleet for extra income
- Enables training of Boats

Shipwright (Third Tier)

- Grants two sea-trade fleets for extra income
- Enables training of Boats
- Enables training of Large Boats

Farm-Class Buildings

Land Clearance (First Tier)

- Improved farms and food production: +1

Communal Farming (Second Tier)

- Improved farms and food production: +2

Roads

Roads (First Tier)

- Improved roads and trade

Tavern-Class Buildings

Tavern (Second Tier)

- Public Order bonus due to happiness: 5%

Bardic Circle (Third Tier)

- Public Order bonus due to happiness: 10%

Temple-Class Buildings

Shrine to Brigantia (First Tier)

- Public Order bonus due to happiness: 5%
- Public health bonus: 5%

Sacred Grove of Brigantia (Second Tier)

- Public Order bonus due to happiness: 10%
- Public health bonus: 10%

Sacred Circle of Brigantia (Third Tier)

- Public Order bonus due to happiness: 15%
- Population Growth bonus: 1.5%

Shrine to Britannia (First Tier)

- Public Order bonus due to happiness: 5%
- Increase in tradable goods

Sacred Grove of Britannia (Second Tier)

- Public Order bonus due to happiness: 10%
- Increase in tradable goods

Sacred Circle of Britannia (Third Tier)

- Public Order bonus due to happiness: 15%
- Increase in tradable goods

Shrine to Andrasta (First Tier)

- Public Order bonus due to happiness: 5%
- Enables training of Woad Warriors

Sacred Grove of Andrasta (Second Tier)

- Public Order bonus due to happiness: 10%
- Experience bonus to troops trained here: +1
- Enables training of Woad Warriors
- Enables training of Head Hurlers

Sacred Circle of Andrasta (Third Tier)

- Public Order bonus due to happiness: 15%
- Experience bonus to troops trained here: +2
- Enables training of Woad Warriors (Experience 1)
- Enables training of Head Hurlers (Experience 1)

Carthaginian Military Units

Artillery Units

Heavy Onagers

STATS

SOLDIERS: 32	ARMOR: 0
ATTACK VS. TROOPS: 63	DEFENSE SKILL: 3
ATTACK VS. BUILDINGS: 55	SHIELD: 0
CHARGE BONUS: 0	HIT POINTS: 1
WEAPON TYPE: Light	RECRUITMENT COST: 1830
TOTAL DEFENSE: 3	UPKEEP: 180

The Heavy Onager is a siege engine capable of reducing even stone ramparts to rubble, but can be vulnerable to enemy catapults.

ABILITIES

- Area attack
- Very long range missiles
- Can use Flaming Missiles
- Can't hide
- Inaccurate against troops

Onagers

STATS

SOLDIERS: 32	ARMOR: 0
ATTACK VS. TROOPS: 53	DEFENSE SKILL: 3
ATTACK VS. BUILDINGS: 35	SHIELD: 0
CHARGE BONUS: 0	HIT POINTS: 1
WEAPON TYPE: Light	RECRUITMENT COST: 1390
TOTAL DEFENSE: 3	UPKEEP: 180

The Onager is a versatile catapult that can launch boulders or incendiary firepots at enemy troops and fortifications.

ABILITIES

- Area attack
- Very long range missiles
- Can use Flaming Missiles
- Can't hide
- Inaccurate against troops

Cavalry Units (Light)

Long Shield Cavalry

STATS

SOLDIERS: 27	DEFENSE SKILL: 6
ATTACK: 9	SHIELD: 4
CHARGE BONUS: 8	HIT POINTS: 1
WEAPON TYPE: Light	RECRUITMENT COST: 460
TOTAL DEFENSE: 13	UPKEEP: 140
ARMOR: 3	

Long Shield Cavalry are spear-armed light cavalry, who can be used to break enemy formations, drive off skirmishers, and pursue fleeing foes.

ABILITIES

- Can form wedge
- Good morale
- Powerful charge

Round Shield Cavalry

STATS

SOLDIERS: 27	DEFENSE SKILL: 4
ATTACK: 7	SHIELD: 2
CHARGE BONUS: 2	HIT POINTS: 1
WEAPON TYPE: Light	RECRUITMENT COST: 280
TOTAL DEFENSE: 8	UPKEEP: 110
ARMOR: 2	

Round Shield Cavalry are best used to ride down skirmishers and pursue fleeing enemies.

ABILITIES

• Can form wedge

Cavalry Units (Heavy)

Armored Elephants

STATS

SOLDIERS: 19	ARMOR: 16
MELEE ATTACK: 7	DEFENSE SKILL: 3
MISSILE ATTACK: 10	SHIELD: 0
CHARGE BONUS: 11	HIT POINTS: 15
WEAPON TYPE: Missile	RECRUITMENT COST: 3200
TOTAL DEFENSE: 19	UPKEEP: 590

Armored Elephants are the most fearsome creatures to be found on a battlefield. Little can stand before these armored giants.

ABILITIES

• Special attack • Good morale
• Bonus fighting cavalry • Animals may run amok
• Frighten nearby enemy • Can't hide

Elephants

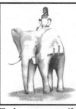

STATS

SOLDIERS: 6	ARMOR: 10
ATTACK: 5	DEFENSE SKILL: 2
CHARGE BONUS: 11	SHIELD: 0
WEAPON TYPE: Cannot be upgraded	HIT POINTS: 12
	RECRUITMENT COST: 1520
TOTAL DEFENSE: 12	UPKEEP: 280

Elephants are a terrifying spectacle to opposing troops, well able to smash battle lines and toss men aside like dogs with rats.

ABILITIES

• Special attack • Good morale
• Bonus fighting cavalry • Animals may run amok
• Frighten nearby enemy • Can't hide

Sacred Band Cavalry

STATS

SOLDIERS: 27	DEFENSE SKILL: 7
ATTACK: 12	SHIELD: 0
CHARGE BONUS: 9	HIT POINTS: 1
WEAPON TYPE: Light	RECRUITMENT COST: 700
TOTAL DEFENSE: 18	UPKEEP: 340
ARMOR: 11	

The Sacred Band fight as heavy cavalry, armed with spears and swords and well armored to boot. They are an elite in Carthaginian warfare and society.

ABILITIES

• Can form wedge • Powerful charge
• Good morale • Good stamina

War Elephants

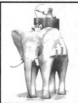

STATS

SOLDIERS: 18	ARMOR: 13
MELEE ATTACK: 7	DEFENSE SKILL: 3
MISSILE ATTACK: 10	SHIELD: 0
CHARGE BONUS: 11	HIT POINTS: 15
WEAPON TYPE: Missile	RECRUITMENT COST: 2880
TOTAL DEFENSE: 16	UPKEEP: 490

War Elephants are fierce and terrible beasts, able to trample men and horses into the dirt.

ABILITIES

• Special attack • Good morale
• Bonus fighting cavalry • Animals may run amok
• Frighten nearby enemy • Can't hide

Infantry Units (Light)

Iberian Infantry

STATS

SOLDIERS: 40	DEFENSE SKILL: 4
ATTACK: 7	SHIELD: 2
CHARGE BONUS: 2	HIT POINTS: 1
WEAPON TYPE: Light	RECRUITMENT COST: 240
TOTAL DEFENSE: 8	UPKEEP: 170
ARMOR: 2	

These infantry are the steady backbone of the armies of Carthage and Spain. Reliable, well-armed, and tough, they are armed with falcatas to cut a path into an enemy line.

ABILITIES

• Can sap

Peasants

STATS

SOLDIERS: 61	DEFENSE SKILL: 3
ATTACK: 3	SHIELD: 0
CHARGE BONUS: 2	HIT POINTS: 1
WEAPON TYPE: Light	RECRUITMENT COST: 120
TOTAL DEFENSE: 3	UPKEEP: 100
ARMOR: 0	

Peasants are reluctant warriors, at best. Going to war is just one more burden of a hard life.

ABILITIES

- Poor morale
- Can sap

Town Militia

STATS

SOLDIERS: 40	DEFENSE SKILL: 2
ATTACK: 3	SHIELD: 5
CHARGE BONUS: 4	HIT POINTS: 1
WEAPON TYPE: Light	RECRUITMENT COST: 150
TOTAL DEFENSE: 7	UPKEEP: 100
ARMOR: 0	

Town Militia are trained bands of citizens dragged from their homes and shops, given a spear each and some rudimentary training.

ABILITIES

- Poor morale
- Can sap

Infantry Units (Missile)

Skirmishers

STATS

SOLDIERS: 40	ARMOR: 0
MELEE ATTACK: 3	DEFENSE SKILL: 2
MISSILE ATTACK: 6	SHIELD: 2
CHARGE BONUS: 2	HIT POINTS: 1
WEAPON TYPE: Missile	RECRUITMENT COST: 180
TOTAL DEFENSE: 4	UPKEEP: 170

Skirmishers rush forward to pepper an enemy with javelins, and then withdraw in good order before a counter-attack can be organized.

ABILITIES

- Can hide in long grass
- Bonus vs. elephants and chariots
- Fast moving
- Can sap

Slingers

STATS

SOLDIERS: 40	ARMOR: 0
MELEE ATTACK: 3	DEFENSE SKILL: 2
MISSILE ATTACK: 3	SHIELD: 2
CHARGE BONUS: 2	HIT POINTS: 1
WEAPON TYPE: Missile	RECRUITMENT COST: 150
TOTAL DEFENSE: 4	UPKEEP: 170

Slingers are highly skilled missile troops but are at a huge disadvantage in hand-to-hand combat, especially against cavalry.

ABILITIES

- Fast moving
- Can sap

Spearmen

Libyan Spearmen

STATS

SOLDIERS: 41	DEFENSE SKILL: 4
ATTACK: 5	SHIELD: 5
CHARGE BONUS: 5	HIT POINTS: 1
WEAPON TYPE: Light	RECRUITMENT COST: 400
TOTAL DEFENSE: 16	UPKEEP: 170
ARMOR: 7	

Libyan Spearmen are best when defending against cavalry, but can hold a battle line for a while when required.

ABILITIES

- Bonus fighting cavalry
- Can sap

Poeni Infantry

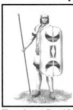

STATS

SOLDIERS: 41	DEFENSE SKILL: 6
ATTACK: 9	SHIELD: 5
CHARGE BONUS: 7	HIT POINTS: 1
WEAPON TYPE: Light	RECRUITMENT COST: 580
TOTAL DEFENSE: 18	UPKEEP: 210
ARMOR: 7	

These heavy Poeni Infantry are drawn from the self-reliant Carthaginian citizenry, and make superior all-round soldiers.

ABILITIES

- Can form phalanx
- Bonus fighting cavalry
- Good morale
- Good stamina
- Can sap

Sacred Band

STATS

SOLDIERS: 41	DEFENSE SKILL: 7
ATTACK: 12	SHIELD: 5
CHARGE BONUS: 8	HIT POINTS: 1
WEAPON TYPE: Light	RECRUITMENT COST: 740
TOTAL DEFENSE: 23	UPKEEP: 270
ARMOR: 11	

The Sacred Band is the elite infantry of any Carthaginian army and can be relied upon to do their duty to the end.

ABILITIES

- Can form phalanx
- Bonus fighting cavalry
- Good morale
- Powerful charge
- Good stamina
- Can sap

Carthaginian Naval Units

Bireme

VESSELS: 20	DEFENSE: 2
ATTACK: 6	

Trireme

VESSELS: 30	DEFENSE: 3
ATTACK: 8	

Quinquireme

VESSELS: 50	DEFENSE: 5
ATTACK: 10	

Carthaginian Buildings

Government-Class Buildings

Governor's House

- Enables training of Peasants
- Enables construction of "First Tier" buildings

Governor's Villa

- Enables training of Peasants
- Enables recruitment of diplomats
- Enables construction of "Second Tier" buildings

Governor's Palace

- Enables training of Peasants
- Enables recruitment of diplomats
- Enables construction of "Third Tier" buildings

Councilor's Chambers

- Enables training of Peasants
- Enables recruitment of diplomats
- Enables construction of "Fourth Tier" buildings

Royal Palace

- Improved Generals' Bodyguards
- Enables training of Peasants
- Enables recruitment of diplomats
- Enables construction of "Fifth Tier" buildings

Wall-Class Buildings

Wooden Palisade (First Tier)

- Extra wall defenses

Wooden Wall (Second Tier)

- Extra wall defenses
- Reinforced gates

Stone Wall (Third Tier)

- Extra wall defenses
- Reinforced gates
- Boiling oil

Large Stone Wall (Fourth Tier)

- Extra wall defenses
- Boiling oil
- Iron gates

Epic Stone Wall (Fifth Tier)

- Extra wall defenses
- Boiling oil
- Iron gates

Barrack-Class Buildings

Barracks (First Tier)

- Enables training of Town Militia

Militia Barracks (Second Tier)

- Enables training of Town Watch
- Enables training of Iberian Infantry

City Barracks (Third Tier)

- Enables training of Town Militia
- Enables training of Iberian Infantry
- Enables training of Libyan Spearmen

Army Barracks (Fourth Tier)

- Enables training of Town Militia
- Enables training of Iberian Infantry
- Enables training of Libyan Spearmen
- Enables training of Poeni Infantry

Stable-Class Buildings

Stables (Second Tier)

- Enables training of Round Shield Cavalry

Cavalry Stables (Third Tier)

- Enables training of Round Shield Cavalry
- Enables training of Long Shield Cavalry
- Enables training of Elephants

Elite Cavalry Stables (Fourth Tier)

- Enables training of Round Shield Cavalry
- Enables training of Long Shield Cavalry
- Enables training of Elephants
- Enables training of War Elephants

Royal Cavalry Stables (Fifth Tier)

- Enables training of Round Shield Cavalry
- Enables training of Long Shield Cavalry
- Enables training of Elephants
- Enables training of War Elephants
- Enables training of Armored Elephants
- Enables training of Sacred Band Cavalry

Range-Class Buildings

Practice Range (Second Tier)

- Enables training of Skirmishers

Archery Range (Third Tier)

- Enables training of Skirmishers
- Enables training of Slingers

Catapult Range (Fourth Tier)

- Enables training of Skirmishers
- Enables training of Onagers
- Enables training of Slingers

Siege Engineer (Fifth Tier)

- Enables training of Skirmishers
- Enables training of Onagers
- Enables training of Slingers
- Enables training of Heavy Onagers

Trader-Class Buildings

Trader (First Tier)

- Increase in tradable goods
- Population Growth bonus: 0.5%

Market (Second Tier)

- Increase in tradable goods
- Enables recruitment of spies
- Population Growth bonus: 0.5%

Bazaar (Third Tier)

- Increase in tradable goods
- Enables recruitment of spies
- Population Growth bonus: 0.5%
- Enables recruitment of assassins

Grand Bazaar (Fourth Tier)

- Increase in tradable goods
- Enables recruitment of spies
- Population Growth bonus: 1%
- Enables recruitment of assassins

Merchants' Quarter (Fifth Tier)

- Increase in tradable goods
- Population Growth bonus: 1%
- Enables recruitment of spies
- Enables recruitment of assassins
- Public Order bonus due to happiness: 10%

Smith-Class Buildings

Blacksmith (Second Tier)

- SPECIAL REQUIREMENT: Trader Building
- Upgrades light weapons +1
- Upgrades heavy weapons +1

Armourer (Third Tier)

- SPECIAL REQUIREMENT: Market Building
- Upgrades light weapons +1
- Upgrades heavy weapons +1
- Upgrades missile weapons +1
- Upgrades armor +1

Foundry (Fifth Tier)

- SPECIAL REQUIREMENT: Grand Bazaar Building
- Upgrades light weapons +2
- Upgrades heavy weapons +2
- Upgrades missile weapons +2
- Upgrades armor +2

Port-Class Buildings

Port (Second Tier)

- Grants one sea-trade fleet for extra income
- Enables training of Biremes

Shipwright (Third Tier)

- Grants two sea-trade fleets for extra income
- Enables training of Biremes
- Enables training of Triremes

Dockyard (Fourth Tier)

- Grants three sea-trade fleets for extra income
- Enables training of Biremes
- Enables training of Triremes
- Enables training of Quinquiremes

Water Supply-Class Buildings

Sewers (Second Tier)

- SPECIAL REQUIREMENT: Trader Building
- Public health bonus: 5%

Public Baths (Third Tier)

- SPECIAL REQUIREMENT: Market Building
- Public health bonus: 10%

Farm-Class Buildings

Land Clearance (First Tier)

- Improved farms and food production: +1

Communal Farming (Second Tier)

- Improved farms and food production: +2

Crop Rotation (Third Tier)

- Improved farms and food production: +3

Irrigation (Fourth Tier)

- Improved farms and food production: +4

Great Estates (Fifth Tier)

- Improved farms and food production: +5

Road-Class Buildingss

Roads (First Tier)

- Improved roads and trade

Paved Roads (Second Tier)

- Improved roads and trade

Academy-Class Buildings

Academy (Third Tier)

- SPECIAL REQUIREMENT: Market Building
- Governors gain skills and knowledge

Scriptorium (Fourth Tier)

- SPECIAL REQUIREMENT: Bazaar Building
- Governors gain skills and knowledge

Ludus Magna (Fifth Tier)

- SPECIAL REQUIREMENT: Grand Bazaar Building
- Governors gain skills and knowledge

Execution Square (Third Tier)

- Public Order bonus due to law: 5%

Secret Police HQ (Fourth Tier)

- Public Order bonus due to law: 10%

Secret Police Network (Fifth Tier)

- Public Order bonus due to law: 15%

Temple-Class Buildings

Shrine to Baal (First Tier)

- Public Order bonus due to happiness: 5%
- Public Order bonus due to law: 5%

Temple of Baal (Second Tier)

- Public Order bonus due to happiness: 10%
- Public Order bonus due to law: 10%

Large Temple of Baal (Third Tier)

- Public Order bonus due to happiness: 15%
- Public Order bonus due to law: 15%

Awesome Temple of Baal (Fourth Tier)

- Public Order bonus due to happiness: 20%
- Public Order bonus due to law: 20%
- Enables training of Sacred Band

Dacian Military Units
Animal Units (Heavy)
Warhounds

STATS

SOLDIERS: 12	DEFENSE SKILL: 1
ATTACK: 14	SHIELD: 0
CHARGE BONUS: 4	HIT POINTS: 1
WEAPON TYPE: Light	RECRUITMENT COST: 570
TOTAL DEFENSE: 3	UPKEEP: 40
ARMOR: 2	

Warhounds are bred for a savage nature and great size, but then hunting men is only a little more dangerous than hunting wild boar!

ABILITIES

- Frighten nearby enemy
- Fast moving
- Combat bonus in woods or snow

Artillery Units
Ballistae

STATS

SOLDIERS: 24	ARMOR: 0
ATTACK VS. TROOPS: 53	DEFENSE SKILL: 3
ATTACK VS. BUILDINGS: 12	SHIELD: 2
CHARGE BONUS: 0	HIT POINTS: 1
WEAPON TYPE: Light	RECRUITMENT COST: 420
TOTAL DEFENSE: 5	UPKEEP: 150

A Ballista is a sinew-powered weapon that looks like an enormous crossbow. It has tremendous range and can skewer files of men with a single bolt!

ABILITIES

- Missiles can impale several men
- Can use Flaming Missiles
- Long range missiles
- Can't hide

Onagers

STATS

SOLDIERS: 32	ARMOR: 0
ATTACK VS. TROOPS: 53	DEFENSE SKILL: 3
ATTACK VS. BUILDINGS: 35	SHIELD: 2
CHARGE BONUS: 0	HIT POINTS: 1
WEAPON TYPE: Light	RECRUITMENT COST: 1410
TOTAL DEFENSE: 5	UPKEEP: 180

The Onager is a versatile catapult that can launch boulders or incendiary firepots at enemy troops and fortifications.

ABILITIES

- Area attack
- Can't hide
- Very long range missiles
- Inaccurate against troops
- Can use Flaming Missiles

Cavalry Units (Light)

Barbarian Cavalry

STATS

SOLDIERS: 27	DEFENSE SKILL: 3
ATTACK: 9	SHIELD: 4
CHARGE BONUS: 9	HIT POINTS: 1
WEAPON TYPE: Light	RECRUITMENT COST: 370
TOTAL DEFENSE: 10	UPKEEP: 90
ARMOR: 3	

Barbarian Cavalry are lightly armored and carry spears. They are best used as scouts and in pursuit of fleeing enemies.

ABILITIES

- Combat bonus in snow
- Can form wedge
- May charge without orders
- Powerful charge

Cavalry Units (Heavy)

Barbarian Noble Cavalry

STATS

SOLDIERS: 27	DEFENSE SKILL: 5
ATTACK: 10	SHIELD: 4
CHARGE BONUS: 10	HIT POINTS: 1
WEAPON TYPE: Light	RECRUITMENT COST: 530
TOTAL DEFENSE: 15	UPKEEP: 160
ARMOR: 6	

Noble Cavalry are an elite in society as well as war, and fight bravely to justify their status.

ABILITIES

- Combat bonus in snow
- Can form wedge
- May charge without orders
- Good morale
- Powerful charge

Infantry Units (Light)

Barbarian Peasants

STATS

SOLDIERS: 61	DEFENSE SKILL: 1
ATTACK: 1	SHIELD: 0
CHARGE BONUS: 1	HIT POINTS: 1
WEAPON TYPE: Light	RECRUITMENT COST: 150
TOTAL DEFENSE: 4	UPKEEP: 100
ARMOR: 3	

Peasants are reluctant warriors, but Barbarian Peasants are better fighters than most: hard lives produce hard men.

ABILITIES

- Warcry improves attack
- Expert at hiding in woods
- Combat bonus in woods or snow
- Poor morale

Warband

STATS

SOLDIERS: 61	DEFENSE SKILL: 2
ATTACK: 7	SHIELD: 5
CHARGE BONUS: 7	HIT POINTS: 1
WEAPON TYPE: Light	RECRUITMENT COST: 420
TOTAL DEFENSE: 10	UPKEEP: 200
ARMOR: 3	

Warbands are bound to the service of a strongman or petty village head. They fight well as personal glory is the way to status, but are often difficult to control.

ABILITIES

- Warcry improves attack
- Expert at hiding in woods
- Combat bonus in woods or snow
- May charge without orders

Infantry Units (Heavy)

Chosen Swordsmen

STATS

SOLDIERS: 41	DEFENSE SKILL: 5
ATTACK: 13	SHIELD: 5
CHARGE BONUS: 5	HIT POINTS: 1
WEAPON TYPE: Light	RECRUITMENT COST: 640
TOTAL DEFENSE: 17	UPKEEP: 210
ARMOR: 7	

Chosen Swordsmen are the best fighting individuals in their tribe, and armed with the finest swords available.

ABILITIES

- Warcry improves attack
- Expert at hiding in woods
- Combat bonus in woods or snow
- Excellent morale
- May charge without orders
- Good stamina

Falxmen

STATS

SOLDIERS: 41	DEFENSE SKILL: 7
ATTACK: 13	SHIELD: 0
CHARGE BONUS: 7	HIT POINTS: 1
WEAPON TYPE: Heavy	RECRUITMENT COST: 460
TOTAL DEFENSE: 10	UPKEEP: 170
ARMOR: 3	

Falxmen are used to carve a path into enemy formations. They are superior, but somewhat ill-disciplined warriors.

ABILITIES

- Warcry improves attack
- Expert at hiding in woods
- Combat bonus in woods or snow
- May charge without orders
- Good morale
- Fast moving

Naked Fanatics

STATS

SOLDIERS: 40	DEFENSE SKILL: 2
ATTACK: 13	SHIELD: 5
CHARGE BONUS: 6	HIT POINTS: 1
WEAPON TYPE: Light	RECRUITMENT COST: 380
TOTAL DEFENSE: 7	UPKEEP: 130
ARMOR: 0	

Wild and savage, Naked Fanatics are always a threat but are at a disadvantage when fighting cavalry.

ABILITIES

- Warcry improves attack
- Expert at hiding in woods
- Combat bonus in woods or snow
- May charge without orders
- Good morale
- Good stamina

Infantry Units (Missile)

Archer Warband

STATS

SOLDIERS: 40	ARMOR: 3
MELEE ATTACK: 3	DEFENSE SKILL: 2
MISSILE ATTACK: 7	SHIELD: 0
CHARGE BONUS: 2	HIT POINTS: 1
WEAPON TYPE: Missile	RECRUITMENT COST: 260
TOTAL DEFENSE: 5	UPKEEP: 170

Archer Warbands are used to harass and break up enemy formations, so that other warriors can then get in among their enemies.

ABILITIES

- Expert at hiding in woods
- Combat bonus in woods or snow
- Can use Flaming Missiles
- Fast moving

Chosen Archer Warband

STATS

SOLDIERS: 41	ARMOR: 7
MELEE ATTACK: 10	DEFENSE SKILL: 4
MISSILE ATTACK: 12	SHIELD: 0
CHARGE BONUS: 5	HIT POINTS: 1
WEAPON TYPE: Missile	RECRUITMENT COST: 600
TOTAL DEFENSE: 11	UPKEEP: 180

Chosen Archers are highly prized for their superior skills in war. They are the best archers available to barbarian warlords.

ABILITIES

- Expert at hiding in woods
- Combat bonus in woods or snow
- Long range missiles
- Can use Flaming Missiles
- Good morale
- Good stamina

Dacian Naval Units

Boats

VESSELS: 15	DEFENSE: 1
ATTACK: 6	

Large Boats

VESSELS: 30	DEFENSE: 3
ATTACK: 8	

NOTE

You cannot play as the Dacians in the Imperial Campaign mode, so their buildings are not listed in this guide.

Egyptian Military Units

Artillery Units

Heavy Onagers

STATS

SOLDIERS: 33	ARMOR: 0
ATTACK VS. TROOPS: 63	DEFENSE SKILL: 3
ATTACK VS. BUILDINGS: 55	SHIELD: 0
CHARGE BONUS: 0	HIT POINTS: 1
WEAPON TYPE: Light	RECRUITMENT COST: 1830
TOTAL DEFENSE: 3	UPKEEP: 180

The Heavy Onager is a siege engine capable of reducing even stone ramparts to rubble, but can be vulnerable to enemy catapults.

ABILITIES

- Area attack
- Very long range missiles
- Can use Flaming Missiles
- Can't hide
- Inaccurate against troops

Onagers

STATS

SOLDIERS: 32	ARMOR: 0
ATTACK VS. TROOPS: 53	DEFENSE SKILL: 3
ATTACK VS. BUILDINGS: 35	SHIELD: 0
CHARGE BONUS: 0	HIT POINTS: 1
WEAPON TYPE: Light	RECRUITMENT COST: 1390
TOTAL DEFENSE: 3	UPKEEP: 180

The Onager is a versatile catapult that can launch boulders or incendiary firepots at enemy troops and fortifications.

ABILITIES

- Area attack
- Very long range missiles
- Can use Flaming Missiles
- Can't hide
- Inaccurate against troops

Cavalry Units (Light)

Desert Cavalry

STATS

SOLDIERS: 27	DEFENSE SKILL: 4
ATTACK: 7	SHIELD: 4
CHARGE BONUS: 3	HIT POINTS: 1
WEAPON TYPE: Light	RECRUITMENT COST: 490
TOTAL DEFENSE: 11	UPKEEP: 170
ARMOR: 3	

Desert Cavalry are fast moving horsemen armed with axes for close combat.

ABILITIES

- Effective against armor
- Combat bonus in deserts
- Can form wedge
- Fast moving

Nubian Cavalry

STATS

SOLDIERS: 27	DEFENSE SKILL: 6
ATTACK: 9	SHIELD: 4
CHARGE BONUS: 8	HIT POINTS: 1
WEAPON TYPE: Light	RECRUITMENT COST: 370
TOTAL DEFENSE: 10	UPKEEP: 140
ARMOR: 0	

Nubian Cavalry are lightly equipped raiders who are perfect for flanking attacks on an enemy line.

ABILITIES

- Combat bonus in deserts
- Can form wedge
- Good morale
- Powerful charge

Cavalry Units (Heavy)

Egyptian Chariots

STATS

SOLDIERS: 27	DEFENSE SKILL: 1
ATTACK: 12	SHIELD: 0
CHARGE BONUS: 7	HIT POINTS: 3
WEAPON TYPE: Heavy	RECRUITMENT COST: 640
TOTAL DEFENSE: 1	UPKEEP: 330
ARMOR: 0	

Chariots are fearsome devices, and the mail-armored, elite crews carry swords to cut down opponents.

ABILITIES

- Special attack
- Combat bonus in deserts
- Frighten nearby enemy infantry
- Good morale

Nile Cavalry

STATS

SOLDIERS: 27	DEFENSE SKILL: 6
ATTACK: 9	SHIELD: 0
CHARGE BONUS: 8	HIT POINTS: 1
WEAPON TYPE: Light	RECRUITMENT COST: 510
TOTAL DEFENSE: 13	UPKEEP: 140
ARMOR: 7	

Nile Cavalry are mail-armored spearmen capable of delivering a decisive blow.

ABILITIES

- Combat bonus in deserts
- Can form wedge
- Good morale
- Powerful charge

Cavalry Units (Missile)

Camel Archers

STATS

SOLDIERS: 27	ARMOR: 0
MELEE ATTACK: 9	DEFENSE SKILL: 1
MISSILE ATTACK: 13	SHIELD: 0
CHARGE BONUS: 6	HIT POINTS: 2
WEAPON TYPE: Missile	RECRUITMENT COST: 470
TOTAL DEFENSE: 1	UPKEEP: 330

These camel-mounted archers are effective skirmishers, especially in deserts. The very smell of camels can upset horses in battle.

ABILITIES

- Special attack
- Can form Cantabrian circle
- Combat bonus in deserts
- Frighten nearby enemy infantry
- Good morale

Egyptian Chariot Archers

STATS

SOLDIERS: 27	ARMOR: 0
MELEE ATTACK: 3	DEFENSE SKILL: 2
MISSILE ATTACK: 7	SHIELD: 0
CHARGE BONUS: 2	HIT POINTS: 1
WEAPON TYPE: Missile	RECRUITMENT COST: 230
TOTAL DEFENSE: 2	UPKEEP: 110

Chariot Archers are highly skilled—they can hit targets while the chariots are moving at high speed.

ABILITIES

- Can form Cantabrian circle
- Combat bonus in deserts
- Scare horses
- Good morale

Infantry Units (Light)

Peasants

STATS

SOLDIERS: 61	DEFENSE SKILL: 3
ATTACK: 3	SHIELD: 0
CHARGE BONUS: 2	HIT POINTS: 1
WEAPON TYPE: Light	RECRUITMENT COST: 120
TOTAL DEFENSE: 3	UPKEEP: 100
ARMOR: 0	

Peasants are reluctant warriors, at best. Going to war is just one more burden of a hard life.

ABILITIES

- Combat bonus in deserts
- Poor morale
- Can sap

Infantry Units (Heavy)

Desert Axemen

STATS

SOLDIERS: 41	DEFENSE SKILL: 5
ATTACK: 10	SHIELD: 2
CHARGE BONUS: 5	HIT POINTS: 1
WEAPON TYPE: Heavy	RECRUITMENT COST: 550
TOTAL DEFENSE: 18	UPKEEP: 210
ARMOR: 11	

These superior soldiers are recruited from among desert dwellers, and are equipped with sharp axes and good quality armor.

ABILITIES

- Combat bonus in deserts
- Good morale
- Can sap

Infantry Units (Missile)

Bowmen

STATS

SOLDIERS: 60	ARMOR: 0
MELEE ATTACK: 3	DEFENSE SKILL: 2
MISSILE ATTACK: 7	SHIELD: 0
CHARGE BONUS: 2	HIT POINTS: 1
WEAPON TYPE: Missile	RECRUITMENT COST: 240
TOTAL DEFENSE: 2	UPKEEP: 250

Archers are rightly feared for the casualties they can inflict, but they are vulnerable in hand-to-hand combat.

ABILITIES

- Combat bonus in deserts
- Can use Flaming Missiles
- Fast moving
- Can sap

Pharaoh's Bowmen

STATS

SOLDIERS: 41	ARMOR: 7
MELEE ATTACK: 9	DEFENSE SKILL: 6
MISSILE ATTACK: 14	SHIELD: 0
CHARGE BONUS: 4	HIT POINTS: 1
WEAPON TYPE: Missile	RECRUITMENT COST: 600
TOTAL DEFENSE: 13	UPKEEP: 330

Pharaoh's Bowmen are skilled archers, the finest to be found in Egyptian armies.

ABILITIES

- Combat bonus in deserts
- Long range missiles
- Can use Flaming Missiles
- Good morale
- Good stamina
- Can sap

Skirmishers

STATS

SOLDIERS: 40	ARMOR: 0
MELEE ATTACK: 3	DEFENSE SKILL: 2
MISSILE ATTACK: 6	SHIELD: 2
CHARGE BONUS: 2	HIT POINTS: 1
WEAPON TYPE: Missile	RECRUITMENT COST: 180
TOTAL DEFENSE: 4	UPKEEP: 170

Egyptian Skirmishers rush forward to pepper an enemy with javelins, and then withdraw in good order before a counter-attack can be organized.

ABILITIES

- Can hide in long grass
- Bonus vs. elephants and chariots
- Combat bonus in deserts
- Fast moving
- Can sap

Slingers

STATS

SOLDIERS: 40	ARMOR: 0
MELEE ATTACK: 3	DEFENSE SKILL: 2
MISSILE ATTACK: 3	SHIELD: 2
CHARGE BONUS: 2	HIT POINTS: 1
WEAPON TYPE: Missile	RECRUITMENT COST: 150
TOTAL DEFENSE: 4	UPKEEP: 170

Slingers are highly skilled missile troops but are at a huge disadvantage in hand-to-hand combat, especially against cavalry.

ABILITIES

- Combat bonus in deserts
- Fast moving
- Can sap

Spearmen

Nile Spearmen

STATS

SOLDIERS: 40	DEFENSE SKILL: 5
ATTACK: 7	SHIELD: 5
CHARGE BONUS: 6	HIT POINTS: 1
WEAPON TYPE: Light	RECRUITMENT COST: 410
TOTAL DEFENSE: 13	UPKEEP: 170
ARMOR: 3	

These well-trained spearmen are the mainstay of many Egyptian armies, thanks to their all-round defensive abilities.

ABILITIES

- Can form phalanx
- Bonus fighting cavalry
- Combat bonus in deserts
- Can sap

Nubian Spearmen

STATS

SOLDIERS: 40	DEFENSE SKILL: 3
ATTACK: 5	SHIELD: 5
CHARGE BONUS: 5	HIT POINTS: 1
WEAPON TYPE: Light	RECRUITMENT COST: 270
TOTAL DEFENSE: 8	UPKEEP: 100
ARMOR: 0	

These militia-like Nubian Spearmen can fight in harsh conditions and are cheap defensive troops for the Pharaoh's armies.

ABILITIES

- Can form phalanx
- Bonus fighting cavalry
- Combat bonus in deserts
- Poor morale
- Can sap

Pharaoh's Guards

STATS

SOLDIERS: 41	DEFENSE SKILL: 7
ATTACK: 12	SHIELD: 5
CHARGE BONUS: 8	HIT POINTS: 1
WEAPON TYPE: Light	RECRUITMENT COST: 640
TOTAL DEFENSE: 19	UPKEEP: 330
ARMOR: 7	

The Pharaoh's Guards are the true elite of any Egyptian army, armored spearmen sworn to defend the Twin Crowns to the death!

ABILITIES

- Can form phalanx
- Bonus fighting cavalry
- Combat bonus in deserts
- Good morale
- Powerful charge
- Good stamina
- Can sap

Egyptian Naval Units

Bireme

VESSELS: 20	DEFENSE: 2
ATTACK: 6	

Trireme

VESSELS: 30   DEFENSE: 3
ATTACK: 8

Quinquireme

VESSELS: 50   DEFENSE: 5
ATTACK: 10

Egyptian Buildings
Government-Class Buildings

Governor's House

- Enables training of Peasants
- Enables construction of "First Tier" buildings

Governor's Villa

- Enables training of Peasants
- Enables recruitment of diplomats
- Enables construction of "Second Tier" buildings

Governor's Palace

- Enables training of Peasants
- Enables recruitment of diplomats
- Enables construction of "Third Tier" buildings

Councilor's Chambers

- Enables training of Peasants
- Enables recruitment of diplomats
- Enables construction of "Fourth Tier" buildings

Pharaoh's Palace

- Improved Generals' Bodyguards
- Enables training' of Peasants
- Enables recruitment of diplomats
- Enables construction of "Fifth Tier" buildings

Wall-Class Buildings
Wooden Palisade (First Tier)

- Extra wall defenses

Wooden Wall (Second Tier)

- Extra wall defenses
- Reinforced gates

Stone Wall (Third Tier)

- Extra wall defenses
- Boiling oil
- Reinforced gates

Large Stone Wall (Fourth Tier)

- Extra wall defenses
- Iron gates
- Boiling oil

Epic Stone Wall (Fifth Tier)

- Extra wall defenses
- Iron gates
- Boiling oil

Barrack-Class Buildings

Barracks (First Tier)

- Enables training of Nubian Spearmen

Militia Barracks (Second Tier)

- Enables training of Nubian Spearmen
- Enables training of Nile Spearmen

City Barracks (Third Tier)

- Enables training of Nubian Spearmen
- Enables training of Desert Axemen
- Enables training of Nile Spearmen

Army Barracks (Fourth Tier)

- Enables training of Nubian Spearmen
- Enables training of Desert Axemen
- Enables training of Nile Spearmen
- Enables training of Pharaoh's Guards

Stable-Class Buildings

Stables (Second Tier)

- Enables training of Desert Cavalry

Cavalry Stables (Third Tier)

- Enables training of Desert Cavalry
- Enables training of Nubian Cavalry

Elite Cavalry Stables (Fourth Tier)

- Enables training of Desert Cavalry
- Enables training of Nubian Cavalry
- Enables training of Nile Cavalry
- Enables training of Camel Archers

Range-Class Buildings

Practice Range (Second Tier)

- Enables training of Skirmishers
- Enables training of Slingers

Archery Range (Third Tier)

- Enables training of Skirmishers
- Enables training of Slingers
- Enables training of Bowmen

Catapult Range (Fourth Tier)

- Enables training of Skirmishers
- Enables training of Slingers
- Enables training of Bowmen
- Enables training of Pharaoh's Bowmen
- Enables training of Onagers

Siege Engineer (Fifth Tier)

- Enables training of Skirmishers
- Enables training of Slingers
- Enables training of Bowmen
- Enables training of Pharaoh's Bowmen
- Enables training of Onagers
- Enables training of Heavy Onagers

Trader-Class Buildings

Trader (First Tier)

- Increase in tradable goods
- Population Growth bonus: 0.5%

Market (Second Tier)

- Increase in tradable goods
- Population Growth bonus: 0.5%
- Enables recruitment of spies

Bazaar (Third Tier)

- Increase in tradable goods
- Population Growth bonus: 0.5%
- Enables recruitment of spies
- Enables recruitment of assassins

Grand Bazaar (Fourth Tier)

- Increase in tradable goods
- Population Growth bonus: 1%
- Enables recruitment of spies
- Enables recruitment of assassins

Merchants' Quarter (Fifth Tier)

- Increase in tradable goods
- Population Growth bonus: 1%
- Enables recruitment of spies
- Enables recruitment of assassins
- Public Order bonus due to happiness: 10%

Smith-Class Buildings

Blacksmith (Second Tier)

- SPECIAL REQUIREMENT: Trader Building
- Upgrades light weapons +1
- Upgrades heavy weapons +1
- Enables training of Egyptian Chariots

Armourer (Third Tier)

- SPECIAL REQUIREMENT: Market Building
- Upgrades light weapons +1
- Upgrades heavy weapons +1
- Upgrades missile weapons +1
- Upgrades armor +1
- Enables training of Egyptian Chariots
- Enables training of Egyptian Chariot Archers

Foundry (Fifth Tier)

- SPECIAL REQUIREMENT: Grand Bazaar Building
- Upgrades light weapons +2
- Upgrades heavy weapons +2
- Upgrades missile weapons +2
- Upgrades armor +2
- Enables training of Egyptian Chariots
- Enables training of Egyptian Chariot Archers

Port-Class Buildings

Port (Second Tier)

- Grants one sea-trade fleet for extra income
- Enables training of Biremes

Shipwright (Third Tier)

- Grants two sea-trade fleets for extra income
- Enables training of Biremes
- Enables training of Triremes

Water Supply-Class Buildings

Sewers (Second Tier)

- SPECIAL REQUIREMENT: Trader Building
- Public health bonus: 5%

Public Baths (Third Tier)

- SPECIAL REQUIREMENT: Market Building
- Public health bonus: 10%

Farm-Class Buildings

Land Clearance (First Tier)

- Improved farms and food production: +1

Communal Farming (Second Tier)

- Improved farms and food production: +2

Crop Rotation (Third Tier)

- Improved farms and food production: +3

Irrigation (Fourth Tier)

- Improved farms and food production: +4

Great Estates (Fifth Tier)

- Improved farms and food production: +5

Roads

Roads (First Tier)

- Improved roads and trade

Paved Roads (Second Tier)

- Improved roads and trade

Academy-Class Buildings

Academy (Third Tier)

- SPECIAL REQUIREMENT: Market Building
- Governors gain skills and knowledge

Scriptorium (Fourth Tier)

- SPECIAL REQUIREMENT: Bazaar Building
- Governors gain skills and knowledge

Ludus Magna (Fifth Tier)

- SPECIAL REQUIREMENT: Grand Bazaar Building
- Governors gain skills and knowledge

Execution Square (Third Tier)

- Public Order bonus due to law: 5%

Secret Police HQ (Fourth Tier)

- Public Order bonus due to law: 10%

Secret Police Network (Fifth Tier)

- Public Order bonus due to law: 15%

Temple-Class Buildings

Shrine to Horus (First Tier)

- Public Order bonus due to happiness: 5%
- Public Order bonus due to law: 5%

Temple of Horus (Second Tier)

- Public Order bonus due to happiness: 10%
- Public Order bonus due to law: 10%

Large Temple of Horus (Third Tier)

- Public Order bonus due to happiness: 15%
- Public Order bonus due to law: 15%

Awesome Temple of Horus (Fourth Tier)

- Public Order bonus due to happiness: 20%
- Public Order bonus due to law: 20%

Temple City (Horus, Fifth Tier)

- Public Order bonus due to happiness: 25%
- Public Order bonus due to law: 25%
- Upgrades light weapons: +1
- Upgrades heavy weapons: +1
- Upgrades ARMOR: +1

Gaulish Military Units

Animal Units (Heavy)

Warhounds

STATS

SOLDIERS: 12	DEFENSE SKILL: 1
ATTACK: 14	SHIELD: 0
CHARGE BONUS: 4	HIT POINTS: 1
WEAPON TYPE: Light	RECRUITMENT COST: 570
TOTAL DEFENSE: 3	UPKEEP: 40
ARMOR: 2	

Warhounds are bred for a savage nature and great size, but then hunting men is only a little more dangerous than hunting wild boar!

ABILITIES

- Frighten nearby enemy
- Fast moving
- Combat bonus in woods or snow

Cavalry Units (Light)

Barbarian Cavalry

STATS

SOLDIERS: 27	DEFENSE SKILL: 3
ATTACK: 9	SHIELD: 4
CHARGE BONUS: 9	HIT POINTS: 1
WEAPON TYPE: Light	RECRUITMENT COST: 370
TOTAL DEFENSE: 10	UPKEEP: 90
ARMOR: 3	

Barbarian Cavalry are lightly armored and carry spears. They are best used as scouts and in pursuit of fleeing enemies.

ABILITIES

- Combat bonus in snow
- May charge without orders
- Can form wedge
- Powerful charge

Cavalry Units (Heavy)

Barbarian Noble Cavalry

STATS

SOLDIERS: 27	DEFENSE SKILL: 5
ATTACK: 10	SHIELD: 4
CHARGE BONUS: 10	HIT POINTS: 1
WEAPON TYPE: Light	RECRUITMENT COST: 530
TOTAL DEFENSE: 15	UPKEEP: 160
ARMOR: 6	

Noble Cavalry are an elite in society as well as war, and fight bravely to justify their status.

ABILITIES

- Combat bonus in snow
- Good morale
- Can form wedge
- Powerful charge
- May charge without orders

Infantry Units (Light)

Barbarian Peasants

STATS

SOLDIERS: 61	DEFENSE SKILL: 1
ATTACK: 1	SHIELD: 0
CHARGE BONUS: 1	HIT POINTS: 1
WEAPON TYPE: Light	RECRUITMENT COST: 150
TOTAL DEFENSE: 4	UPKEEP: 100
ARMOR: 3	

Peasants are reluctant warriors, but Barbarian Peasants are better fighters than most: hard lives produce hard men.

ABILITIES

- Warcry improves attack
- Combat bonus in woods or snow
- Expert at hiding in woods
- Poor morale

Druids

STATS

SOLDIERS: 16	DEFENSE SKILL: 5
ATTACK: 13	SHIELD: 2
CHARGE BONUS: 5	HIT POINTS: 1
WEAPON TYPE: Light	RECRUITMENT COST: 450
TOTAL DEFENSE: 14	UPKEEP: 90
ARMOR: 7	

Druids are spiritual leaders with practical fighting skills who instill confidence in nearby friendly warriors.

ABILITIES

- Chanting inspires nearby troops
- Excellent morale
- Expert at hiding in woods
- Very good stamina
- Combat bonus in woods or snow

Warband

STATS

SOLDIERS: 61	DEFENSE SKILL: 2
ATTACK: 7	SHIELD: 5
CHARGE BONUS: 7	HIT POINTS: 1
WEAPON TYPE: Light	RECRUITMENT COST: 420
TOTAL DEFENSE: 10	UPKEEP: 200
ARMOR: 3	

Warbands are bound to the service of a strongman or petty village head. They fight well as personal glory is the way to status, but are often difficult to control.

ABILITIES

- Warcry improves attack
- Combat bonus in woods or snow
- Expert at hiding in woods
- May charge without orders

Infantry Units (Heavy)

Chosen Swordsmen

STATS	
SOLDIERS: 41	DEFENSE SKILL: 5
ATTACK: 13	SHIELD: 5
CHARGE BONUS: 5	HIT POINTS: 1
WEAPON TYPE: Light	RECRUITMENT COST: 640
TOTAL DEFENSE: 17	UPKEEP: 210
ARMOR: 7	

Chosen Swordsmen are the best fighting individuals in their tribe, and armed with the finest swords available.

ABILITIES
- Warcry improves attack
- Expert at hiding in woods
- Combat bonus in woods or snow
- Excellent morale
- May charge without orders
- Good stamina

Naked Fanatics

STATS	
SOLDIERS: 40	DEFENSE SKILL: 2
ATTACK: 13	SHIELD: 5
CHARGE BONUS: 6	HIT POINTS: 1
WEAPON TYPE: Light	RECRUITMENT COST: 380
TOTAL DEFENSE: 7	UPKEEP: 130
ARMOR: 0	

Wild and savage, Naked Fanatics are always a threat but are at a disadvantage when fighting cavalry.

ABILITIES
- Warcry improves attack
- Expert at hiding in woods
- Combat bonus in woods or snow
- May charge without orders
- Good morale
- Good stamina

Swordsmen

STATS	
SOLDIERS: 41	DEFENSE SKILL: 4
ATTACK: 10	SHIELD: 5
CHARGE BONUS: 5	HIT POINTS: 1
WEAPON TYPE: Light	RECRUITMENT COST: 440
TOTAL DEFENSE: 12	UPKEEP: 170
ARMOR: 3	

Swordsmen are steadfast and aggressive warriors, the 'infantry of the line' for barbarian warlords.

ABILITIES
- Warcry improves attack
- Expert at hiding in woods
- Combat bonus in woods or snow
- May charge without orders
- Good morale

Infantry Units (Missile)

Forester Warband

STATS	
SOLDIERS: 40	ARMOR: 3
MELEE ATTACK: 11	DEFENSE SKILL: 5
MISSILE ATTACK: 15	SHIELD: 0
CHARGE BONUS: 2	HIT POINTS: 1
WEAPON TYPE: Missile	RECRUITMENT COST: 820
TOTAL DEFENSE: 8	UPKEEP: 200

A life spent hunting is an excellent training for war. Personal courage, skill and the readiness to take a life can all be learned during a hunt.

ABILITIES
- Can hide anywhere
- Combat bonus in woods or snow
- Long range missiles
- Excellent morale
- Can use Flaming Missiles
- Very good stamina
- Fast moving

Skirmisher Warband

STATS	
SOLDIERS: 40	ARMOR: 0
MELEE ATTACK: 6	DEFENSE SKILL: 1
MISSILE ATTACK: 9	SHIELD: 2
CHARGE BONUS: 4	HIT POINTS: 1
WEAPON TYPE: Missile	RECRUITMENT COST: 220
TOTAL DEFENSE: 3	UPKEEP: 130

Skirmishers rush forward to pepper an enemy with javelins, and then withdraw in good order before a counter-attack can be organized.

ABILITIES
- Can hide in long grass
- Bonus vs. elephants and chariots
- Combat bonus in woods or snow
- Fast moving

Gaulish Naval Units

Boats

VESSELS: 15	DEFENSE: 1
ATTACK: 6	

Large Boats

VESSELS: 30   DEFENSE: 3
ATTACK: 8

Gaulish Buildings

Government-Class Buildings

Warrior's Hold

- Enables training of Barbarian Peasants
- Enables construction of "First Tier" buildings

Warlord's Hold

- Enables training of Barbarian Peasants
- Enables recruitment of diplomats
- Enables construction of "Second Tier" buildings

High King's Hall

- Improved Generals' Bodyguards
- Enables training of Barbarian Peasants
- Enables recruitment of diplomats
- Enables construction of "Third Tier" buildings

Wall-Class Buildings

Wooden Palisade (First Tier)

- Extra wall defenses

Stockade (Second Tier)

- Extra wall defenses
- Reinforced gates

Barrack-Class Buildings

Muster Field (First Tier)

- Enables training of Warband

Meeting Hall (Second Tier)

- Enables training of Warband
- Enables training of Swordsmen

Hall of Heroes (Third Tier)

- Enables training of Warband
- Enables training of Swordsmen
- Enables training of Chosen Swordsmen

Stable-Class Buildings

Stables (Second Tier)

- Enables training of Barbarian Cavalry
- Enables training of Warhounds

Warlord's Stables (Third Tier)

- Enables training of Barbarian Cavalry
- Enables training of Warhounds
- Enables training of Barbarian Noble Cavalry

Range-Class Buildings

Practice Range (Second Tier)

- Enables training of Skirmisher Warband

Archery Range (Third Tier)

- Enables training of Skirmisher Warband
- Enables training of Forester Warband

Trader-Class Buildings

Trader (First Tier)

- Increase in tradable goods
- Population Growth bonus: 0.5%

Market (Second Tier)

- Increase in tradable goods
- Population Growth bonus: 0.5%
- Enables recruitment of spies

Great Market (Third Tier)

- Increase in tradable goods
- Population Growth bonus: 0.5%
- Enables recruitment of spies
- Enables recruitment of assassins

Smith-Class Buildings

Blacksmith (Second Tier)

- SPECIAL REQUIREMENT: Trader Building
- Upgrades light weapons: +1
- Upgrades heavy weapons: +1

Weaponsmith (Third Tier)

- SPECIAL REQUIREMENT: Market Building
- Upgrades light weapons: +1
- Upgrades heavy weapons: +1
- Upgrades missile weapons: +1
- Upgrades Armor: +1

Port-Class Buildings

Port (Second Tier)

- Grants one sea-trade fleet for extra income
- Enables training of Boats

Shipwright (Third Tier)

- Grants two sea-trade fleets for extra income
- Enables training of Boats
- Enables training of Large Boats

Farm-Class Buildings

Land Clearance (First Tier)

- Improved farms and food production: +1

Communal Farming (Second Tier)

- Improved farms and food production: +2

Roads

Roads (First Tier)

- Improved roads and trade

Tavern-Class Buildings

Tavern (Second Tier)

- Public Order bonus due to happiness: 5%

Bardic Circle (Third Tier)

- Public Order bonus due to happiness: 10%

Temple-Class Buildings

Shrine to Teutatis (First Tier)

- Public Order bonus due to happiness: 5%
- Experience bonus to troops trained here: +1

Sacred Grove of Teutatis (Second Tier)

- Public Order bonus due to happiness: 10%
- Upgrades light weapons: +1
- Experience bonus to troops

trained here: +1
- Enables training of Naked Fanatics

Sacred Circle of Teutatis (Third Tier)

- Public Order bonus due to happiness: 15%
- Upgrades light weapons: +1
- Experience bonus to troops

trained here: +2
- Enables training of Naked Fanatics (Experience 1)

Shrine to Epona (First Tier)

- Public Order bonus due to happiness: 5%
- Experience bonus to troops trained here: +1

Sacred Grove of Epona (Second Tier)

- Public Order bonus due to happiness: 10%
- Experience bonus to troops trained here: +2

Sacred Circle of Epona (Third Tier)

- Public Order bonus due to happiness: 15%
- Experience bonus to troops trained here: +3

Shrine to Abnoba (First Tier)

- Public Order bonus due to happiness: 5%
- Upgrades missile weapons: +1

Sacred Grove of Abnoba (Second Tier)

- Public Order bonus due to happiness: 10%
- Upgrades missile weapons: +2

Sacred Circle of Abnoba (Third Tier)

- Public Order bonus due to happiness: 15%
- Upgrades missile weapons: +3

Shrine to Esus (First Tier)

- Public Order bonus due to happiness: 5%
- Public Order bonus due to law: 5%

Sacred Grove of Esus (Second Tier)

- Public Order bonus due to happiness: 10%
- Public Order bonus due to law: 10%

Sacred Circle of Esus (Third Tier)

- Public Order bonus due to happiness: 15%
- Public Order bonus due to law: 15%
- Enables training of Druids

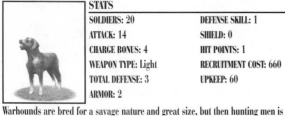

German Military Units

Animal Units (Heavy)

Warhounds

STATS

SOLDIERS: 20	DEFENSE SKILL: 1
ATTACK: 14	SHIELD: 0
CHARGE BONUS: 4	HIT POINTS: 1
WEAPON TYPE: Light	RECRUITMENT COST: 660
TOTAL DEFENSE: 3	UPKEEP: 60
ARMOR: 2	

Warhounds are bred for a savage nature and great size, but then hunting men is only a little more dangerous than hunting wild boar!

ABILITIES

- Frighten nearby enemy
- Fast moving
- Combat bonus in woods or snow

Cavalry Units (Light)

Barbarian Cavalry

STATS

SOLDIERS: 27	DEFENSE SKILL: 3
ATTACK: 9	SHIELD: 4
CHARGE BONUS: 9	HIT POINTS: 1
WEAPON TYPE: Light	RECRUITMENT COST: 370
TOTAL DEFENSE: 10	UPKEEP: 90
ARMOR: 3	

Barbarian Cavalry are lightly armored and carry spears. They are best used as scouts and in pursuit of fleeing enemies.

ABILITIES

- Combat bonus in snow
- May charge without orders
- Can form wedge
- Powerful charge

Cavalry Units (Heavy)

Barbarian Noble Cavalry

STATS

SOLDIERS: 27	DEFENSE SKILL: 5
ATTACK: 10	SHIELD: 4
CHARGE BONUS: 10	HIT POINTS: 1
WEAPON TYPE: Light	RECRUITMENT COST: 530
TOTAL DEFENSE: 15	UPKEEP: 160
ARMOR: 6	

Noble Cavalry are an elite in society as well as war, and fight bravely to justify their status.

ABILITIES

- Combat bonus in snow
- Good morale
- Can form wedge
- Powerful charge
- May charge without orders

Gothic Cavalry

STATS

SOLDIERS: 27	DEFENSE SKILL: 6
ATTACK: 13	SHIELD: 4
CHARGE BONUS: 10	HIT POINTS: 1
WEAPON TYPE: Light	RECRUITMENT COST: 700
TOTAL DEFENSE: 19	UPKEEP: 190
ARMOR: 9	

Gothic Cavalry are an aristocratic—if such a word can be applied to barbarians - heavy cavalry elite of the German tribes.

ABILITIES

- Combat bonus in snow
- May charge without orders
- Excellent morale
- Powerful charge
- Can form wedge

Infantry Units (Light)

Barbarian Peasants

STATS

SOLDIERS: 61	DEFENSE SKILL: 1
ATTACK: 1	SHIELD: 0
CHARGE BONUS: 1	HIT POINTS: 1
WEAPON TYPE: Light	RECRUITMENT COST: 150
TOTAL DEFENSE: 4	UPKEEP: 100
ARMOR: 3	

Peasants are reluctant warriors, but Barbarian Peasants are better fighters than most: hard lives produce hard men.

ABILITIES

- Warcry improves attack
- Combat bonus in woods or snow
- Expert at hiding in woods
- Poor morale

Berserkers

STATS

SOLDIERS: 12	DEFENSE SKILL: 5
ATTACK: 19	SHIELD: 0
CHARGE BONUS: 8	HIT POINTS: 3
WEAPON TYPE: Heavy	RECRUITMENT COST: 760
TOTAL DEFENSE: 5	UPKEEP: 120
ARMOR: 0	

Berserkers are extremely ferocious, aggressive, indomitable warriors with no thought for personal safety once the rage of battle comes upon them.

ABILITIES

- Warcry improves attack
- May charge without orders
- Combat bonus in woods or snow
- Powerful charge
- Frighten nearby enemy infantry
- Very good stamina
- Excellent morale

Screeching Women

STATS

SOLDIERS: 40	DEFENSE SKILL: 1
ATTACK: 11	SHIELD: 0
CHARGE BONUS: 7	HIT POINTS: 1
WEAPON TYPE: Heavy	RECRUITMENT COST: 310
TOTAL DEFENSE: 1	UPKEEP: 130
ARMOR: 0	

German Screeching Women think nothing of participating in a battle, wailing encouragement to their own men as they fight, and screaming defiance at the enemy to unnerve them.

ABILITIES

- Screeching dismays enemy
- Expert at hiding in woods
- Combat bonus in woods or snow
- Good morale

Infantry Units (Heavy)

Axemen

STATS

SOLDIERS: 41	DEFENSE SKILL: 4
ATTACK: 11	SHIELD: 2
CHARGE BONUS: 7	HIT POINTS: 1
WEAPON TYPE: Heavy	RECRUITMENT COST: 430
TOTAL DEFENSE: 9	UPKEEP: 170
ARMOR: 3	

Axemen are steadfast and aggressive warriors, the 'infantry of the line' for barbarian warlords.

ABILITIES

- Warcry improves attack
- Expert at hiding in woods
- Combat bonus in woods or snow
- May charge without orders
- Good morale

Chosen Axemen

STATS

SOLDIERS: 41	DEFENSE SKILL: 6
ATTACK: 18	SHIELD: 0
CHARGE BONUS: 9	HIT POINTS: 1
WEAPON TYPE: Heavy	RECRUITMENT COST: 520
TOTAL DEFENSE: 6	UPKEEP: 200
ARMOR: 0	

Double-handed axes are intimidating weapons, especially in the hands of Chosen Axemen. These men can hack a hole in almost any enemy battle line.

ABILITIES

- Warcry improves attack
- Expert at hiding in woods
- Effective against armor
- Combat bonus in woods or snow
- Excellent morale
- May charge without orders
- Powerful charge

Naked Fanatics

STATS

SOLDIERS: 40	DEFENSE SKILL: 2
ATTACK: 13	SHIELD: 5
CHARGE BONUS: 6	HIT POINTS: 1
WEAPON TYPE: Light	RECRUITMENT COST: 380
TOTAL DEFENSE: 7	UPKEEP: 130
ARMOR: 0	

Wild and savage, Naked Fanatics are always a threat but are at a disadvantage when fighting cavalry.

ABILITIES

- Warcry improves attack
- Expert at hiding in woods
- Combat bonus in woods or snow
- May charge without orders
- Good morale
- Good stamina

Night Raiders

STATS

SOLDIERS: 40	DEFENSE SKILL: 2
ATTACK: 14	SHIELD: 5
CHARGE BONUS: 8	HIT POINTS: 1
WEAPON TYPE: Heavy	RECRUITMENT COST: 500
TOTAL DEFENSE: 10	UPKEEP: 130
ARMOR: 3	

Night Raiders are lightly armed shock troops whose appearance alone is fearful!

ABILITIES

- Warcry improves attack
- Combat bonus in woods or snow
- Frighten nearby enemy infantry
- May charge without orders
- Good morale
- Powerful charge
- Good stamina

Infantry Units (Missile)

Chosen Archer Warband

STATS

SOLDIERS: 41	ARMOR: 7
MELEE ATTACK: 10	DEFENSE SKILL: 4
MISSILE ATTACK: 12	SHIELD: 0
CHARGE BONUS: 5	HIT POINTS: 1
WEAPON TYPE: Missile	RECRUITMENT COST: 600
TOTAL DEFENSE: 11	UPKEEP: 180

Chosen Archers are highly prized for their superior skills in war. They are the best archers available to barbarian warlords.

ABILITIES

- Expert at hiding in woods
- Combat bonus in woods or snow
- Long range missiles
- Can use Flaming Missiles
- Good morale
- Good stamina

Skirmisher Warband

STATS

SOLDIERS: 40	ARMOR: 0
MELEE ATTACK: 6	DEFENSE SKILL: 1
MISSILE ATTACK: 9	SHIELD: 2
CHARGE BONUS: 4	HIT POINTS: 1
WEAPON TYPE: Missile	RECRUITMENT COST: 220
TOTAL DEFENSE: 3	UPKEEP: 130

Skirmishers rush forward to pepper an enemy with javelins, and then withdraw in good order before a counter-attack can be organized.

ABILITIES

- Can hide in long grass
- Bonus vs. elephants and chariots
- Combat bonus in woods or snow
- Fast moving

Spearmen

Spear Warband

STATS

SOLDIERS: 61	DEFENSE SKILL: 3
ATTACK: 8	SHIELD: 5
CHARGE BONUS: 8	HIT POINTS: 1
WEAPON TYPE: Light	RECRUITMENT COST: 570
TOTAL DEFENSE: 11	UPKEEP: 200
ARMOR: 3	

The men of a Spear Warband are effective against cavalry and most infantry, but lack the discipline of more 'civilized' troops.

ABILITIES

- Can form phalanx
- Expert at hiding in woods
- Bonus fighting cavalry
- Combat bonus in woods or snow
- May charge without orders
- Powerful charge

German Naval Units

Boats

VESSELS: 15	DEFENSE: 1
ATTACK: 6	

Large Boats

VESSELS: 30	DEFENSE: 3
ATTACK: 8	

German Buildings

Government-Class Buildings

Warrior's Hold

- Enables training of Barbarian Peasants
- Enables construction of "First Tier" buildings

Warlord's Hold

- Enables training of Barbarian Peasants
- Enables recruitment of diplomats
- Enables construction of "Second Tier" buildings

High King's Hall

- Improved Generals' Bodyguards
- Enables training of Barbarian Peasants
- Enables recruitment of diplomats
- Enables construction of "Third Tier" buildings

Wall-Class Buildings

Wooden Palisade (First Tier)

- Extra wall defenses

Stockade (Second Tier)

- Extra wall defenses
- Reinforced gates

Barrack-Class Buildings

Muster Field (First Tier)

- Enables training of Spear Warband

Meeting Hall (Second Tier)

- Enables training of Spear Warband
- Enables training of Axemen

Hall of Heroes (Third Tier)

- Enables training of Spear Warband
- Enables training of Axemen
- Enables training of Chosen Axemen

Stable-Class Buildings

Stables (Second Tier)

- Enables training of Barbarian Cavalry
- Enables training of Warhounds

Warlord's Stables (Third Tier)

- Enables training of Barbarian Cavalry
- Enables training of Warhounds
- Enables training of Barbarian Noble Cavalry

Range-Class Buildings

Practice Range (Second Tier)

- Enables training of Skirmisher Warband

Archery Range (Third Tier)

- Enables training of Skirmisher Warband
- Enables training of Chosen Archer Warband

Trader-Class Buildings

Trader (First Tier)

- Increase in tradable goods
- Population Growth bonus: 0.5%

Market (Second Tier)

- Increase in tradable goods
- Population Growth bonus: 0.5%
- Enables recruitment of spies

Great Market (Third Tier)

- Increase in tradable goods
- Population Growth bonus: 0.5%
- Enables recruitment of spies
- Enables recruitment of assassins

Smith-Class Buildings

Blacksmith (Second Tier)

- SPECIAL REQUIREMENT: Trader Building
- Upgrades light weapons: +1
- Upgrades heavy weapons: +1

Weaponsmith (Third Tier)

- SPECIAL REQUIREMENT: Market Building
- Upgrades light weapons: +1
- Upgrades heavy weapons: +1
- Upgrades missile weapons: +1
- Upgrades ARMOR: +1

Port-Class Buildings

Port (Second Tier)

- Grants one sea-trade fleet for extra income
- Enables training of Boats

Shipwright (Third Tier)

- Grants two sea-trade fleets for extra income
- Enables training of Boats
- Enables training of Large Boats

Farm-Class Buildings

Land Clearance (First Tier)

- Improved farms and food production: +1

Communal Farming (Second Tier)

- Improved farms and food production: +2

Roads

Roads (First Tier)

- Improved roads and trade

Tavern-Class Buildings

Tavern (Second Tier)

- Public Order bonus due to happiness: 5%

Bardic Circle (Third Tier)

- Public Order bonus due to happiness: 10%
- Enables training of Night Raiders

Temple-Class Buildings

Shrine to Freyja (First Tier)

- Public Order bonus due to happiness: 5%
- Population Growth bonus: 0.5%
- Enables training of Screeching Women

Sacred Grove of Freyja (Second Tier)

- Public Order bonus due to happiness: 10%
- Population Growth bonus: 1%
- Enables training of Screeching Women

Sacred Circle of Freyja (Third Tier)

- Public Order bonus due to happiness: 15%
- Population Growth bonus: 1.5%
- Enables training of Screeching Women

Shrine to Donar (First Tier)

- Public Order bonus due to happiness: 5%

Sacred Grove of Donar (Second Tier)

- Public Order bonus due to happiness: 10%
- Experience bonus to troops trained here: +1

Sacred Circle of Donar (Third Tier)

- Public Order bonus due to happiness: 15%
- Experience bonus to troops trained here: +2
- Enables training of Berserkers

Shrine to Woden (First Tier)

- Public Order bonus due to happiness: 5%
- Experience bonus to troops trained here: +1

Sacred Grove of Woden (Second Tier)

- Public Order bonus due to happiness: 10%
- Experience bonus to troops trained here: +2
- Enables training of Naked Fanatics

Sacred Circle of Woden (Third Tier)

- Public Order bonus due to happiness: 15%
- Experience bonus to troops trained here: +3
- Enables training of Naked Fanatics
- Enables training of Gothic Cavalry

Greek Military Units

Animal Units (Incendiary Pigs)

Incendiary Pigs

STATS		
SOLDIERS: 12	DEFENSE SKILL: 1	
ATTACK: 7	SHIELD: 0	
CHARGE BONUS: 2	HIT POINTS: 1	
WEAPON TYPE: Light	RECRUITMENT COST: 140	
TOTAL DEFENSE: 1	UPKEEP: 60	
ARMOR: 0		

Incendiary Pigs are 'one shot' weapons intended to spread panic and terror amongst enemies, particularly elephants.

ABILITIES

- Frighten elephants
- Fast moving

Artillery Units

Ballistas

STATS		
SOLDIERS: 24	ARMOR: 0	
ATTACK VS. TROOPS: 53	DEFENSE SKILL: 3	
ATTACK VS. BUILDINGS: 12	SHIELD: 0	
CHARGE BONUS: 0	HIT POINTS: 1	
WEAPON TYPE: Light	RECRUITMENT COST: 410	
TOTAL DEFENSE: 3	UPKEEP: 150	

A Ballista is a sinew-powered weapon that looks like an enormous crossbow. It has tremendous range and can skewer files of men with a single bolt!

ABILITIES

- Missiles can impale several men
- Long range missiles
- Can use Flaming Missiles
- Can't hide

Heavy Onagers

STATS		
SOLDIERS: 32	ARMOR: 0	
ATTACK VS. TROOPS: 63	DEFENSE SKILL: 3	
ATTACK VS. BUILDINGS: 55	SHIELD: 0	
CHARGE BONUS: 0	HIT POINTS: 1	
WEAPON TYPE: Light	RECRUITMENT COST: 1830	
TOTAL DEFENSE: 3	UPKEEP: 180	

The Heavy Onager is a siege engine capable of reducing even stone ramparts to rubble, but can be vulnerable to enemy catapults.

ABILITIES

- Area attack
- Very long range missiles
- Can use Flaming Missiles
- Can't hide
- Inaccurate against troops

Onagers

STATS		
SOLDIERS: 32	ARMOR: 0	
ATTACK VS. TROOPS: 53	DEFENSE SKILL: 3	
ATTACK VS. BUILDINGS: 35	SHIELD: 0	
CHARGE BONUS: 0	HIT POINTS: 1	
WEAPON TYPE: Light	RECRUITMENT COST: 1390	
TOTAL DEFENSE: 3	UPKEEP: 180	

The Onager is a versatile catapult that can launch boulders or incendiary firepots at enemy troops and fortifications.

ABILITIES

- Area attack
- Very long range missiles
- Can use Flaming Missiles
- Can't hide
- Inaccurate against troops

Cavalry Units (Light)

Greek Cavalry

STATS		
SOLDIERS: 27	DEFENSE SKILL: 5	
ATTACK: 7	SHIELD: 0	
CHARGE BONUS: 7	HIT POINTS: 1	
WEAPON TYPE: Light	RECRUITMENT COST: 300	
TOTAL DEFENSE: 8	UPKEEP: 110	
ARMOR: 3		

Greek Cavalry are fast moving horsemen armed with spears for maximum impact in a charge.

ABILITIES

- Can form wedge

Cavalry Units (Missile)

Militia Cavalry

STATS		
SOLDIERS: 27	ARMOR: 0	
MELEE ATTACK: 6	DEFENSE SKILL: 2	
MISSILE ATTACK: 6	SHIELD: 4	
CHARGE BONUS: 2	HIT POINTS: 1	
WEAPON TYPE: Missile	RECRUITMENT COST: 320	
TOTAL DEFENSE: 6	UPKEEP: 110	

Militia cavalry are javelin-armed mounted skirmishers who can strike quickly and be gone before the enemy reacts.

ABILITIES

- Can form Cantabrian circle
- Fast moving

Infantry Units (Light)

Peasants

STATS

SOLDIERS: 61	DEFENSE SKILL: 1
ATTACK: 1	SHIELD: 0
CHARGE BONUS: 1	HIT POINTS: 1
WEAPON TYPE: Light	RECRUITMENT COST: 60
TOTAL DEFENSE: 1	UPKEEP: 100
ARMOR: 0	

Peasants are reluctant warriors, at best. Going to war is just one more burden of a hard life.

ABILITIES

- Poor morale
- Can sap

Infantry Units (Missile)

Archers

STATS

SOLDIERS: 40	ARMOR: 0
MELEE ATTACK: 3	DEFENSE SKILL: 2
MISSILE ATTACK: 7	SHIELD: 0
CHARGE BONUS: 2	HIT POINTS: 1
WEAPON TYPE: Missile	RECRUITMENT COST: 180
TOTAL DEFENSE: 2	UPKEEP: 170

Archers are rightly feared for the casualties they can inflict, but they are vulnerable in hand-to-hand combat.

ABILITIES

- Combat bonus in woods
- Fast moving
- Can use Flaming Missiles
- Can sap

Heavy Peltasts

STATS

SOLDIERS: 40	ARMOR: 3
MELEE ATTACK: 5	DEFENSE SKILL: 3
MISSILE ATTACK: 7	SHIELD: 5
CHARGE BONUS: 2	HIT POINTS: 1
WEAPON TYPE: Missile	RECRUITMENT COST: 350
TOTAL DEFENSE: 11	UPKEEP: 170

A combination of protection and mobility make Heavy Peltasts suitable for skirmishing duties as well as for taking a stand as part of the main battle line.

ABILITIES

- Can hide in long grass
- Fast moving
- Bonus vs. elephants and chariots
- Can sap
- Combat bonus in woods

Peltasts

STATS

SOLDIERS: 40	ARMOR: 0
MELEE ATTACK: 3	DEFENSE SKILL: 2
MISSILE ATTACK: 6	SHIELD: 2
CHARGE BONUS: 2	HIT POINTS: 1
WEAPON TYPE: Missile	RECRUITMENT COST: 180
TOTAL DEFENSE: 4	UPKEEP: 170

Greek Peltasts advance at speed to pepper an enemy with javelins, and then withdraw in good order before a counter-attack can be organized.

ABILITIES

- Can hide in long grass
- Fast moving
- Bonus vs. elephants and chariots
- Can sap
- Combat bonus in woods

Spearmen

Armored Hoplites

STATS

SOLDIERS: 41	DEFENSE SKILL: 6
ATTACK: 9	SHIELD: 5
CHARGE BONUS: 7	HIT POINTS: 1
WEAPON TYPE: Light	RECRUITMENT COST: 680
TOTAL DEFENSE: 22	UPKEEP: 210
ARMOR: 11	

Armored Hoplites are an elite among Greek soldiery, carefully selected and given the best training to make them superior spearmen.

ABILITIES

- Can form phalanx
- Good stamina
- Bonus fighting cavalry
- Can sap
- Good morale

Hoplites

STATS

SOLDIERS: 40	DEFENSE SKILL: 5
ATTACK: 7	SHIELD: 5
CHARGE BONUS: 6	HIT POINTS: 1
WEAPON TYPE: Light	RECRUITMENT COST: 480
TOTAL DEFENSE: 16	UPKEEP: 170
ARMOR: 6	

Hoplites are well equipped infantry that are most effective in the formidable, if slightly inflexible, phalanx formation.

ABILITIES

- Can form phalanx
- Can sap
- Bonus fighting cavalry

Militia Hoplites

STATS

SOLDIERS: 40	DEFENSE SKILL: 3
ATTACK: 5	SHIELD: 5
CHARGE BONUS: 5	HIT POINTS: 1
WEAPON TYPE: Light	RECRUITMENT COST: 280
TOTAL DEFENSE: 8	UPKEEP: 100
ARMOR: 0	

Militia Hoplites are levies drawn from cities and thrust into battle with a little training.

ABILITIES

- Can form phalanx
- Bonus fighting cavalry
- Poor morale
- Can sap

Spartan Hoplites

STATS

SOLDIERS: 40	DEFENSE SKILL: 9
ATTACK: 16	SHIELD: 5
CHARGE BONUS: 8	HIT POINTS: 2
WEAPON TYPE: Light	RECRUITMENT COST: 1270
TOTAL DEFENSE: 17	UPKEEP: 460
ARMOR: 3	

Spartan Hoplites are trained from infancy to be nothing but soldiers. They are 'perfect soldiers' and nothing else.

ABILITIES

- Can form phalanx
- Bonus fighting cavalry
- Excellent morale
- Powerful charge
- Very good stamina
- Can sap

Greek Naval Units

Bireme

VESSELS: 20 ATTACK: 6 DEFENSE: 2

Trireme

VESSELS: 30 ATTACK: 8 DEFENSE: 3

Quinquireme

VESSELS: 50 ATTACK: 10 DEFENSE: 5

Greek Buildings

Government-Class Buildings

Governor's House

- Enables training of Peasants
- Enables construction of "First Tier" buildings

Governor's Villa

- Enables training of Peasants
- Enables recruitment of diplomats
- Enables construction of "Second Tier" buildings

Governor's Palace

- Enables training of Peasants
- Enables recruitment of diplomats
- Enables construction of "Third Tier" buildings

Councilor's Chambers

- Enables training of Peasants
- Enables recruitment of diplomats
- Enables construction of "Fourth Tier" buildings

Royal Palace • Improved Generals' Bodyguards

- Enables training of Peasants
- Enables training of Praetorian Cohort
- Enables recruitment of diplomats
- Enables construction of "Fifth Tier" buildings

Wall-Class Buildings

Wooden Palisade (First Tier)

- Extra wall defenses

Wooden Wall (Second Tier)

- Extra wall defenses
- Reinforced gates

Stone Wall (Third Tier)

- Extra wall defenses
- Reinforced gates
- Boiling oil

Large Stone Wall (Fourth Tier)

- Extra wall defenses
- Boiling oil
- Iron gates

Epic Stone Wall (Fifth Tier)

- Extra wall defenses
- Boiling oil
- Iron gates

Barrack-Class Buildings

Barracks (First Tier)

- Enables training of Militia Hoplites

Militia Barracks (Second Tier)

- Enables training of Militia Hoplites
- Enables training of Hoplites

City Barracks (Third Tier)

- Enables training of Militia Hoplites
- Enables training of Hoplites
- Enables training of Armored Hoplites

Army Barracks (Fourth Tier)

- Enables training of Militia Hoplites
- Enables training of Hoplites (Experience 1)
- Enables training of Armored Hoplites
- Enables training of Spartan Hoplites

Stable-Class Buildings

Stables (Second Tier)

- Enables training of Militia Cavalry

Cavalry Stables (Third Tier)

- Enables training of Militia Cavalry
- Enables training of Greek Cavalry

Elite Cavalry Stables (Fourth Tier)

- Enables training of Militia Cavalry
- Enables training of Greek Cavalry
- Enables training of Incendiary Pigs

Range-Class Buildings

Practice Range (Second Tier)

- Enables training of Peltasts

Archery Range (Third Tier)

- Enables training of Peltasts
- Enables training of Archers
- Enables training of Ballistae

Catapult Range (Fourth Tier)

- Enables training of Peltasts
- Enables training of Archers
- Enables training of Ballistae
- Enables training of Heavy Peltasts
- Enables training of Onagers

Siege Engineer (Fifth Tier)

- Enables training of Peltasts
- Enables training of Archers
- Enables training of Ballistae
- Enables training of Heavy Peltasts
- Enables training of Onagers
- Enables training of Heavy Onagers

Trader-Class Buildings

Trader (First Tier)

- Increase in tradable goods
- Population Growth bonus: 0.5%

Market (Second Tier)

- Increase in tradable goods
- Population Growth bonus: 0.5%
- Enables recruitment of spies

Agora (Third Tier)

- Increase in tradable goods
- Population Growth bonus: 0.5%
- Enables recruitment of spies
- Enables recruitment of assassins

Great Agora (Fourth Tier)

- Increase in tradable goods
- Population Growth bonus: 1%
- Enables recruitment of spies
- Enables recruitment of assassins

Merchants' Quarter (Fifth Tier)

- Increase in tradable goods
- Population Growth bonus: 1%
- Enables recruitment of spies
- Enables recruitment of assassins
- Public Order bonus due to happiness: 10%

Smith-Class Buildings

Blacksmith (Second Tier)

- SPECIAL REQUIREMENT: Trader Building
- Upgrades light weapons: +1
- Upgrades heavy weapons: +1

Armourer (Third Tier)

- SPECIAL REQUIREMENT: Market Building
- Upgrades light weapons: +1
- Upgrades heavy weapons: +1
- Upgrades missile weapons: +1
- Upgrades Armor: +1

Foundry (Fifth Tier)

- SPECIAL REQUIREMENT: Great Agora Building
- Upgrades light weapons +2
- Upgrades heavy weapons +2
- Upgrades missile weapons +2
- Upgrades armor +2

Port-Class Buildings

Port (Second Tier)

- Grants one sea-trade fleet for extra income
- Enables training of Biremes

Shipwright (Third Tier)

- Grants two sea-trade fleets for extra income
- Enables training of Biremes
- Enables training of Triremes

Dockyard (Fourth Tier)

- Grants three sea-trade fleets for extra income
- Enables training of Biremes
- Enables training of Triremes
- Enables training of Quinquiremes

Water Supply-Class Buildings

Sewers (Second Tier)

- SPECIAL REQUIREMENT: Trader Building
- Public health bonus: 5%

Public Baths (Third Tier)

- SPECIAL REQUIREMENT: Market Building
- Public health bonus: 10%

Aqueduct (Fourth Tier)

- SPECIAL REQUIREMENT: Forum Building
- Public health bonus: 15%

Farm-Class Buildings

Land Clearance (First Tier)

- Improved farms and food production: +1

Communal Farming (Second Tier)

- Improved farms and food production: +2

Crop Rotation (Third Tier)

- Improved farms and food production: +3

Irrigation (Fourth Tier)

- Improved farms and food production: +4

Roads

Roads (First Tier)

- Improved roads and trade

Paved Roads (Second Tier)

- Improved roads and trade

Academy-Class Buildings

Academy (Third Tier)

- SPECIAL REQUIREMENT: Market Building
- Governors gain skills and knowledge

Scriptorium (Fourth Tier)

- SPECIAL REQUIREMENT: Agora Building
- Governors gain skills and knowledge

Ludus Magna (Fifth Tier)

- SPECIAL REQUIREMENT: Great Agora Building
- Governors gain skills and knowledge

Theater-Class Buildings

Odeon (Third Tier)

- Public Order bonus due to happiness: 5%

Lyceum (Fourth Tier)

- Public Order bonus due to happiness: 10%

Theater (Fifth Tier)

- Public Order bonus due to happiness: 15%

Temple-Class Buildings

Shrine to Nike (First Tier)

- Public Order bonus due to happiness: 5%

Temple of Nike (Second Tier)

- Public Order bonus due to happiness: 10%
- Experience bonus to troops trained here: +1

Large Temple of Nike (Third Tier)

- Public Order bonus due to happiness: 15%
- Experience bonus to troops trained here: +2

Awesome Temple of Nike (Fourth Tier)

- Public Order bonus due to happiness: 20%
- Experience bonus to troops trained here: +3

Pantheon of Nike (Fifth Tier)

- Public Order bonus due to happiness: 25%
- Experience bonus to troops trained here: +3
- Population Growth bonus: 1%
- Public Order bonus due to law: 10%
- Increase in tradable goods

Macedonian Military Units

Artillery Units

Ballistae

STATS	
SOLDIERS: 24	ARMOR: 0
ATTACK VS. TROOPS: 53	DEFENSE SKILL: 3
ATTACK VS. BUILDINGS: 12	SHIELD: 0
CHARGE BONUS: 0	HIT POINTS: 1
WEAPON TYPE: Light	RECRUITMENT COST: 410
TOTAL DEFENSE: 3	UPKEEP: 150

A Ballista is a sinew-powered weapon that looks like an enormous crossbow. It has tremendous range and can skewer files of men with a single bolt!

ABILITIES

- Missiles can impale several men
- Long range missiles
- Can use Flaming Missiles
- Can't hide

Heavy Onagers

STATS	
SOLDIERS: 32	ARMOR: 0
ATTACK VS. TROOPS: 63	DEFENSE SKILL: 3
ATTACK VS. BUILDINGS: 55	SHIELD: 0
CHARGE BONUS: 0	HIT POINTS: 1
WEAPON TYPE: Light	RECRUITMENT COST: 1830
TOTAL DEFENSE: 3	UPKEEP: 180

The Heavy Onager is a siege engine capable of reducing even stone ramparts to rubble, but can be vulnerable to enemy catapults.

ABILITIES

- Area attack
- Very long range missiles
- Can use Flaming Missiles
- Can't hide
- Inaccurate against troops

Onagers

STATS	
SOLDIERS: 32	ARMOR: 0
ATTACK VS. TROOPS: 53	DEFENSE SKILL: 3
ATTACK VS. BUILDINGS: 35	SHIELD: 0
CHARGE BONUS: 0	HIT POINTS: 1
WEAPON TYPE: Light	RECRUITMENT COST: 1390
TOTAL DEFENSE: 3	UPKEEP: 180

The Onager is a versatile catapult that can launch boulders or incendiary firepots at enemy troops and fortifications.

ABILITIES

- Area attack
- Very long range missiles
- Can use Flaming Missiles
- Can't hide
- Inaccurate against troops

Cavalry Units (Light)

Greek Cavalry

STATS

SOLDIERS: 27	DEFENSE SKILL: 5
ATTACK: 7	SHIELD: 0
CHARGE BONUS: 7	HIT POINTS: 1
WEAPON TYPE: Light	RECRUITMENT COST: 300
TOTAL DEFENSE: 8	UPKEEP: 110
ARMOR: 3	

Greek Cavalry are fast moving horsemen armed with spears for maximum impact in a charge.

ABILITIES

- Can form wedge

Light Lancers

STATS

SOLDIERS: 27	DEFENSE SKILL: 5
ATTACK: 7	SHIELD: 0
CHARGE BONUS: 15	HIT POINTS: 1
WEAPON TYPE: Heavy	RECRUITMENT COST: 330
TOTAL DEFENSE: 5	UPKEEP: 140
ARMOR: 0	

Light Lancers are fast, lightly-equipped cavalrymen who rely on hit-and-run charges where the killing power of their lances is maximized.

ABILITIES

- Can form wedge
- Good morale
- Powerful charge
- Fast moving

Cavalry Units (Heavy)

Companion Cavalry

STATS

SOLDIERS: 27	DEFENSE SKILL: 6
ATTACK: 10	SHIELD: 0
CHARGE BONUS: 16	HIT POINTS: 1
WEAPON TYPE: Heavy	RECRUITMENT COST: 690
TOTAL DEFENSE: 17	UPKEEP: 240
ARMOR: 11	

Companion Cavalry are a social and military elite, and fight as heavy cavalry using shock and mass to break enemy units.

ABILITIES

- Can form wedge
- Good morale
- Powerful charge
- Good stamina

Macedonian Cavalry

STATS

SOLDIERS: 27	DEFENSE SKILL: 6
ATTACK: 9	SHIELD: 0
CHARGE BONUS: 8	HIT POINTS: 1
WEAPON TYPE: Light	RECRUITMENT COST: 630
TOTAL DEFENSE: 17	UPKEEP: 140
ARMOR: 11	

Macedonian Cavalry are armored spear-armed horsemen capable of delivering a decisive blow.

ABILITIES

- Can form wedge
- Good morale
- Powerful charge
- Good stamina

Infantry Units (Light)

Peasants

STATS

SOLDIERS: 61	DEFENSE SKILL: 1
ATTACK: 1	SHIELD: 0
CHARGE BONUS: 1	HIT POINTS: 1
WEAPON TYPE: Light	RECRUITMENT COST: 60
TOTAL DEFENSE: 1	UPKEEP: 100
ARMOR: 0	

Peasants are reluctant warriors, at best. Going to war is just one more burden of a hard life.

ABILITIES

- Poor morale
- Can sap

Infantry Units (Missile)

Archers

STATS

SOLDIERS: 40	ARMOR: 0
MELEE ATTACK: 3	DEFENSE SKILL: 2
MISSILE ATTACK: 7	SHIELD: 0
CHARGE BONUS: 2	HIT POINTS: 1
WEAPON TYPE: Missile	RECRUITMENT COST: 180
TOTAL DEFENSE: 2	UPKEEP: 170

Archers are rightly feared for the casualties they can inflict, but they are vulnerable in hand-to-hand combat.

ABILITIES

- Combat bonus in woods
- Can use Flaming Missiles
- Fast moving
- Can sap

Peltasts

STATS

SOLDIERS: 40	ARMOR: 0
MELEE ATTACK: 3	DEFENSE SKILL: 2
MISSILE ATTACK: 6	SHIELD: 2
CHARGE BONUS: 2	HIT POINTS: 1
WEAPON TYPE: Missile	RECRUITMENT COST: 180
TOTAL DEFENSE: 4	UPKEEP: 170

Macedonian Peltasts advance at speed to pepper an enemy with javelins, and then withdraw in good order before a counter-attack can be organized.

ABILITIES

- Can hide in long grass
- Bonus vs. elephants and chariots
- Combat bonus in woods
- Fast moving
- Can sap

Spearmen

Levy Pikemen

STATS

SOLDIERS: 60	DEFENSE SKILL: 3
ATTACK: 6	SHIELD: 2
CHARGE BONUS: 5	HIT POINTS: 1
WEAPON TYPE: Heavy	RECRUITMENT COST: 390
TOTAL DEFENSE: 5	UPKEEP: 150
ARMOR: 0	

Levy Pikemen are best used as defensive infantry, but their lack of armor leaves them vulnerable in battle.

ABILITIES

- Can form phalanx
- Bonus fighting cavalry
- Poor morale
- Very long spears
- Can sap

Militia Hoplites

STATS

SOLDIERS: 40	DEFENSE SKILL: 3
ATTACK: 5	SHIELD: 5
CHARGE BONUS: 5	HIT POINTS: 1
WEAPON TYPE: Light	RECRUITMENT COST: 280
TOTAL DEFENSE: 8	UPKEEP: 100
ARMOR: 0	

Militia Hoplites are levies drawn from cities and thrust into battle with a little training.

ABILITIES

- Can form phalanx
- Bonus fighting cavalry
- Poor morale
- Can sap

Phalanx Pikemen

STATS

SOLDIERS: 60	DEFENSE SKILL: 5
ATTACK: 8	SHIELD: 2
CHARGE BONUS: 6	HIT POINTS: 1
WEAPON TYPE: Heavy	RECRUITMENT COST: 660
TOTAL DEFENSE: 13	UPKEEP: 250
ARMOR: 6	

Phalanx Pikemen form the backbone of Macedonian and Seleucid battle lines, and are used to engage and hold the enemy's main force.

ABILITIES

- Can form phalanx
- Bonus fighting cavalry
- Very long spears
- Can sap

Royal Pikemen

STATS

SOLDIERS: 61	DEFENSE SKILL: 6
ATTACK: 9	SHIELD: 5
CHARGE BONUS: 7	HIT POINTS: 1
WEAPON TYPE: Light	RECRUITMENT COST: 740
TOTAL DEFENSE: 17	UPKEEP: 360
ARMOR: 6	

Well disciplined, led by high-ranking officers and carrying large shields, Royal Pikemen are the bulwark of the Macedonian battle line.

ABILITIES

- Can form phalanx
- Bonus fighting cavalry
- Good morale
- Good stamina
- Can sap

Macedonian Naval Units

Bireme

VESSELS: 20	DEFENSE: 2
ATTACK: 6	

Trireme

VESSELS: 30   **DEFENSE:** 3
ATTACK: 8

Quinquireme

VESSELS: 50   **DEFENSE:** 5
ATTACK: 10

NOTE

You cannot play as the Macedonians in the Imperial Campaign mode, so their buildings are not listed in this guide.

Mercenary Units

NOTE

Mercenaries aren't a faction in and of themselves. They're units that can be hired by Generals in the Imperial Campaign mode. For details, please see the Field Recruitment section of Chapter IV: Imperial Campaign.

Cavalry Units (Light)

Arab Cavalry

STATS

SOLDIERS: 27	DEFENSE SKILL: 4
ATTACK: 7	SHIELD: 4
CHARGE BONUS: 2	HIT POINTS: 1
WEAPON TYPE: Light	RECRUITMENT COST: Varies
TOTAL DEFENSE: 11	UPKEEP: 110
ARMOR: 3	

Desert-dwelling cavalry make excellent scouts, especially in harsh conditions, but they are not equipped for prolonged combat.

ABILITIES

- Combat bonus in deserts
- Can form wedge
- Good stamina
- Fast moving

Barbarian Cavalry Mercenaries

STATS

SOLDIERS: 28	DEFENSE SKILL: 3
ATTACK: 9	SHIELD: 4
CHARGE BONUS: 9	HIT POINTS: 1
WEAPON TYPE: Light	RECRUITMENT COST: Varies
TOTAL DEFENSE: 10	UPKEEP: 90
ARMOR: 3	

Mercenary barbarian cavalry ride sturdy and sure-footed horses, and are excellent light cavalry, useful as scouts and to pursue fleeing enemies.

ABILITIES

- Combat bonus in snow
- Can form wedge
- May charge without orders
- Powerful charge

Bedouin Warriors

STATS

SOLDIERS: 27	DEFENSE SKILL: 4
ATTACK: 7	SHIELD: 4
CHARGE BONUS: 2	HIT POINTS: 1
WEAPON TYPE: Light	RECRUITMENT COST: Varies
TOTAL DEFENSE: 11	UPKEEP: 110
ARMOR: 3	

These mercenaries are light camel riders from the nomadic tribes of Arabia. They are rugged men used to hard conditions and neither they nor their camel steeds tire quickly.

ABILITIES

- Combat bonus in deserts
- Scare horses
- Can form wedge
- Good stamina

Cavalry Units (Heavy)

Mercenary War Elephants

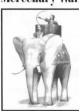

STATS

SOLDIERS: 18	ARMOR: 13
MELEE ATTACK: 7	DEFENSE SKILL: 3
MISSILE ATTACK: 10	SHIELD: 0
CHARGE BONUS: 11	HIT POINTS: 13
WEAPON TYPE: Missile	RECRUITMENT COST: Varies
TOTAL DEFENSE: 16	UPKEEP: 490

War Elephants are large, fierce and unpredictable beasts, and terrifying in battle. They are the ultimate shock troops available to any commander.

ABILITIES

- Special attack
- Bonus fighting cavalry
- Frighten nearby enemy
- Good morale
- Animals may run amok
- Can't hide

Cavalry Units (Missile)

Bedouin Archers

STATS

SOLDIERS: 27	ARMOR: 3
MELEE ATTACK: 3	DEFENSE SKILL: 2
ATTACK: 7	SHIELD: 4
CHARGE BONUS: 2	HIT POINTS: 1
WEAPON TYPE: Missile	RECRUITMENT COST: Varies
TOTAL DEFENSE: 9	UPKEEP: 110

These mercenaries are light camel archers from the nomadic tribes of Arabia. They are rugged men used to harsh conditions.

ABILITIES

- Can form Cantabrian circle
- Combat bonus in desert
- Scare horses
- Good stamina

Numidian Mercenaries

STATS

SOLDIERS: 27	ARMOR: 0
MELEE ATTACK: 6	DEFENSE SKILL: 4
ATTACK: 9	SHIELD: 4
CHARGE BONUS: 3	HIT POINTS: 1
WEAPON TYPE: Missile	RECRUITMENT COST: Varies
TOTAL DEFENSE: 8	UPKEEP: 130

Numidian Cavalry are superb mounted skirmishers who weaken the enemy with javelins.

ABILITIES

- Can form Cantabrian circle
- Good morale
- Good stamina
- Fast moving

Scythian Mercenaries

STATS

SOLDIERS: 27	ARMOR: 0
MELEE ATTACK: 3	DEFENSE SKILL: 2
ATTACK: 7	SHIELD: 0
CHARGE BONUS: 2	HIT POINTS: 1
WEAPON TYPE: Missile	RECRUITMENT COST: Varies
TOTAL DEFENSE: 2	UPKEEP: 110

Scythian Mercenaries are superb horse archers, well able to inflict losses as they harass enemies.

ABILITIES

- Can form Cantabrian circle
- Good stamina
- Fast moving

Infantry Units (Light)

Cilician Pirates

STATS

SOLDIERS: 40	ARMOR: 0
MELEE ATTACK: 10	DEFENSE SKILL: 5
MISSILE ATTACK: 13	SHIELD: 0
CHARGE BONUS: 3	HIT POINTS: 1
WEAPON TYPE: Heavy	RECRUITMENT COST: Varies
TOTAL DEFENSE: 5	UPKEEP: 200

These Cilician mercenaries are excellent and well-armed skirmishers, if somewhat hot-headed!

ABILITIES

- Javelins thrown before charge
- May charge without orders
- Good morale
- Fast moving
- Can sap

Spanish Mercenaries

STATS

SOLDIERS: 40	ARMOR: 3
MELEE ATTACK: 7	DEFENSE SKILL: 4
MISSILE ATTACK: 11	SHIELD: 5
CHARGE BONUS: 2	HIT POINTS: 1
WEAPON TYPE: Heavy	RECRUITMENT COST: Varies
TOTAL DEFENSE: 12	UPKEEP: 170

Spanish Mercenaries are general purpose light infantry, although they can skirmish if necessary.

ABILITIES

- Javelins thrown before charge
- Can sap

Thracian Mercenaries

STATS

SOLDIERS: 40	DEFENSE SKILL: 2
ATTACK: 10	SHIELD: 2
CHARGE BONUS: 6	HIT POINTS: 1
WEAPON TYPE: Heavy	RECRUITMENT COST: Varies
TOTAL DEFENSE: 6	UPKEEP: 130
ARMOR: 2	

Thracian barbarians are best used to hack through enemy infantry. They are not subtle warriors!

ABILITIES

- Expert at hiding in woods
- Combat bonus in woods
- May charge without orders
- Fast moving

Infantry Units (Missile)

Balearic Slingers

STATS

SOLDIERS: 40	ARMOR: 0
MELEE ATTACK: 6	DEFENSE SKILL: 4
MISSILE ATTACK: 9	SHIELD: 2
CHARGE BONUS: 3	HIT POINTS: 1
WEAPON TYPE: Missile	RECRUITMENT COST: Varies
TOTAL DEFENSE: 6	UPKEEP: 200

Mercenary slingers from the Balearic isles are famed as superior missile troops, although they are vulnerable in hand-to-hand combat.

ABILITIES

- Good morale
- Good stamina
- Fast moving
- Can sap

Cretan Archers

STATS

SOLDIERS: 40	ARMOR: 0
MELEE ATTACK: 6	DEFENSE SKILL: 5
MISSILE ATTACK: 11	SHIELD: 0
CHARGE BONUS: 3	HIT POINTS: 1
WEAPON TYPE: Missile	RECRUITMENT COST: Varies
TOTAL DEFENSE: 5	UPKEEP: 200

The archers of Crete are famed for their abilities. They can rain arrows on their opponents, not just bombard them!

ABILITIES

- Combat bonus in woods
- Long range missiles
- Can use Flaming Missiles
- Good morale
- Good stamina
- Fast moving
- Can sap

Illyrian Mercenaries

STATS

SOLDIERS: 40	ARMOR: 2
MELEE ATTACK: 7	DEFENSE SKILL: 1
MISSILE ATTACK: 9	SHIELD: 5
CHARGE BONUS: 4	HIT POINTS: 1
WEAPON TYPE: Missile	RECRUITMENT COST: Varies
TOTAL DEFENSE: 8	UPKEEP: 130

Illyrian Mercenaries are aggressive barbarian skirmishers accustomed to operating in rough terrain who are liable to attack without orders.

ABILITIES

- Expert at hiding in woods
- Combat bonus in woods or snow
- May charge without orders
- Fast moving

Rhodian Slingers

STATS

SOLDIERS: 40	ARMOR: 0
MELEE ATTACK: 6	DEFENSE SKILL: 4
MISSILE ATTACK: 9	SHIELD: 2
CHARGE BONUS: 3	HIT POINTS: 1
WEAPON TYPE: Missile	RECRUITMENT COST: Varies
TOTAL DEFENSE: 6	UPKEEP: 200

Mercenary slingers from Rhodes are famed as superior missile troops, although they are vulnerable in hand-to-hand combat.

ABILITIES

- Combat bonus in woods
- Good morale
- Good stamina
- Fast moving
- Can sap

Numidian Military Units

Artillery Units

Onagers

STATS	
SOLDIERS: 32	ARMOR: 0
ATTACK VS. TROOPS: 53	DEFENSE SKILL: 3
ATTACK VS. BUILDINGS: 35	SHIELD: 0
CHARGE BONUS: 0	HIT POINTS: 1
WEAPON TYPE: Light	RECRUITMENT COST: 1390
TOTAL DEFENSE: 3	UPKEEP: 180

The Onager is a versatile catapult that can launch boulders or incendiary firepots at enemy troops and fortifications.

ABILITIES
- Area attack
- Can't hide
- Very long range missiles
- Inaccurate against troops
- Can use Flaming Missiles

Cavalry Units (Light)

Long Shield Cavalry

STATS	
SOLDIERS: 27	DEFENSE SKILL: 6
ATTACK: 9	SHIELD: 4
CHARGE BONUS: 8	HIT POINTS: 1
WEAPON TYPE: Light	RECRUITMENT COST: 460
TOTAL DEFENSE: 13	UPKEEP: 140
ARMOR: 3	

Long Shield Cavalry are spear-armed light cavalry, who can be used to break enemy formations, drive off skirmishers, and pursue fleeing foes.

ABILITIES
- Can form wedge
- Powerful charge
- Good morale

Numidian Camel Riders

STATS	
SOLDIERS: 27	DEFENSE SKILL: 6
ATTACK: 9	SHIELD: 4
CHARGE BONUS: 8	HIT POINTS: 1
WEAPON TYPE: Light	RECRUITMENT COST: 450
TOTAL DEFENSE: 13	UPKEEP: 140
ARMOR: 3	

These tough desert warriors are camel lancers, exploiting the speed of their mounts and the fear effect that camels cause to horses.

ABILITIES
- Combat bonus in deserts
- Powerful charge
- Scare horses
- Good stamina
- Good morale

Cavalry Units (Missile)

Numidian Cavalry

STATS	
SOLDIERS: 27	ARMOR: 0
MELEE ATTACK: 6	DEFENSE SKILL: 4
MISSILE ATTACK: 9	SHIELD: 4
CHARGE BONUS: 3	HIT POINTS: 1
WEAPON TYPE: Missile	RECRUITMENT COST: 380
TOTAL DEFENSE: 8	UPKEEP: 130

Numidian Cavalry are superb skirmish cavalry that weakens the enemy with javelins.

ABILITIES
- Can form Cantabrian circle
- Good stamina
- Good morale
- Fast moving

Infantry Units (Light)

Peasants

STATS	
SOLDIERS: 61	DEFENSE SKILL: 3
ATTACK: 3	SHIELD: 0
CHARGE BONUS: 2	HIT POINTS: 1
WEAPON TYPE: Light	RECRUITMENT COST: 120
TOTAL DEFENSE: 3	UPKEEP: 100
ARMOR: 0	

Peasants are reluctant warriors, at best. Going to war is just one more burden of a hard life.

ABILITIES
- Poor morale
- Can sap

Infantry Units (Heavy)

Numidian Legionaries

STATS	
SOLDIERS: 41	ARMOR: 7
MELEE ATTACK: 7	DEFENSE SKILL: 4
MISSILE ATTACK: 11	SHIELD: 5
CHARGE BONUS: 2	HIT POINTS: 1
WEAPON TYPE: Light	RECRUITMENT COST: 490
TOTAL DEFENSE: 16	UPKEEP: 220

Numidian Legionaries are local copies of Roman Legionaries, but lack the truly awesome discipline of the originals. This still makes them dangerous foes.

ABILITIES
- Javelins thrown before charge
- Can sap
- Good stamina

Infantry Units (Missile)

Archers

STATS

SOLDIERS: 40	ARMOR: 0
MELEE ATTACK: 3	DEFENSE SKILL: 2
MISSILE ATTACK: 7	SHIELD: 0
CHARGE BONUS: 2	HIT POINTS: 1
WEAPON TYPE: Missile	RECRUITMENT COST: 180
TOTAL DEFENSE: 2	UPKEEP: 170

Archers are rightly feared for the casualties they can inflict, but they are vulnerable in hand-to-hand combat.

ABILITIES

- Can use Flaming Missiles
- Fast moving
- Can sap

Numidian Javelinmen

STATS

SOLDIERS: 40	ARMOR: 0
MELEE ATTACK: 3	DEFENSE SKILL: 2
MISSILE ATTACK: 6	SHIELD: 2
CHARGE BONUS: 2	HIT POINTS: 1
WEAPON TYPE: Missile	RECRUITMENT COST: 180
TOTAL DEFENSE: 4	UPKEEP: 170

Numidian Javelinmen are fast moving skirmishers trained from infancy in the use of the javelin.

ABILITIES

- Bonus vs. elephants and chariots
- Fast moving
- Can sap

Slingers

STATS

SOLDIERS: 40	ARMOR: 0
MELEE ATTACK: 3	DEFENSE SKILL: 2
MISSILE ATTACK: 3	SHIELD: 2
CHARGE BONUS: 2	HIT POINTS: 1
WEAPON TYPE: Missile	RECRUITMENT COST: 150
TOTAL DEFENSE: 4	UPKEEP: 170

Slingers are highly skilled missile troops but are at a huge disadvantage in hand-to-hand combat, especially against cavalry.

ABILITIES

- Fast moving
- Can sap

Spearmen

Desert Infantry

STATS

SOLDIERS: 40	DEFENSE SKILL: 5
ATTACK: 7	SHIELD: 5
CHARGE BONUS: 6	HIT POINTS: 1
WEAPON TYPE: Light	RECRUITMENT COST: 380
TOTAL DEFENSE: 13	UPKEEP: 200
ARMOR: 3	

These hardy folk from the fringes of the Sahara make excellent spearmen, well suited to defending against cavalry.

ABILITIES

- Bonus fighting cavalry
- Combat bonus in deserts
- Good morale
- Good stamina
- Can sap

Numidian Naval Units

Bireme

VESSELS: 20	DEFENSE: 2
ATTACK: 6	

Trireme

VESSELS: 30	DEFENSE: 3
ATTACK: 8	

Quinquireme

VESSELS: 50	DEFENSE: 5
ATTACK: 10	

Parthian Military Units

Artillery Units

Onagers

STATS

SOLDIERS: 32	ARMOR: 2
ATTACK VS. TROOPS: 53	DEFENSE SKILL: 3
ATTACK VS. BUILDINGS: 35	SHIELD: 0
CHARGE BONUS: 0	HIT POINTS: 1
WEAPON TYPE: Light	RECRUITMENT COST: 1440
TOTAL DEFENSE: 5	UPKEEP: 180

The Onager is a versatile catapult that can launch boulders or incendiary firepots at enemy troops and fortifications.

ABILITIES

- Area attack
- Very long range missiles
- Can use Flaming Missiles
- Can't hide
- Inaccurate against troops

Cavalry Units (Heavy)

Cataphracts

STATS

SOLDIERS: 27	DEFENSE SKILL: 5
ATTACK: 7	SHIELD: 0
CHARGE BONUS: 15	HIT POINTS: 1
WEAPON TYPE: Heavy	RECRUITMENT COST: 810
TOTAL DEFENSE: 23	UPKEEP: 140
ARMOR: 18	

Cataphracts are extremely heavily-armored shock cavalry who can turn a battle with one thunderous charge.

ABILITIES

- Can form wedge
- Good morale
- Powerful charge

Cataphract Camels

STATS

SOLDIERS: 27	DEFENSE SKILL: 5
ATTACK: 7	SHIELD: 0
CHARGE BONUS: 15	HIT POINTS: 1
WEAPON TYPE: Heavy	RECRUITMENT COST: 810
TOTAL DEFENSE: 23	UPKEEP: 140
ARMOR: 18	

Cataphract Camels are well armored - camel and rider both - shock cavalry who use weight and speed to cause additional disruption.

ABILITIES

- Combat bonus in deserts
- Scare horses
- Can form wedge
- Good morale
- Powerful charge

War Elephants

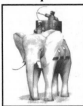

STATS

SOLDIERS: 18	ARMOR: 13
MELEE ATTACK: 7	DEFENSE SKILL: 3
MISSILE ATTACK: 10	SHIELD: 0
CHARGE BONUS: 11	HIT POINTS: 15
WEAPON TYPE: Missile	RECRUITMENT COST: 2880
TOTAL DEFENSE: 16	UPKEEP: 490

War Elephants are fierce and terrible beasts, able to trample men and horses into the dirt.

ABILITIES

- Special attack
- Bonus fighting cavalry
- Frighten nearby enemy
- Good morale
- Animals may run amok
- Can't hide

Cavalry Units (Missile)

Horse Archers

STATS

SOLDIERS: 27	ARMOR: 0
MELEE ATTACK: 3	DEFENSE SKILL: 2
MISSILE ATTACK: 7	SHIELD: 0
CHARGE BONUS: 2	HIT POINTS: 1
WEAPON TYPE: Missile	RECRUITMENT COST: 260
TOTAL DEFENSE: 2	UPKEEP: 110

Horse Archers are a specialty of the East: swift horses and expert marksmen make a deadly combination.

ABILITIES

- Can form Cantabrian circle
- Fast moving

Persian Cavalry

STATS

SOLDIERS: 27	ARMOR: 6
MELEE ATTACK: 9	DEFENSE SKILL: 4
MISSILE ATTACK: 10	SHIELD: 0
CHARGE BONUS: 3	HIT POINTS: 1
WEAPON TYPE: Missile	RECRUITMENT COST: 570
TOTAL DEFENSE: 10	UPKEEP: 140

Persian Cavalry can fight well with either bow or sword, making them valuable skirmishers and general purpose horsemen.

ABILITIES

- Can form Cantabrian circle
- Good morale

Infantry Units (Light)

Hillmen

STATS

SOLDIERS: 40	DEFENSE SKILL: 4
ATTACK: 5	SHIELD: 2
CHARGE BONUS: 5	HIT POINTS: 1
WEAPON TYPE: Light	RECRUITMENT COST: 290
TOTAL DEFENSE: 9	UPKEEP: 170
ARMOR: 3	

The Hillmen are a wild, savage people but they are skilled hunters, making them superb ambushers.

ABILITIES

- Can hide in long grass
- May charge without orders
- Good stamina
- Fast moving
- Can sap

Peasants

STATS

SOLDIERS: 61	DEFENSE SKILL: 3
ATTACK: 3	SHIELD: 0
CHARGE BONUS: 2	HIT POINTS: 1
WEAPON TYPE: Light	RECRUITMENT COST: 120
TOTAL DEFENSE: 3	UPKEEP: 100
ARMOR: 0	

Peasants are reluctant warriors, at best. Going to war is just one more burden of a hard life.

ABILITIES

- Poor morale
- Can sap

Infantry Units (Missile)

Archers

STATS

SOLDIERS: 40	ARMOR: 0
MELEE ATTACK: 3	DEFENSE SKILL: 2
MISSILE ATTACK: 7	SHIELD: 0
CHARGE BONUS: 2	HIT POINTS: 1
WEAPON TYPE: Missile	RECRUITMENT COST: 180
TOTAL DEFENSE: 2	UPKEEP: 170

Archers are rightly feared for the casualties they can inflict, but they are vulnerable in hand-to-hand combat.

ABILITIES

- Can use Flaming Missiles
- Fast moving
- Can sap

Slingers

STATS

SOLDIERS: 40	ARMOR: 0
MELEE ATTACK: 3	DEFENSE SKILL: 2
MISSILE ATTACK: 3	SHIELD: 2
CHARGE BONUS: 2	HIT POINTS: 1
WEAPON TYPE: Missile	RECRUITMENT COST: 150
TOTAL DEFENSE: 4	UPKEEP: 170

Slingers are highly skilled missile troops but are at a huge disadvantage in hand-to-hand combat, especially against cavalry.

ABILITIES

- Fast moving
- Can sap

Spearmen

Eastern Infantry

STATS

SOLDIERS: 60	DEFENSE SKILL: 2
ATTACK: 3	SHIELD: 5
CHARGE BONUS: 4	HIT POINTS: 1
WEAPON TYPE: Light	RECRUITMENT COST: 330
TOTAL DEFENSE: 10	UPKEEP: 150
ARMOR: 3	

Eastern Infantry are easily recruited militia-spearmen, who are good for defense against less able opponents.

ABILITIES

- Bonus fighting cavalry
- Poor morale
- Can sap

Parthian Naval Units

Bireme

VESSELS: 20   DEFENSE: 2
ATTACK: 6

Trireme

VESSELS: 30   DEFENSE: 3
ATTACK: 8

Quinquireme

VESSELS: 50   DEFENSE: 5
ATTACK: 10

Parthian Buildings

Government-Class Buildings

Governor's House

- Enables training of Peasants
- Enables construction of "First Tier" buildings

Governor's Villa

- Enables training of Peasants
- Enables recruitment of diplomats
- Enables construction of "Second Tier" buildings

Governor's Palace

- Enables training of Peasants
- Enables recruitment of diplomats
- Enables construction of "Third Tier" buildings

Councilor's Chambers

- Enables training of Peasants
- Enables recruitment of diplomats
- Enables construction of "Fourth Tier" buildings

Royal Palace

- Improved Generals' Bodyguards
- Enables training of Peasants
- Enables training of Praetorian Cohort
- Enables recruitment of diplomats
- Enables construction of "Fifth Tier" buildings

Wall-Class Buildings

Wooden Palisade (First Tier)

- Extra wall defenses

Wooden Wall (Second Tier)

- Extra wall defenses
- Reinforced gates

Stone Wall (Third Tier)

- Extra wall defenses
- Reinforced gates
- Boiling oil

Large Stone Wall (Fourth Tier)

- Extra wall defenses
- Boiling oil
- Iron gates

Epic Stone Wall (Fifth Tier)

- Extra wall defenses
- Boiling oil
- Iron gates

Barrack-Class Buildings

Barracks (First Tier)

- Enables training of Eastern Infantry

Militia Barracks (Second Tier)

- Enables training of Eastern Infantry
- Enables training of Hillmen

Stable-Class Buildings

Stables (Second Tier)

- Enables training of Horse Archers

Cavalry Stables (Third Tier)

- Enables training of Horse Archers
- Enables training of Persian Cavalry

Elite Cavalry Stables (Fourth Tier)

- Enables training of Horse Archers
- Enables training of Persian Cavalry
- Enables training of Cataphracts
- Enables training of War Elephants

Royal Cavalry Stables (Fifth Tier)

- Enables training of Horse Archers
- Enables training of Persian Cavalry
- Enables training of Cataphracts
- Enables training of War Elephants
- Enables training of Incendiary Pigs
- Enables training of Cataphract Camels

Range-Class Buildings

Practice Range (Second Tier)

- Enables training of Slingers

Archery Range (Third Tier)

- Enables training of Slingers
- Enables training of Archers

Catapult Range (Fourth Tier)

- Enables training of Slingers
- Enables training of Archers
- Enables training of Onagers

Trader-Class Buildings

Trader (First Tier)

- Increase in tradable goods
- Population Growth bonus: 0.5%

Market (Second Tier)

- Increase in tradable goods
- Population Growth bonus: 0.5%
- Enables recruitment of spies

Bazaar (Third Tier)

- Increase in tradable goods
- Population Growth bonus: 0.5%
- Enables recruitment of spies
- Enables recruitment of assassins

Grand Bazaar (Fourth Tier)

- Increase in tradable goods
- Population Growth bonus: 1%
- Enables recruitment of spies
- Enables recruitment of assassins

Merchants' Quarters (Fifth Tier)

- Increase in tradable goods
- Population Growth bonus: 1%
- Enables recruitment of spies
- Enables recruitment of assassins
- Public Order bonus due to happiness: 10%

Smith-Class Buildings

Blacksmith (Second Tier)

- SPECIAL REQUIREMENT: Trader Building
- Upgrades light weapons: +1
- Upgrades heavy weapons: +1

Armourer (Third Tier)

- SPECIAL REQUIREMENT: Market Building
- Upgrades light weapons: +1
- Upgrades heavy weapons: +1
- Upgrades missile weapons: +1
- Upgrades armor: +1

Foundry (Fifth Tier)

- SPECIAL REQUIREMENT: Grand Bazaar Building
- Upgrades light weapons: +2
- Upgrades heavy weapons: +2
- Upgrades missile weapons: +2
- Upgrades armor: +2

Port-Class Buildings

Port (Second Tier)

- Grants one sea-trade fleet for extra income
- Enables training of Biremes

Shipwright (Third Tier)

- Grants two sea-trade fleets for extra income
- Enables training of Biremes
- Enables training of Triremes

Dockyard (Fourth Tier)

- Grants three sea-trade fleets for extra income
- Enables training of Biremes
- Enables training of Triremes
- Enables training of Quinquiremes

Farm-Class Buildings

Land Clearance (First Tier)

- Improved farms and food production: +1

Communal Farming (Second Tier)

- Improved farms and food production: +2

Crop Rotation (Third Tier)

- Improved farms and food production: +3

Irrigation (Fourth Tier)

- Improved farms and food production: +4

Roads

Roads (First Tier)

- Improved roads and trade

Academy-Class Buildings

Academy (Third Tier)

- SPECIAL REQUIREMENT: Market Building
- Governors gain skills and knowledge

Scriptorium (Fourth Tier)

- SPECIAL REQUIREMENT: Bazaar Building
- Governors gain skills and knowledge

Ludus Magna (Fifth Tier)

- SPECIAL REQUIREMENT: Grand Bazaar Building
- Governors gain skills and knowledge

Law Enforcement-Class Buildings

Execution Square (Third Tier)

- Public Order bonus due to law: 5%

Secret Police HQ (Fourth Tier)

- Public Order bonus due to law: 10%

Secret Police Network (Fifth Tier)

- Public Order bonus due to happiness: 15%

Caravan-Class Buildings

Trade Caravan (Third Tier)

- Increase in tradable goods

Spice Road (Fourth Tier)

- Increase in tradable goods

Silk Road (Fifth Tier)

- Increase in tradable goods

Temple-Class Buildings

Shrine to Zoroastra (First Tier)

- Public Order bonus due to happiness: 5%
- Public Order bonus due to law: 5%

Temple of Zoroastra (Second Tier)

- Public Order bonus due to happiness: 10%
- Public Order bonus due to law: 10%

Large Temple of Zoroastra (Third Tier)

- Public Order bonus due to happiness: 15%
- Public Order bonus due to law: 15%

Awesome Temple of Zoroastra (Fourth Tier)

- Public Order bonus due to happiness: 20%
- Public Order bonus due to law: 20%

Temple Complex of Zoroastra (Fifth Tier)

- Public Order bonus due to happiness: 25%
- Public Order bonus due to law: 25%

Pontic Military Units
Artillery
Onagers

STATS	
SOLDIERS: 32	ARMOR: 2
ATTACK VS. TROOPS: 53	DEFENSE SKILL: 3
ATTACK VS. BUILDINGS: 35	SHIELD: 0
CHARGE BONUS: 0	HIT POINTS: 1
WEAPON TYPE: Light	RECRUITMENT COST: 1440
TOTAL DEFENSE: 5	UPKEEP: 180

The Onager is a versatile catapult that can launch boulders or incendiary firepots at enemy troops and fortifications.

ABILITIES

- Area attack
- Very long range missiles
- Can use Flaming Missiles
- Can't hide
- Inaccurate against troops

Cavalry Units (Heavy)

Cappadocian Cavalry

STATS	
SOLDIERS: 27	DEFENSE SKILL: 5
ATTACK: 7	SHIELD: 0
CHARGE BONUS: 15	HIT POINTS: 1
WEAPON TYPE: Heavy	RECRUITMENT COST: 560
TOTAL DEFENSE: 14	UPKEEP: 140
ARMOR: 9	

Cappadocian lancers are excellent horsemen, best suited to charging into and breaking through enemy formations.

ABILITIES
- Can form wedge
- Good morale
- Powerful charge

Pontic Heavy Cavalry

STATS	
SOLDIERS: 27	ARMOR: 6
MELEE ATTACK: 9	DEFENSE SKILL: 4
MISSILE ATTACK: 9	SHIELD: 4
CHARGE BONUS: 3	HIT POINTS: 1
WEAPON TYPE: Missile	RECRUITMENT COST: 570
TOTAL DEFENSE: 14	UPKEEP: 140

Pontic Heavy Cavalry are javelin-armed horsemen who can also fight hand-to-hand - a potent combination in one force!

ABILITIES
- Can form Cantabrian circle
- Good morale

Scythed Chariots

STATS	
SOLDIERS: 9	DEFENSE SKILL: 1
ATTACK: 15	SHIELD: 0
CHARGE BONUS: 8	HIT POINTS: 4
WEAPON TYPE: Light	RECRUITMENT COST: 910
TOTAL DEFENSE: 1	UPKEEP: 210
ARMOR: 0	

Scythed Chariots are fearsome devices, covered in scythe blades to cut down any infantry foolish enough to stand still when charged.

ABILITIES
- Special attack
- Frighten nearby enemy infantry
- May charge without orders
- Good morale
- Animals may run amok

Cavalry Units (Missile)

Chariot Archers

STATS	
SOLDIERS: 27	ARMOR: 0
MELEE ATTACK: 9	DEFENSE SKILL: 1
MISSILE ATTACK: 13	SHIELD: 0
CHARGE BONUS: 6	HIT POINTS: 2
WEAPON TYPE: Missile	RECRUITMENT COST: 870
TOTAL DEFENSE: 1	UPKEEP: 330

Chariot Archers are highly skilled - they can hit targets while their chariots are moving at high speed.

ABILITIES
- Special attack
- Can form Cantabrian circle
- Frighten nearby enemy infantry
- Good morale

Pontic Light Cavalry

STATS	
SOLDIERS: 27	ARMOR: 0
MELEE ATTACK: 7	DEFENSE SKILL: 3
MISSILE ATTACK: 7	SHIELD: 4
CHARGE BONUS: 2	HIT POINTS: 1
WEAPON TYPE: Missile	RECRUITMENT COST: 350
TOTAL DEFENSE: 7	UPKEEP: 110

Pontic Light Cavalry are javelin-armed mounted skirmishers who can strike quickly and be gone before the enemy reacts.

ABILITIES
- Can form Cantabrian circle
- Fast moving

Infantry Units (Light)

Hillmen

STATS	
SOLDIERS: 40	DEFENSE SKILL: 4
ATTACK: 5	SHIELD: 2
CHARGE BONUS: 5	HIT POINTS: 1
WEAPON TYPE: Light	RECRUITMENT COST: 290
TOTAL DEFENSE: 9	UPKEEP: 170
ARMOR: 3	

The Hillmen are a wild, savage people but they are skilled hunters, making them superb ambushers.

ABILITIES
- Can hide in long grass
- May charge without orders
- Good stamina
- Fast moving
- Can sap

Peasants

STATS

SOLDIERS: 61	DEFENSE SKILL: 3
ATTACK: 3	SHIELD: 0
CHARGE BONUS: 2	HIT POINTS: 1
WEAPON TYPE: Light	RECRUITMENT COST: 120
TOTAL DEFENSE: 3	UPKEEP: 100
ARMOR: 0	

Peasants are reluctant warriors, at best. Going to war is just one more burden of a hard life.

ABILITIES

- Poor morale
- Can sap

Infantry Units (Missile)

Archers

STATS

SOLDIERS: 40	ARMOR: 0
MELEE ATTACK: 3	DEFENSE SKILL: 2
MISSILE ATTACK: 7	SHIELD: 0
CHARGE BONUS: 2	HIT POINTS: 1
WEAPON TYPE: Missile	RECRUITMENT COST: 180
TOTAL DEFENSE: 2	UPKEEP: 170

Archers are rightly feared for the casualties they can inflict, but they are vulnerable in hand-to-hand combat.

ABILITIES

- Can use Flaming Missiles
- Can sap
- Fast moving

Peltasts

STATS

SOLDIERS: 40	ARMOR: 0
MELEE ATTACK: 3	DEFENSE SKILL: 2
MISSILE ATTACK: 6	SHIELD: 2
CHARGE BONUS: 2	HIT POINTS: 1
WEAPON TYPE: Missile	RECRUITMENT COST: 180
TOTAL DEFENSE: 4	UPKEEP: 170

Eastern Peltasts rush forward to pepper an enemy with javelins, and then withdraw in good order before a counter-attack can be organized.

ABILITIES

- Can hide in long grass
- Fast moving
- Bonus vs. elephants and chariots
- Can sap

Spearmen

Bronze Shields

STATS

SOLDIERS: 61	DEFENSE SKILL: 6
ATTACK: 10	SHIELD: 2
CHARGE BONUS: 7	HIT POINTS: 1
WEAPON TYPE: Heavy	RECRUITMENT COST: 760
TOTAL DEFENSE: 14	UPKEEP: 360
ARMOR: 6	

Bronze Shields are the elite of the army of Pontus, among the heirs of the world-conquering phalanxes of Alexander!

ABILITIES

- Can form phalanx
- Good stamina
- Bonus fighting cavalry
- Very long spears
- Good morale
- Can sap

Eastern Infantry

STATS

SOLDIERS: 60	DEFENSE SKILL: 2
ATTACK: 3	SHIELD: 5
CHARGE BONUS: 4	HIT POINTS: 1
WEAPON TYPE: Light	RECRUITMENT COST: 330
TOTAL DEFENSE: 10	UPKEEP: 150
ARMOR: 3	

Eastern Infantry are easily recruited militia-spearmen, who are good for defense against less able opponents.

ABILITIES

- Bonus fighting cavalry
- Can sap
- Poor morale

Phalanx Pikemen

STATS

SOLDIERS: 40	DEFENSE SKILL: 5
ATTACK: 8	SHIELD: 5
CHARGE BONUS: 6	HIT POINTS: 1
WEAPON TYPE: Heavy	RECRUITMENT COST: 530
TOTAL DEFENSE: 16	UPKEEP: 170
ARMOR: 6	

Phalanx Pikemen, or phalangites, are well-drilled infantry who fight best as a solid mass of men.

ABILITIES

- Can form phalanx
- Very long spears
- Bonus fighting cavalry
- Can sap

Pontic Naval Units

Bireme

VESSELS: 20　　　DEFENSE: 2
ATTACK: 6

Trireme

VESSELS: 30　　　DEFENSE: 3
ATTACK: 8

Quinquireme

VESSELS: 50　　　DEFENSE: 5
ATTACK: 10

NOTE

You cannot play as the People of Pontus in the Imperial Campaign mode, so their buildings are not listed in this guide.

Scythian Military Units

Animal Units (Heavy)

Warhounds

STATS

SOLDIERS: 20	DEFENSE SKILL: 1
ATTACK: 14	SHIELD: 0
CHARGE BONUS: 4	HIT POINTS: 1
WEAPON TYPE: Light	RECRUITMENT COST: 660
TOTAL DEFENSE: 3	UPKEEP: 60
ARMOR: 2	

Warhounds are bred for a savage nature and great size, but then hunting men is only a little more dangerous than hunting wild boar!

ABILITIES

- Frighten nearby enemy
- Fast moving
- Combat bonus in woods or snow

Artillery Units

Onagers

STATS

SOLDIERS: 32	ARMOR: 0
ATTACK VS. TROOPS: 53	DEFENSE SKILL: 3
ATTACK VS. BUILDINGS: 35	SHIELD: 2
CHARGE BONUS: 0	HIT POINTS: 1
WEAPON TYPE: Light	RECRUITMENT COST: 1410
TOTAL DEFENSE: 5	UPKEEP: 180

The Onager is a versatile catapult that can launch boulders or incendiary firepots at enemy troops and fortifications.

ABILITIES

- Area attack
- Can't hide
- Very long range missiles
- Inaccurate against troops
- Can use Flaming Missiles

Cavalry Units (Light)

Barbarian Cavalry

STATS

SOLDIERS: 27	DEFENSE SKILL: 3
ATTACK: 9	SHIELD: 4
CHARGE BONUS: 9	HIT POINTS: 1
WEAPON TYPE: Light	RECRUITMENT COST: 370
TOTAL DEFENSE: 10	UPKEEP: 90
ARMOR: 3	

Barbarian Cavalry are lightly armored and carry spears. They are best used as scouts and in pursuit of fleeing enemies.

ABILITIES

- Combat bonus in snow
- May charge without orders
- Can form wedge
- Powerful charge

Head Hunting Maidens

STATS

SOLDIERS: 27	DEFENSE SKILL: 1
ATTACK: 10	SHIELD: 4
CHARGE BONUS: 6	HIT POINTS: 1
WEAPON TYPE: Light	RECRUITMENT COST: 540
TOTAL DEFENSE: 11	UPKEEP: 140
ARMOR: 6	

Head Hunting Maidens are hot-headed light cavalry who are useful against skirmisher and missile troops.

ABILITIES

- Effective against armor
- Combat bonus in snow
- Can form wedge
- May charge without orders
- Good morale
- Fast moving

Cavalry Units (Heavy)

Scythian Nobles

STATS

SOLDIERS: 27	DEFENSE SKILL: 4
ATTACK: 8	SHIELD: 0
CHARGE BONUS: 17	HIT POINTS: 1
WEAPON TYPE: Heavy	RECRUITMENT COST: 560
TOTAL DEFENSE: 13	UPKEEP: 170
ARMOR: 9	

Scythian Nobles are superb horsemen: armored lancers who can put many infantry units to flight.

ABILITIES

- Combat bonus in snow
- Can form wedge
- May charge without orders
- Good morale
- Powerful charge

Cavalry Units (Missile)

Scythian Horse Archers

STATS

SOLDIERS: 27	ARMOR: 3
MELEE ATTACK: 3	DEFENSE SKILL: 2
MISSILE ATTACK: 7	SHIELD: 0
CHARGE BONUS: 2	HIT POINTS: 1
WEAPON TYPE: Missile	RECRUITMENT COST: 350
TOTAL DEFENSE: 5	UPKEEP: 110

Deadly with a bow and highly mobile, Scythian Horse Archers are thorns in the side of many opponents.

ABILITIES

- Can form Cantabrian circle
- Combat bonus in snow
- Good stamina
- Fast moving

Scythian Noble Archers

STATS

SOLDIERS: 27	ARMOR: 9
MELEE ATTACK: 10	DEFENSE SKILL: 3
MISSILE ATTACK: 11	SHIELD: 0
CHARGE BONUS: 5	HIT POINTS: 1
WEAPON TYPE: Missile	RECRUITMENT COST: 660
TOTAL DEFENSE: 12	UPKEEP: 170

These Scythian nobles are armored horse archers who are also well able to fight in melee.

ABILITIES

- Can form Cantabrian circle
- Combat bonus in snow
- Good morale
- Good stamina

Scythian Noble Women

STATS

SOLDIERS: 18	ARMOR: 6
MELEE ATTACK: 7	DEFENSE SKILL: 3
MISSILE ATTACK: 11	SHIELD: 0
CHARGE BONUS: 5	HIT POINTS: 1
WEAPON TYPE: Missile	RECRUITMENT COST: 460
TOTAL DEFENSE: 9	UPKEEP: 130

Scythian Noble Women are excellent and well-armored horse archers, but they are vulnerable in close combat.

ABILITIES

- Can form Cantabrian circle
- Combat bonus in snow
- Good morale
- Fast moving

Infantry Units (Light)

Barbarian Peasants

STATS

SOLDIERS: 61	DEFENSE SKILL: 1
ATTACK: 1	SHIELD: 0
CHARGE BONUS: 1	HIT POINTS: 1
WEAPON TYPE: Light	RECRUITMENT COST: 150
TOTAL DEFENSE: 4	UPKEEP: 100
ARMOR: 3	

Peasants are reluctant warriors, but Barbarian Peasants are better fighters than most: hard lives produce hard men.

ABILITIES

- Warcry improves attack
- Expert at hiding in woods
- Combat bonus in woods or snow
- Poor morale

Infantry Units (Heavy)

Axemen

STATS

SOLDIERS: 61	DEFENSE SKILL: 1
ATTACK: 1	SHIELD: 0
CHARGE BONUS: 1	HIT POINTS: 1
WEAPON TYPE: Light	RECRUITMENT COST: 150
TOTAL DEFENSE: 4	UPKEEP: 100
ARMOR: 3	

Axemen are steadfast and aggressive warriors, the 'infantry of the line' for barbarian warlords.

ABILITIES

- Warcry improves attack
- Expert at hiding in woods
- Combat bonus in woods or snow
- Poor morale

Infantry Units (Missile)

Archer Warband

STATS

SOLDIERS: 40	ARMOR: 3
MELEE ATTACK: 3	DEFENSE SKILL: 2
MISSILE ATTACK: 7	SHIELD: 0
CHARGE BONUS: 2	HIT POINTS: 1
WEAPON TYPE: Missile	RECRUITMENT COST: 260
TOTAL DEFENSE: 5	UPKEEP: 170

Archer Warbands are used to harass and break up enemy formations, so that other warriors can then get in amongst their enemies.

ABILITIES

- Expert at hiding in woods
- Combat bonus in woods or snow
- Can use Flaming Missiles
- Fast moving

Chosen Archer Warband

STATS

SOLDIERS: 41	ARMOR: 7
MELEE ATTACK: 10	DEFENSE SKILL: 4
MISSILE ATTACK: 12	SHIELD: 0
CHARGE BONUS: 5	HIT POINTS: 1
WEAPON TYPE: Missile	RECRUITMENT COST: 600
TOTAL DEFENSE: 11	UPKEEP: 180

Chosen Archers are highly prized for their superior skills in war. They are the best archers available to barbarian warlords.

ABILITIES

- Expert at hiding in woods
- Combat bonus in woods or snow
- Long range missiles
- Can use Flaming Missiles
- Good morale
- Good stamina

Scythian Naval Units

Boats

VESSELS: 15	DEFENSE: 1	
ATTACK: 6		

Large Boats

VESSELS: 30	DEFENSE: 3	
ATTACK: 8		

Bireme

VESSELS: 20	DEFENSE: 2	
ATTACK: 6		

Trireme

VESSELS: 30	DEFENSE: 3	
ATTACK: 8		

Quinquireme

VESSELS: 50	DEFENSE: 5	
ATTACK: 10		

NOTE

You cannot play as the Scythians in the Imperial Campaign mode, so their buildings are not listed in this guide.

Seleucid Military Units

Artillery Units

Onagers

STATS

SOLDIERS: 32	ARMOR: 0
ATTACK VS. TROOPS: 53	DEFENSE SKILL: 3
ATTACK VS. BUILDINGS: 35	SHIELD: 0
CHARGE BONUS: 0	HIT POINTS: 1
WEAPON TYPE: Light	RECRUITMENT COST: 1390
TOTAL DEFENSE: 3	UPKEEP: 180

The Onager is a versatile catapult that can launch boulders or incendiary firepots at enemy troops and fortifications.

ABILITIES

- Area attack
- Very long range missiles
- Can use Flaming Missiles
- Can't hide
- Inaccurate against troops

Cavalry Units (Light)

Greek Cavalry

STATS

SOLDIERS: 27	DEFENSE SKILL: 5
ATTACK: 7	SHIELD: 0
CHARGE BONUS: 7	HIT POINTS: 1
WEAPON TYPE: Light	RECRUITMENT COST: 300
TOTAL DEFENSE: 8	UPKEEP: 110
ARMOR: 3	

Greek Cavalry are fast moving horsemen armed with spears for maximum impact in a charge.

ABILITIES

- Can form wedge

Cavalry Units (Heavy)

Armored Elephants

STATS

SOLDIERS: 18	ARMOR: 16
MELEE ATTACK: 7	DEFENSE SKILL: 3
MISSILE ATTACK: 10	SHIELD: 0
CHARGE BONUS: 11	HIT POINTS: 15
WEAPON TYPE: Missile	RECRUITMENT COST: 3420
TOTAL DEFENSE: 19	UPKEEP: 590

Armored Elephants are the most fearsome creatures to be found on a battlefield. Little can stand before these armored giants.

ABILITIES

- Special attack
- Bonus fighting cavalry
- Frighten nearby enemy
- Good morale
- Animals may run amok
- Can't hide

Cataphracts

STATS

SOLDIERS: 27	DEFENSE SKILL: 5
ATTACK: 7	SHIELD: 0
CHARGE BONUS: 15	HIT POINTS: 1
WEAPON TYPE: Heavy	RECRUITMENT COST: 810
TOTAL DEFENSE: 23	UPKEEP: 140
ARMOR: 18	

Cataphracts are extremely heavily-armored shock cavalry who can turn a battle with one thunderous charge.

ABILITIES

- Can form wedge
- Good morale
- Powerful charge

Companion Cavalry

STATS

SOLDIERS: 27	DEFENSE SKILL: 6
ATTACK: 10	SHIELD: 0
CHARGE BONUS: 16	HIT POINTS: 1
WEAPON TYPE: Heavy	RECRUITMENT COST: 690
TOTAL DEFENSE: 17	UPKEEP: 240
ARMOR: 11	

Companion Cavalry are a social and military elite, and fight as heavy cavalry using shock and mass to break enemy units.

ABILITIES

- Can form wedge
- Good morale
- Powerful charge
- Good stamina

Elephants

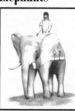

STATS

SOLDIERS: 6	ARMOR: 10
ATTACK: 3	DEFENSE SKILL: 2
CHARGE BONUS: 10	SHIELD: 0
WEAPON TYPE: Cannot be upgraded	HIT POINTS: 12
	RECRUITMENT COST: 1560
TOTAL DEFENSE: 12	UPKEEP: 270

Elephants are a terrifying spectacle to opposing troops, well able to smash battle lines and toss men aside like dogs with rats.

ABILITIES

- Special attack
- Bonus fighting cavalry
- Frighten nearby enemy
- Animals may run amok
- Can't hide

Scythed Chariots

STATS

SOLDIERS: 9	DEFENSE SKILL: 1
ATTACK: 15	SHIELD: 0
CHARGE BONUS: 8	HIT POINTS: 4
WEAPON TYPE: Light	RECRUITMENT COST: 970
TOTAL DEFENSE: 1	UPKEEP: 160
ARMOR: 0	

Scythed Chariots are fearsome devices, covered in scythe blades to cut down any infantry foolish enough to stand still when charged. They are, however, somewhat uncontrollable!

ABILITIES

- Special attack
- Frighten nearby enemy infantry
- May charge without orders
- Good morale
- Animals may run amok

War Elephants

STATS

SOLDIERS: 19	ARMOR: 13
MELEE ATTACK: 7	DEFENSE SKILL: 3
MISSILE ATTACK: 10	SHIELD: 0
CHARGE BONUS: 11	HIT POINTS: 15
WEAPON TYPE: Missile	RECRUITMENT COST: 3080
TOTAL DEFENSE: 16	UPKEEP: 490

War Elephants are fierce and terrible beasts, able to trample men and horses into the dirt.

ABILITIES

- Special attack
- Bonus fighting cavalry
- Frighten nearby enemy
- Good morale
- Animals may run amok
- Can't hide

Cavalry Units (Missile)

Militia Cavalry

STATS

SOLDIERS: 27	ARMOR: 0
MELEE ATTACK: 6	DEFENSE SKILL: 2
MISSILE ATTACK: 6	SHIELD: 4
CHARGE BONUS: 2	HIT POINTS: 1
WEAPON TYPE: Missile	RECRUITMENT COST: 320
TOTAL DEFENSE: 6	UPKEEP: 110

Militia Cavalry are javelin-armed mounted skirmishers who can strike quickly and be gone before the enemy reacts.

ABILITIES

- Can form Cantabrian circle
- Fast moving

Infantry Units (Light)

Peasants

STATS

SOLDIERS: 61	DEFENSE SKILL: 1
ATTACK: 1	SHIELD: 0
CHARGE BONUS: 1	HIT POINTS: 1
WEAPON TYPE: Light	RECRUITMENT COST: 60
TOTAL DEFENSE: 1	UPKEEP: 100
ARMOR: 0	

Peasants are reluctant warriors, at best. Going to war is just one more burden of a hard life.

ABILITIES

- Poor morale
- Can sap

Infantry Units (Heavy)

Silver Shield Legionaries

STATS

SOLDIERS: 41	ARMOR: 12
MELEE ATTACK: 9	DEFENSE SKILL: 5
MISSILE ATTACK: 13	SHIELD: 5
CHARGE BONUS: 3	HIT POINTS: 1
WEAPON TYPE: Heavy	RECRUITMENT COST: 680
TOTAL DEFENSE: 22	UPKEEP: 260

The Seleucid talent for adopting good ideas is given solidity in the shape of these Legionaries - copies of the Roman originals!

ABILITIES

- Can form testudo
- Javelins thrown before charge
- Good morale
- Good stamina
- Can sap

Infantry Units (Missile)

Archers

STATS

SOLDIERS: 40	ARMOR: 0
MELEE ATTACK: 3	DEFENSE SKILL: 2
MISSILE ATTACK: 7	SHIELD: 0
CHARGE BONUS: 2	HIT POINTS: 1
WEAPON TYPE: Missile	RECRUITMENT COST: 180
TOTAL DEFENSE: 2	UPKEEP: 170

Archers are rightly feared for the casualties they can inflict, but they are vulnerable in hand-to-hand combat.

ABILITIES

- Combat bonus in woods
- Can use Flaming Missiles
- Fast moving
- Can sap

Peltasts

STATS

SOLDIERS: 40	ARMOR: 0
MELEE ATTACK: 3	DEFENSE SKILL: 2
MISSILE ATTACK: 6	SHIELD: 2
CHARGE BONUS: 2	HIT POINTS: 1
WEAPON TYPE: Missile	RECRUITMENT COST: 180
TOTAL DEFENSE: 4	UPKEEP: 170

Seleucid Peltasts advance at speed to pepper an enemy with javelins, and then withdraw in good order before a counter-attack can be organized.

ABILITIES

- Can hide in long grass
- Bonus vs. elephants and chariots
- Combat bonus in woods
- Fast moving
- Can sap

Spearmen

Levy Pikemen

STATS

SOLDIERS: 60	DEFENSE SKILL: 3
ATTACK: 6	SHIELD: 2
CHARGE BONUS: 5	HIT POINTS: 1
WEAPON TYPE: Heavy	RECRUITMENT COST: 390
TOTAL DEFENSE: 5	UPKEEP: 150
ARMOR: 0	

Levy Pikemen are best used as defensive infantry, but their lack of armor leaves them vulnerable in battle.

ABILITIES

- Can form phalanx
- Bonus fighting cavalry
- Poor morale
- Very long spears
- Can sap

Militia Hoplites

STATS

SOLDIERS: 40	DEFENSE SKILL: 3
ATTACK: 5	SHIELD: 5
CHARGE BONUS: 5	HIT POINTS: 1
WEAPON TYPE: Light	RECRUITMENT COST: 280
TOTAL DEFENSE: 8	UPKEEP: 100
ARMOR: 0	

Militia Hoplites are levies drawn from cities and thrust into battle with a little training.

ABILITIES

- Can form phalanx
- Bonus fighting cavalry
- Poor morale
- Can sap

Phalanx Pikemen

STATS

SOLDIERS: 60	DEFENSE SKILL: 5
ATTACK: 8	SHIELD: 2
CHARGE BONUS: 6	HIT POINTS: 1
WEAPON TYPE: Heavy	RECRUITMENT COST: 660
TOTAL DEFENSE: 13	UPKEEP: 250
ARMOR: 6	

Phalanx Pikemen form the backbone of Macedonian and Seleucid battle lines, and are used to engage and hold the enemy's main force.

ABILITIES

- Can form phalanx
- Bonus fighting cavalry
- Very long spears
- Can sap

Silver Shield Pikemen

STATS

SOLDIERS: 61	DEFENSE SKILL: 6
ATTACK: 10	SHIELD: 2
CHARGE BONUS: 7	HIT POINTS: 1
WEAPON TYPE: Heavy	RECRUITMENT COST: 810
TOTAL DEFENSE: 14	UPKEEP: 360
ARMOR: 6	

Silver Shield Pikemen are the best of the Seleucid Pikemen, well disciplined and not likely to tire quickly.

ABILITIES

- Can form phalanx
- Bonus fighting cavalry
- Good morale
- Good stamina
- Very long spears
- Can sap

Seleucid Naval Units

Bireme

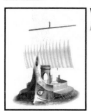

VESSELS: 20   DEFENSE: 2
ATTACK: 6

Trireme

VESSELS: 30   DEFENSE: 3
ATTACK: 8

Quinquireme

VESSELS: 50   DEFENSE: 5
ATTACK: 10

Seleucid Buildings

Government-Class Buildings

Governor's House

- Enables training of Peasants
- Enables construction of "First Tier" buildings

Governor's Villa

- Enables training of Peasants
- Enables recruitment of diplomats
- Enables construction of "Second Tier" buildings

Governor's Palace

- Enables training of Peasants
- Enables recruitment of diplomats
- Enables construction of "Third Tier" buildings

Councilor's Chambers

- Enables training of Peasants
- Enables recruitment of diplomats
- Enables construction of "Fourth Tier" buildings

Royal Palace

- Improved Generals' Bodyguards
- Enables training of Peasants
- Enables recruitment of diplomats
- Enables construction of "Fifth Tier" buildings

Wall-Class Buildings

Wooden Palisade (First Tier)

- Extra wall defenses

Wooden Wall (Second Tier)

- Extra wall defenses
- Reinforced gates

Stone Wall (Third Tier)

- Extra wall defenses
- Boiling oil
- Reinforced gates

Large Stone Wall (Fourth Tier)

- Extra wall defenses
- Iron gates
- Boiling oil

Epic Stone Wall (Fifth Tier)

- Extra wall defenses
- Iron gates
- Boiling oil

Barrack-Class Buildings

Barracks (First Tier)

- Enables training of Militia Hoplites

Militia Barracks (Second Tier)

- Enables training of Militia Hoplites
- Enables training of Levy Pikemen

City Barracks (Third Tier)

- Enables training of Militia Hoplites
- Enables training of Phalanx Pikemen
- Enables training of Levy Pikemen

Army Barracks (Fourth Tier)

- Enables training of Militia Hoplites
- Enables training of Levy Pikemen
- Enables training of Phalanx Pikemen
- Enables training of Silver Shield Pikemen

Royal Barracks (Fifth Tier)

- Enables training of Militia Hoplites
- Enables training of Levy Pikemen
- Enables training of Phalanx Pikemen
- Enables training of Silver Shield Pikemen
- Enables training of Silver Shield Legionaries

Stable-Class Buildings

Stables (Second Tier)

- Enables training of Militia Cavalry

Cavalry Stables (Third Tier)

- Enables training of Militia Cavalry
- Enables training of Greek Cavalry
- Enables training of Elephants

Elite Cavalry Stables (Fourth Tier)

- Enables training of Militia Cavalry
- Enables training of Greek Cavalry
- Enables training of Elephants
- Enables training of Cataphracts
- Enables training of War Elephants

Circus Maximus (Fifth Tier)

- Enables training of Militia Cavalry
- Enables training of Greek Cavalry
- Enables training of Elephants
- Enables training of Cataphracts
- Enables training of War Elephants
- Enables training of Companion Cavalry
- Enables training of Armored Elephants

Range-Class Buildings

Practice Range (Second Tier)

- Enables training of Peltasts

Archery Range (Third Tier)

- Enables training of Peltasts
- Enables training of Archers

Catapult Range (Fourth Tier)

- Enables training of Peltasts
- Enables training of Onagers
- Enables training of Archers

Trader-Class Buildings

Trader (First Tier)

- Increase in tradable goods
- Population Growth bonus: 0.5%

Market (Second Tier)

- Increase in tradable goods
- Enables recruitment of spies
- Population Growth bonus: 0.5%

Agora (Third Tier)

- Increase in tradable goods
- Enables recruitment of spies
- Population Growth bonus: 0.5%
- Enables recruitment of assassins

Great Agora (Fourth Tier)

- Increase in tradable goods
- Enables recruitment of spies
- Population Growth bonus: 1%
- Enables recruitment of assassins

Merchants' Quarter (Fifth Tier)

- Increase in tradable goods
- Enables recruitment of assassins
- Population Growth bonus: 1%
- Public Order bonus due to happiness: 10%
- Enables recruitment of spies

Smith-Class Buildings

Blacksmith (Second Tier)

- SPECIAL REQUIREMENT: Trader Building
- Upgrades light weapons: +1
- Upgrades heavy weapons: +1
- Enables training of Scythed Chariots

Armourer (Third Tier)

- SPECIAL REQUIREMENT: Market Building
- Upgrades light weapons: +1
- Upgrades heavy weapons: +1
- Upgrades missile weapons: +1
- Upgrades armor: +1
- Enables training of Scythed Chariots

Foundry (Fifth Tier)

- SPECIAL REQUIREMENT: Great Agora Building
- Upgrades light weapons: +2
- Upgrades heavy weapons: +2
- Upgrades missile weapons: +2
- Upgrades armor: +2
- Enables training of Scythed Chariots

Port-Class Buildings

Port (Second Tier)

- Grants one sea-trade fleet for extra income
- Enables training of Biremes

Shipwright (Third Tier)

- Grants two sea-trade fleets for extra income
- Enables training of Biremes
- Enables training of Triremes

Dockyard (Fourth Tier)

- Grants three sea-trade fleets for extra income
- Enables training of Biremes
- Enables training of Triremes
- Enables training of Quinquiremes

Water Supply-Class Buildings

Sewers (Second Tier)

- SPECIAL REQUIREMENT: Trader Building
- Public health bonus: 5%

Public Baths (Third Tier)

- SPECIAL REQUIREMENT: Market Building
- Public health bonus: 10%

Aqueduct (Fourth Tier)

- SPECIAL REQUIREMENT: Agora Building
- Public health bonus: 15%

Farm-Class Buildings

Land Clearance (First Tier)

- Improved farms and food production: +1

Communal Farming (Second Tier)

- Improved farms and food production: +2

Crop Rotation (Third Tier)

- Improved farms and food production: +3

Irrigation (Fourth Tier)

- Improved farms and food production: +4

Roads

Roads (First Tier)

- Improved roads and trade

Paved Roads (Second Tier)

- Improved roads and trade

Academy-Class Buildings

Academy (Third Tier)

- SPECIAL REQUIREMENT: Market Building
- Governors gain skills and knowledge

Scriptorium (Fourth Tier)

- SPECIAL REQUIREMENT: Agora Building
- Governors gain skills and knowledge

Ludus Magna (Fifth Tier)

- SPECIAL REQUIREMENT: Great Agora Building
- Governors gain skills and knowledge

Theater-Class Buildings

Odeon (Third Tier)

- Public Order bonus due to happiness: 5%

Lyceum (Fourth Tier)

- Public Order bonus due to happiness: 10%

Theater (Fifth Tier)

- Public Order bonus due to happiness: 15%

Temple-Class Buildings

Shrine to Hephaestus (First Tier)

- Public Order bonus due to happiness: 5%
- Upgrades light weapons: +1

Temple of Hephaestus (Second Tier)

- Public Order bonus due to happiness: 10%
- Upgrades light weapons: +1
- Upgrades heavy weapons: +1

Large Temple of Hephaestus (Third Tier)

- Public Order bonus due to happiness: 15%
- Upgrades light weapons: +1
- Upgrades heavy weapons: +1
- Upgrades armor: +1

Awesome Temple of Hephaestus (Fourth Tier)

- Public Order bonus due to happiness: 20%
- Upgrades light weapons: +1
- Upgrades heavy weapons: +1
- Upgrades armor: +1
- Experience bonus to troops trained here: +1

Pantheon (Ceres, Fifth Tier)

- Public Order bonus due to happiness: 25%
- Upgrades light weapons: +1
- Upgrades heavy weapons: +1
- Upgrades armor: +1
- Experience bonus to troops trained here: +2
- Public Order bonus due to law: 10%

Shrine to Dionysus (First Tier)

- Public Order bonus due to happiness: 10%

Temple of Dionysus (Second Tier)

- Public Order bonus due to happiness: 20%

Large Temple of Dionysus (Third Tier)

- Public Order bonus due to happiness: 30%

Awesome Temple of Dionysus (Fourth Tier)

- Public Order bonus due to happiness: 40%

Pantheon (Dionysus, Fifth Tier)

- Public Order bonus due to happiness: 50%
- Public Order bonus due to law: 10%
- Population Growth bonus: 1%

Shrine to Asklepios (First Tier)

- Public Order bonus due to happiness: 5%
- Public health bonus: 5%

Temple of Asklepios (Second Tier)

- Public Order bonus due to happiness: 10%
- Public health bonus: 10%

Large Temple of Asklepios (Third Tier)

- Public Order bonus due to happiness: 15%
- Public health bonus: 15%

Awesome Temple of Asklepios (Fourth Tier)

- Public Order bonus due to happiness: 20%
- Public health bonus: 5%

Pantheon (Asklepios, Fifth Tier)

- Public Order bonus due to happiness: 25%
- Public health bonus: 25%
- Increase in tradable goods
- Experience bonus to troops trained here: +2

Spanish Military Units

Animal Units (Heavy)

Warhounds

STATS	
SOLDIERS: 12	DEFENSE SKILL: 1
ATTACK: 12	SHIELD: 0
CHARGE BONUS: 2	HIT POINTS: 1
WEAPON TYPE: Light	RECRUITMENT COST: 490
TOTAL DEFENSE: 3	UPKEEP: 50
ARMOR: 2	

Warhounds are bred for a savage nature and great size, but then hunting men is only a little more dangerous than hunting wild boar!

ABILITIES
- Frighten nearby enemy
- Fast moving

Artillery Units

Onagers

STATS	
SOLDIERS: 32	ARMOR: 0
ATTACK VS. TROOPS: 53	DEFENSE SKILL: 3
ATTACK VS. BUILDINGS: 35	SHIELD: 0
CHARGE BONUS: 0	HIT POINTS: 1
WEAPON TYPE: Light	RECRUITMENT COST: 1390
TOTAL DEFENSE: 3	UPKEEP: 180

The Onager is a versatile catapult that can launch boulders or incendiary firepots at enemy troops and fortifications.

ABILITIES
- Area attack
- Can't hide
- Very long range missiles
- Inaccurate against troops
- Can use Flaming Missiles

Cavalry Units (Light)

Long Shield Cavalry

STATS	
SOLDIERS: 27	DEFENSE SKILL: 6
ATTACK: 9	SHIELD: 4
CHARGE BONUS: 8	HIT POINTS: 1
WEAPON TYPE: Light	RECRUITMENT COST: 460
TOTAL DEFENSE: 13	UPKEEP: 140
ARMOR: 3	

Long Shield Cavalry are spear-armed light cavalry, who can be used to break enemy formations, drive off skirmishers and pursue fleeing foes.

ABILITIES
- Can form wedge
- Powerful charge
- Good morale

Round Shield Cavalry

STATS	
SOLDIERS: 27	DEFENSE SKILL: 4
ATTACK: 7	SHIELD: 2
CHARGE BONUS: 2	HIT POINTS: 1
WEAPON TYPE: Light	RECRUITMENT COST: 280
TOTAL DEFENSE: 8	UPKEEP: 110
ARMOR: 2	

Round Shield Cavalry are best used to ride down skirmishers and pursue fleeing enemies.

ABILITIES
- Can form wedge

Infantry Units (Light)

Iberian Infantry

STATS	
SOLDIERS: 40	DEFENSE SKILL: 4
ATTACK: 7	SHIELD: 2
CHARGE BONUS: 2	HIT POINTS: 1
WEAPON TYPE: Light	RECRUITMENT COST: 240
TOTAL DEFENSE: 8	UPKEEP: 170
ARMOR: 2	

These infantry are the steady backbone of the armies of Carthage and Spain. Reliable, well-armed and tough, they are armed with falcatas to cut a path into an enemy line.

ABILITIES
- Warcry improves attack
- Can sap

Peasants

STATS	
SOLDIERS: 61	DEFENSE SKILL: 3
ATTACK: 3	SHIELD: 0
CHARGE BONUS: 2	HIT POINTS: 1
WEAPON TYPE: Light	RECRUITMENT COST: 120
TOTAL DEFENSE: 3	UPKEEP: 100
ARMOR: 0	

Peasants are reluctant warriors, at best. Going to war is just one more burden of a hard life.

ABILITIES
- Warcry improves attack
- Can sap
- Poor morale

Scutarii

STATS

SOLDIERS: 41	ARMOR: 5
MELEE ATTACK: 9	DEFENSE SKILL: 2
MISSILE ATTACK: 13	SHIELD: 5
CHARGE BONUS: 4	HIT POINTS: 1
WEAPON TYPE: Heavy	RECRUITMENT COST: 420
TOTAL DEFENSE: 12	UPKEEP: 140

Scutarii are well-equipped light infantry armed with swords, shields and heavy javelins.

ABILITIES

- Warcry improves attack
- Expert at hiding in woods
- Javelins thrown before charge
- May charge without orders

Town Militia

STATS

SOLDIERS: 40	DEFENSE SKILL: 2
ATTACK: 3	SHIELD: 5
CHARGE BONUS: 4	HIT POINTS: 1
WEAPON TYPE: Light	RECRUITMENT COST: 150
TOTAL DEFENSE: 7	UPKEEP: 100
ARMOR: 0	

Town Militia are trained bands of citizens dragged from their homes and shops, given a spear each and some rudimentary training.

ABILITIES

- Warcry improves attack
- Poor morale
- Can sap

Infantry Units (Heavy)

Bull Warriors

STATS

SOLDIERS: 41	ARMOR: 5
MELEE ATTACK: 13	DEFENSE SKILL: 5
MISSILE ATTACK: 17	SHIELD: 2
CHARGE BONUS: 5	HIT POINTS: 2
WEAPON TYPE: Heavy	RECRUITMENT COST: 1050
TOTAL DEFENSE: 12	UPKEEP: 200

Bull Warriors are men whose bravery, stamina and skill are unmatched. These elite fighters are shock troops.

ABILITIES

- Warcry improves attack
- Expert at hiding in woods
- Javelins thrown before charge
- Excellent morale
- May charge without orders
- Good stamina
- Fast moving

Naked Fanatics

STATS

SOLDIERS: 40	DEFENSE SKILL: 2
ATTACK: 13	SHIELD: 5
CHARGE BONUS: 6	HIT POINTS: 1
WEAPON TYPE: Light	RECRUITMENT COST: 380
TOTAL DEFENSE: 7	UPKEEP: 130
ARMOR: 0	

Wild and savage, Naked Fanatics are always a threat but are at a disadvantage when fighting cavalry.

ABILITIES

- Warcry improves attack
- Expert at hiding in woods
- Combat bonus in woods or snow
- May charge without orders
- Good morale
- Good stamina

Infantry Units (Missile)

Skirmishers

STATS

SOLDIERS: 40	ARMOR: 0
MELEE ATTACK: 3	DEFENSE SKILL: 2
MISSILE ATTACK: 6	SHIELD: 2
CHARGE BONUS: 2	HIT POINTS: 1
WEAPON TYPE: Missile	RECRUITMENT COST: 180
TOTAL DEFENSE: 4	UPKEEP: 170

Skirmishers rush forward to pepper an enemy with javelins, and then withdraw in good order before a counter-attack can be organized.

ABILITIES

- Can hide in long grass
- Bonus vs. elephants and chariots
- Fast moving
- Can sap

Slingers

STATS

SOLDIERS: 40	ARMOR: 0
MELEE ATTACK: 3	DEFENSE SKILL: 2
MISSILE ATTACK: 3	SHIELD: 2
CHARGE BONUS: 2	HIT POINTS: 1
WEAPON TYPE: Missile	RECRUITMENT COST: 150
TOTAL DEFENSE: 4	UPKEEP: 170

Slingers are highly skilled missile troops but are at a huge disadvantage in hand-to-hand combat, especially against cavalry.

ABILITIES

- Fast moving
- Can sap

Spanish Naval Units

Boats

| VESSELS: 15 | DEFENSE: 1 |
| ATTACK: 6 | |

Large Boats

| VESSELS: 30 | DEFENSE: 3 |
| ATTACK: 8 | |

Bireme

| VESSELS: 20 | DEFENSE: 2 |
| ATTACK: 6 | |

Trireme

| VESSELS: 30 | DEFENSE: 3 |
| ATTACK: 8 | |

Quinquireme

| VESSELS: 50 | DEFENSE: 5 |
| ATTACK: 10 | |

> **NOTE**
> You cannot play as the Spanish in the Imperial Campaign mode, so their buildings are not listed in this guide.

Thracian Military Units

Artillery Units

Onagers

STATS

SOLDIERS: 32	ARMOR: 0
ATTACK VS. TROOPS: 53	DEFENSE SKILL: 3
ATTACK VS. BUILDINGS: 35	SHIELD: 0
CHARGE BONUS: 0	HIT POINTS: 1
WEAPON TYPE: Light	RECRUITMENT COST: 1390
TOTAL DEFENSE: 3	UPKEEP: 180

The Onager is a versatile catapult that can launch boulders or incendiary firepots at enemy troops and fortifications.

ABILITIES

- Area attack
- Very long range missiles
- Can use Flaming Missiles
- Can't hide
- Inaccurate against troops

Cavalry Units (Light)

Greek Cavalry

STATS

SOLDIERS: 27	DEFENSE SKILL: 5
ATTACK: 7	SHIELD: 0
CHARGE BONUS: 7	HIT POINTS: 1
WEAPON TYPE: Light	RECRUITMENT COST: 300
TOTAL DEFENSE: 8	UPKEEP: 110
ARMOR: 3	

Greek Cavalry are fast moving horsemen armed with spears for maximum impact in a charge.

ABILITIES

- Can form wedge

Cavalry Units (Missile)

Militia Cavalry

STATS

SOLDIERS: 27	ARMOR: 0
MELEE ATTACK: 6	DEFENSE SKILL: 2
MISSILE ATTACK: 6	SHIELD: 4
CHARGE BONUS: 2	HIT POINTS: 1
WEAPON TYPE: Missile	RECRUITMENT COST: 320
TOTAL DEFENSE: 6	UPKEEP: 110

Militia Cavalry are javelin-armed mounted skirmishers who can strike quickly and be gone before the enemy reacts.

ABILITIES

- Can form Cantabrian circle
- Fast moving

Infantry Units (Light)

Peasants

STATS

SOLDIERS: 61	DEFENSE SKILL: 1
ATTACK: 1	SHIELD: 0
CHARGE BONUS: 1	HIT POINTS: 1
WEAPON TYPE: Light	RECRUITMENT COST: 60
TOTAL DEFENSE: 1	UPKEEP: 100
ARMOR: 0	

Peasants are reluctant warriors, at best. Going to war is just one more burden of a hard life.

ABILITIES

- Poor morale
- Can sap

Infantry Units (Heavy)

Bastarnae

STATS

SOLDIERS: 40	DEFENSE SKILL: 2
ATTACK: 14	SHIELD: 2
CHARGE BONUS: 8	HIT POINTS: 2
WEAPON TYPE: Heavy	RECRUITMENT COST: 720
TOTAL DEFENSE: 6	UPKEEP: 130
ARMOR: 2	

Fierce warriors adept at close quarters against other infantry, Bastarnae may attack without orders.

ABILITIES

- Expert at hiding in woods
- Good morale
- Combat bonus in woods or snow
- Powerful charge
- May charge without orders
- Fast moving

Falxmen

STATS

SOLDIERS: 41	DEFENSE SKILL: 7
ATTACK: 13	SHIELD: 0
CHARGE BONUS: 7	HIT POINTS: 1
WEAPON TYPE: Heavy	RECRUITMENT COST: 460
TOTAL DEFENSE: 10	UPKEEP: 170
ARMOR: 3	

Falxmen are used to carve a path into enemy formations. They are superior, but somewhat ill-disciplined warriors.

ABILITIES

- Expert at hiding in woods
- Good morale
- Combat bonus in woods or snow
- Fast moving
- May charge without orders

Infantry Units (Missile)

Archers

STATS

SOLDIERS: 40	ARMOR: 0
MELEE ATTACK: 3	DEFENSE SKILL: 2
MISSILE ATTACK: 7	SHIELD: 0
CHARGE BONUS: 2	HIT POINTS: 1
WEAPON TYPE: Missile	RECRUITMENT COST: 180
TOTAL DEFENSE: 2	UPKEEP: 170

Archers are rightly feared for the casualties they can inflict, but they are vulnerable in hand-to-hand combat.

ABILITIES

- Combat bonus in woods
- Fast moving
- Can use Flaming Missiles
- Can sap

Peltasts

STATS

SOLDIERS: 40	ARMOR: 0
MELEE ATTACK: 3	DEFENSE SKILL: 2
MISSILE ATTACK: 6	SHIELD: 2
CHARGE BONUS: 2	HIT POINTS: 1
WEAPON TYPE: Missile	RECRUITMENT COST: 180
TOTAL DEFENSE: 4	UPKEEP: 170

Thracian Peltasts advance at speed to pepper an enemy with javelins, and then withdraw in good order before a counter-attack can be organized.

ABILITIES

- Can hide in long grass
- Fast moving
- Bonus vs. elephants and chariots
- Can sap
- Combat bonus in woods

Spearmen

Militia Hoplites

STATS

SOLDIERS: 40	DEFENSE SKILL: 3
ATTACK: 5	SHIELD: 5
CHARGE BONUS: 5	HIT POINTS: 1
WEAPON TYPE: Light	RECRUITMENT COST: 280
TOTAL DEFENSE: 8	UPKEEP: 100
ARMOR: 0	

Militia Hoplites are levies drawn from cities and thrust into battle with a little training.

ABILITIES

- Can form phalanx
- Bonus fighting cavalry
- Poor morale
- Can sap

Phalanx Pikemen

STATS

SOLDIERS: 60	DEFENSE SKILL: 5
ATTACK: 8	SHIELD: 2
CHARGE BONUS: 6	HIT POINTS: 1
WEAPON TYPE: Heavy	RECRUITMENT COST: 660
TOTAL DEFENSE: 13	UPKEEP: 250
ARMOR: 6	

Phalanx Pikemen form the backbone of Macedonian and Seleucid battle lines, and are used to engage and hold the enemy's main force.

ABILITIES

- Can form phalanx
- Bonus fighting cavalry
- Very long spears
- Can sap

Thracian Naval Units

Bireme

VESSELS: 20	DEFENSE: 2
ATTACK: 6	

Trireme

VESSELS: 30	DEFENSE: 3
ATTACK: 8	

Quinquireme

VESSELS: 50	DEFENSE: 5
ATTACK: 10	

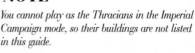

NOTE

You cannot play as the Thracians in the Imperial Campaign mode, so their buildings are not listed in this guide.

TOTAL WAR: FIGHTING (AND WINNING) BATTLES

Picking a Fight

Before you start a fight, you've got to pick it first. If you're playing a Historic Battle, the battle is already determined for you, and you take control of your army at the beginning of the battle. If you are playing the Imperial Campaign, you must choose to attack an enemy army on the Campaign Map (see the Imperial Campaign section of this guide for more information).

Battle Deployment Scroll

At the start of a battle in the Imperial Campaign, the Battle Deployment Scroll appears. This contains some important information about the battle that is about to take place, including a comparison of the two armies' relative strengths and a list of available reinforcements in the area. You can then choose to  manually fight the battle on the battlefield, have the battle automatically resolved, or withdraw from the battle if you can.

Sieges

Sieges are special battles fought against an army defending a settlement. While most battles require you to kill or rout the opposing army, a siege gives you a third option for victory: Occupy the town plaza in the center of the settlement and hold it against all enemy units. You need to have at least one siege weapon to fight a  siege if the enemy has any Wall-Class Buildings defending their settlement. (For more information on sieges, refer to the Siege section at the end of this chapter.)

Reinforcements

Reinforcements are friendly or allied troops in the vicinity of the battle that may be called into action. Having reinforcements nearby dramatically increases an army's chance of victory. (For more information on reinforcements, refer to the Reinforcements section at the end of this chapter.)

Terrain and Weather

Pay attention to the terrain, weather and other physical features of your battlefield, as they all have an effect on your army's performance.

Bridges

Bridges favor defenders. Attacking forces must cross in very narrow columns, which allows for the bridge to be defended by a much smaller force. Flanking a bridge defender is not an option either, unless you do it from a different crossing point. A single unit of strong spearmen in phalanx formation with a few missile troops supporting them might be all you need to hold the bridge and deny an enemy advance.

Cliffs and Valleys

Cliffs and valleys limit your mobility. On the bright side, you can use them to defend one flank of your army. On the down side, you can be backed into them and have your avenues of escape cut off.

Extreme Temperatures

In sweltering summer heat or frigid winter climes, your men will tire especially quickly, so don't exhaust them by running them ragged.

Hills

When fighting on a hill, remember that the high ground is advantageous. If you absolutely must attack uphill, choose the gentlest slope possible to minimize your attack penalty. Use missile units to attack the enemy before clashing in hand-to-hand combat; you might just get lucky and drive them off of the hill!

Moving around behind hills is also an excellent way to hide your actions from your enemy. If you do it carefully, you can set up a crushing flanking maneuver that your rivals will never see coming.

Rain and Snow

Rain and snow negatively affect the stamina and attacking ability of most units (unless specifically mentioned in the unit description). You might wish to press the Wait Button at the start of the battle to delay it in order to wait for the inclement weather to pass.

Scrub

Scrub is dense grass and underbrush that entangles the feet of marching troops. It has an especially negative effect on cavalry.

Woods

Sending units into wooded areas hides them from the enemy, although fighting in the woods also lowers the attack and defense values of any units not specifically trained for woodland combat (it also disrupts formations, which can adversely affect Phalanxes and Legionaries). Hiding your main force in a wooded area and luring the enemy past them with a couple of highly mobile visible units is an excellent way to perform a devastating flanking maneuver.

NOTE

Generals and warlords can never hide in woods, as they must ensure that their troops know where they are at all times. Siege machines and artillery units are too large to move into woods, much less hide in them.

If you see birds rising and circling over a wooded area, there are troops hiding in it.

Before the Battle

Before the battle actually commences, there are several things you should do and pay attention to.

General's Speech

Before most Imperial Campaign battles, your General gives an inspirational speech abut the coming clash. Listen carefully to what he has to say, as he may give you some important clues as to how best to fight and win the battle.

Deploying Troops

Unless you are ambushed, you are allowed to deploy your troops in any configuration you want before a battle by left-clicking on a unit and right-clicking the area where you want to deploy it. Make good use of this opportunity, as nothing improves your odds for success like getting off on the right foot. Make good use of this opportunity, as nothing improves your odds for success like getting off on the right foot.

Military Advisor

If you have enabled it, your military advisor appears in the upper-left corner of the screen and offers context-sensitive advice during the course of the battle. It's recommended that you listen to him until you feel comfortable with the intricacies of combat in *Rome: Total War*.

Viewing the Battlefield

Getting a good look at the battlefield is the first thing you should do at the start of a battle. Press P to pause the game and use the arrow keys or mouse to scroll along the battlefield.

Examine the dust clouds kicked up by your enemy to get a better idea of what troops they're bringing to the fight. High columns of dust indicate cavalry, while low clouds are the result of marching infantry.

Default Camera Controls

Command	Effect
Move cursor to top or bottom edge of screen, or up and down arrow keys	Track forward and backward
Move cursor to left or right edge of screen	Pan right or left
Move cursor to left or right edge of control panel, or right and left arrow keys	Track right and left
Mouse wheel (spin), or / and * on the numeric keypad	Change camera height
Mouse wheel (click and hold)	Zoom in on cursor position
- and + on the numeric keypad	Alter camera tilt without changing height

Battlefield Control Panel

The **battlefield control panel** appears at the bottom of the screen during a battle and contains a variety of useful commands and information. The battlefield control panel is divided into three parts: the Mini-Map, the unit cards and the unit controls.

Mini-Map

The **Mini-Map** shows a zoomed-out view of the entire battlefield, with every visible unit indicated by an arrow. Click the + and – buttons to the right of the Mini-Map to zoom it in and out.

The hourglass next to the Mini-Map represents the time limit of the battle. You must win the battle before the sand is completely gone from the hourglass, or your troops retreat in defeat.

A bar below the Mini-Map represents the relative strength of each army. When a unit is killed or routed, the other army gains strength. The blue bar represents your strength, and the red bar represents your opponent's strength.

Unit Cards

Each unit card represents a single unit in your army. The number on the card represents the number of men in that unit. As your unit takes casualties, this number drops.

Generals and warlords are marked with a gold star. Experienced units or units with improved weapons or armor are labeled with special icons, such as chevrons (experience), swords (weapons), or shields (armor).

Units capable of firing missiles have an additional blue bar at the bottom of their card that represents their ammunition level. If this bar is empty, the unit is out of ammunition and must fight hand-to-hand.

Right-click on a unit card while the game is paused to view expanded information about that unit.

Unit Controls

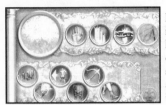

Mouse over the command buttons in the unit controls section of the battlefield control panel to see the commands available to the selected units. Not every unit has all of the following commands at their disposal.

COMMAND BUTTONS

COMMAND	DESCRIPTION
Halt	Cancels unit's current orders and brings it to a stop (see following)
Group	Group selected units (see following)
Link	Link selected units (see following)
AI Assistance	Puts units under AI control (see following)
Withdraw	Command selected units to retreat in orderly fashion (see following)
Unit Formation	Toggle between tight (strong line) or loose (best against missiles) formation
Skirmish	Skirmishing units avoid hand-to-hand combat; best for missile troops
Fire at Will	Automatically shoot at nearby enemies
Special Ability	Use unit's special ability (see the Factions section for more info on special abilities)
Guard	Stops units from pursing; makes units hold formation more effectively; increases units' defense stat slightly, but at the cost of their attack
Walk/Run	Toggle the speed of unit movement (running will tire out units faster)

Managing Your Troops

Strong troop management almost always means the difference between victory and defeat. History is littered with the bodies of great armies wasted under the command of incompetents.

Selecting Units

Before you can order a unit to do anything, you have to select it. There are three main ways to select a unit:

1. **Left-click on the unit's banner or any member of the unit.**
2. **Left-click on the unit's card in the battlefield control panel.**
3. **Hold the left mouse button and drag the mouse to draw a box on the battlefield that selects all of your units within it.**

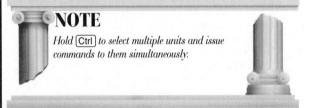

NOTE

Hold Ctrl *to select multiple units and issue commands to them simultaneously.*

Issuing Commands

Once you've selected your units, click on a unit command in the unit controls section of the battlefield control panel to issue a command to it.

AI Assistance

If you're overwhelmed by a battle taking place on several different fronts, highlight a group of units and press the AI Assistance Button (which is also the linking button when a single unit is selected) to appoint an AI captain to take control of the group, leaving you free to focus on other areas of the battle.

Grouping Units

Grouping units creates smaller subdivisions of the selected units in your army and allows you to more easily fight a battle on two fronts, for example. To group units, select all of the units you want to include and then click the Group Selected Units Button. You can then select all of the units in a group by clicking on the group tab in the battlefield control panel.

Importance of the General

Your General (sometimes referred to as a warlord or chieftain) is the most important unit in your army. Not only is he usually one of the most powerful units under your command, his presence improves the morale of your nearby troops and weakens the morale of surrounding enemy troops.

Despite your General's great power, however, you don't want to constantly throw him into the thick of battle. Even the greatest warriors are mortal, and the loss of your General could crush your army's spirit and send them into a rout (see Morale at the end of this section).

Moving and Attacking

Once you have selected one or more units, right-click anywhere on the battlefield map to send them marching toward that point. Double-right-click to send them running.

If you right-click on an enemy unit, your selected unit(s) will move straight toward that enemy and attack it. If you double-right-click on an enemy unit, your selected unit(s) will charge the enemy, moving faster and dealing more damage when they hit, at the cost of some stamina.

The cursor icon that appears when you mouse over an enemy unit describes the attack your forces will use. A sword means hand-to-hand combat, while javelins and arrows represent missile combat.

Setting Waypoints

If you want your selected unit(s) to perform a more elaborate movement—such as running through a breach in a city wall or running past an enemy unit and making a U-turn for a flanking attack—hold down Shift while right-clicking on the battlefield map to set waypoints. Your units will move to each of these waypoints in order.

Charging

Charging toward an enemy army deals greater damage on impact and can smash their defensive line, allowing you to push past their infantry to reach their more vulnerable troops. Counter an enemy charge with a solid line of infantry. When they crash into you, occupy them with your infantry while peppering them with missile fire from a distance, and send cavalry around to their exposed flanks.

If your enemy is charging you, move your troops into a defensive position and let the enemy come. They'll be tired from their advance, giving you the upper hand. The only exception to this rule is if you can send your troops in for a quick and effective counter-charge before the enemy is fully prepared. Knocking them off-balance from the start of the battle is worth sacrificing a bit of stamina. But don't ever try this against an enemy who has already formed into tight battle lines.

Alternate Attack Modes

Some units have both missile and melee attacks. Right-clicking on an enemy causes the unit to attack with its default weapon, but holding down Alt while right-clicking on an enemy employs its alternate attack. Look at the cursor to determine what type of attack the unit is going to use.

Group Formations

Selecting a group of units and pressing a Shift key combination aligns them in a group formation. There are several different group formations to choose from, each with its own distinct tactical advantages.

GROUP FORMATION COMMANDS

COMMAND	GROUP FORMATION
Shift + 1	Single Line
Shift + 2	Sorted Single Line
Shift + 3	Double Line
Shift + 4	Sorted Double Line
Shift + 5	Missile First 3 Line
Shift + 6	Foot First 3 Line
Shift + 7	Cavalry First 3 Line
Shift + 8	Column

NOTE

Artillery (siege machines) and animal handlers are always deployed behind the main force, regardless of formation.

Cavalry First 3 Line

This sets your troops up in three lines: cavalry first, followed by infantry, and then missile. Use this formation only if your enemy's infantry is significantly weaker than your own. Your cavalry will plow through the enemy lines, smashing through and allowing your infantry to follow up on the attack while you pull your cavalry back for another charge. Never use this formation if your enemy has spearmen in his front line!

Column

Intended for attacking or defending a narrow path, such as a bridge or breach in a city wall, the column formation places your troops into single-file lines, sorted by unit. You can also use this formation when space is limited and doesn't allow for a traditional battle line.

Double Line

Similar to the single line formation, a double line simply draws your units into two parallel lines without strategically positioning any of them. Use it for holding or supporting a defensive position.

Foot First 3 Line

Foot first formation places your heavy infantry in the first line, backed up by missile troops in the second line, and cavalry in the third. This formation is best used to counter a charging enemy.

Missile First 3 Line

Like the name implies, missile first formation puts your missile troops at the front of the line, with non-missile infantry in the second line, and cavalry in the third line. Use this formation to pick off distant enemies, and send your infantry and cavalry in for a charge to protect your missile units when the enemy draws near.

Single Line Formation

A single line formation stretches your units into a line without any strategic positioning. It's good for quickly holding a defensive position.

Sorted Double Line

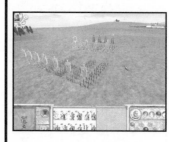

A sorted double line is identical to a sorted single line, except your units are two rows deep instead of one. Like a sorted single line, a sorted double line should be used to surround an enemy force.

Sorted Single Line

Best used for surrounding the enemy, a sorted single line formation places heavy infantry in the center, with light infantry and missile troops stretching out to the sides. Cavalry is placed at the ends, ready to swoop down onto the flanks of engaged enemy troops.

Unit Facing

Generally speaking, the front of a unit—or its **facing** direction—is its best-defended position. If a unit is attacked from any other direction, the unit is **flanked**, which is generally much more damaging than a frontal assault.

To change a unit's facing without moving it, select the unit and use ⟨<⟩ and ⟨>⟩ to rotate its facing. This is best used when you see that an enemy is trying to flank you.

Unit vs. Unit Strengths and Weaknesses

Although there are dozens of different units in *Rome: Total War*, most are broken down into five distinct groups: cavalry, infantry, spearmen, missile, and siege. Each of these units has particular strengths and weaknesses against other units.

Cavalry

Cavalry are fast-moving mounted units that can outmaneuver anything else on the battlefield. They are best used to flank enemy units (especially spearmen) that are tied up in battle with other units. They're also good for luring enemy units out of line for an exhausting chase, countering a rival cavalry charge, or chasing down enemy missile units. Cavalry do significantly more damage while charging, so send them charging in against enemy troops, then withdraw them and repeat the charge.

Generally speaking, use light cavalry against missile units and heavy cavalry against light cavalry.

Cavalry units are generally vulnerable to missile fire and particularly vulnerable to spearmen, especially in phalanx formation. You can also rout them quickly by spooking the mounts with fire, especially Flaming Arrows. All cavalry units are completely wasted in defensive roles. Use them offensively as a rule.

Elephants and camels can frighten and rout horse cavalry. Camels are frightened of elephants as well. Although tough to scare, elephants may run amok and trample friendly troops if frightened in battle. If this happens, use the unit's special ability to kill the elephants before they take out your troops.

NOTE

Javelin-armed troops, such as Velites, are very effective against elephants. Set them to skirmish and lose formation for maximum effectiveness.

Infantry

Infantry are the backbone of any army—think of them as your linebackers. These foot soldiers are best used to engage and occupy enemy forces and set them up for an attack on their flanks by swifter cavalry units. Infantry units equipped with javelins or other thrown missile weapons will automatically fire them just before charging to soften up the enemy line.

NOTE

Some infantry units can sap enemy city walls, creating a breach that opens them up for attack. Consult your individual units' abilities to see if any of them have this ability. Building a sapping point and deploying it against enemy walls is much less obvious than deploying a siege machine.

You're not going to win a battle using only infantry troops. Although they present a fierce front to their enemies, they're not the most tactically versatile troops in your army. All infantry units are best used to hold the line and allow spearmen, missile troops, and calvary to position themselves for maximum effectiveness. Note that heavy calvary will last longer than light calvary (which may fold relatively quickly).

Don't ask infantry to do anything that they're not intended to do, or their limitations will become painfully obvious.

Missile

Missile troops should never be used in hand-to-hand combat, except as a last resort when their ammunition is depleted. They are best used against the distant front line of an advancing army or against light cavalry—just make sure to pull them back behind infantry units when the enemy draws near!

Using flaming ammunition against enemy troops results in fewer kills but has a much greater effect on enemy morale.

Missile units with spears or javelins are more effective against heavily armored troops than missile units that fire slings or arrows. However, slings and arrows have a much longer range than spears and javelins.

Missile troops are generally helpless against infantry or cavalry in hand-to-hand combat, so don't let them get too far ahead of heavier units that they can quickly hide behind. Even if an enemy unit can't catch them, missile units set to **skirmish** mode will continue to back away from any advancing troops, effectively taking them out of the battle. Friendly fire is also an issue for missile troops, as they may accidentally hit their own infantry while firing into massed combat.

The best defense against missile troops is to put your troops into loose formation, which minimizes the effectiveness of the barrage of missiles. Certain units can also form special defensive postures (such as the testudo formation) that limit casualties from missile attacks.

Siege

Siege weapons are primarily designed for—you guessed it—besieging settlements. Make sure you use the right siege weapon for the right job:

- **Ballistae and scorpions fire**

large spears or bolts at tremendous speeds and are most effective against massed units, rather than gates or walls.

- **ONAGERS** are boulder-hurling catapults best used against buildings and walls. They can fire flaming ammunition, which starts fires in any settlement unfortunate enough to be besieged by them.

- Siege towers and ladders should be placed against heavily defended walls. They are vulnerable to enemy artillery.

All siege machines are initially operated by extremely weak and vulnerable soldiers. If your enemy is foolish enough to leave the machines undefended, send out your fastest troops to kill or rout the operators and take their most powerful units out of the battle in one fell swoop.

By the same token, you should always be sure that your siege engines are well defended. If your siege machine operators are killed, you can send another foot unit to take control of the machine by selecting the unit and right-clicking on the machine.

Spearmen

Spearmen are devastating attackers and, in their dreaded phalanx formation, a virtual meat grinder to any foes who charge them from the front. Although slow, they are particularly deadly against charging cavalry. Keeping spearmen at your flanks ensures that you can neutralize any cavalry attempting to flank you, and positioning them in the center of your line creates a virtual battering ram that can plow through the toughest enemy units.

To defeat spearmen, occupy them with infantry troops and send cavalry

CAUTION

Spearmen in a phalanx formation cannot run, so they react very slowly to sudden changes on the battlefield or in their orders.

around to their unprotected flanks—the spearmen won't be able to turn and attack effectively and will be quickly destroyed. You can also use light cavalry to lure them out of formation and send other units in to attack their exposed flanks. The only units you ever want to use for a frontal assault on spearmen in phalanx formation are other phalanxed spearmen.

Withdraw

If you find yourself hopelessly outmatched, click the Withdraw Button immediately. This causes your selected units to retreat from the battlefield in an orderly manner, as opposed to a full-scale rout. Although you lose the battle, any non-routed troops that withdraw from it live to fight another day and remain in your army.

Halt

Click on the Halt Button to cancel all orders for the selected troops. You could also just give them different orders without telling them to halt, but this is a good way to get them to stop quickly and prepare to accept new orders.

Morale

A unit doesn't have to be killed to be taken out of the battle. If a unit's morale is crushed, it will turn and rout, fleeing the field of battle and bringing shame upon its army.

Affecting Factors

A unit's morale is negatively affected by the following factors:

- Significant losses, especially rapid losses
- Being outnumbered by superior troops
- Fire and flaming weapons
- The rout of nearby friendly units
- The death of their General or warlord
- The presence of an enemy General or warlord
- Frightening animals, such as elephants
- The special abilities of certain units (screeching, war drums, etc.)

A unit's morale is positively affected by the following factors:

- The presence of their General or warlord
- Significant gains over local enemies, whether routed or killed
- The special abilities of certain units (carrying standards, chanting, etc.)
- Distance from the enemy

Routed Units

If a unit suffers a critical blow to its morale, it routs; its flags turn white, and it starts running from the battlefield. Routed troops are no longer under anyone's control and are no longer considered a part of their army. If all of an army's troops are simultaneously routed, that army loses the battle as surely as if all of the troops had been destroyed.

Routing is contagious. If you can cause a unit to rout, you have a better chance of routing all nearby enemy units. As more units rout, the remaining non-routed units suffer increasing morale penalties, and it snowballs from there.

If a routed unit cannot escape from the thick of battle because it is surrounded, the unit fights to the death. Battling units in this condition is a foolish mistake. It's far better to let a routed unit run than to dedicate resources to fighting it instead of other non-routed units.

Rallying the Troops

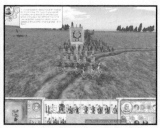

If a unit routs, it runs from the battlefield at top speed, and you lose control over it. Some units will recover their composure after they reach a certain distance from any enemy units. When this happens, their white banners turn back to the standard of your army, and you can control them again.

Each General or warlord also has the special ability to rally his troops. Move your General or warlord close to routing troops and use the Rally Ability to try and convince them to return to the fray. This ability works best on troops that are far removed from any enemy units.

Fatigue

Tired troops suffer penalties to attacking, defending, and morale, so keep your troops as fresh as possible. Don't force them to run when a walk will do. Cavalry units have much higher stamina than foot soldiers, though certain units have unusually high stamina for their class.

Siege Warfare

Siege warfare takes place when you are trying to capture an enemy settlement. Before you can achieve victory, you have to break through the city walls and conquer its defenders.

You have to be careful how you use your artillery. You're not firing precision laser-guided smart bombs; you're using a simple lever to hurl boulders. Siege artillery is infamously inaccurate and may accidentally wind up hitting your own troops if they are standing between the artillery and the target. Artillery is best employed against large, stationary targets (like buildings) or against massed enemy troops, where even a near miss can inflict catastrophic casualties.

Capturing Walls

Many settlements will be encircled by sturdy walls. Before you can take a settlement, you have to get past the walls, which is no easy feat. Use siege machines to batter down doors or sections of the wall, and send your heaviest troops in to the breach to take the wall and secure a beachhead for the invasion of the town. This keeps enemy archers and ballistae from firing on your units.

Some infantry units have the ability to sap walls, which means that they dig a tunnel under the wall and light a fire in the tunnel that collapses a section of the wall. To deploy a sapping point, left-click to select it and then drag it onto a section of the wall. Once battle has started, select an infantry unit and right-click on the sapping point. Sapping is a slightly more subtle way to create a breach in a wall, and you can distract your enemies from your sappers by making a big show of using siege machines elsewhere.

Siege Defense

If you're on the defending side of a siege, there are really only two things you have to do: Send heavy troops to guard any breach in your walls, and keep the enemy occupied until time runs out. Don't leave the city to attack the enemy, unless you're taking a pounding from enemy artillery. Instead, make them come to you and fight on your terms.

Ballista towers mounted on your settlement walls are the best way to destroy enemy siege engines. Of course, they quickly become a prime target for enemy artillery as well.

Conditions for Victory

If you're the attacking force in a siege, you win by either destroying or routing all enemy units (as usual) or by capturing and holding the plaza in the center of town for three minutes. Capturing and holding the town plaza requires you to move at least one unit onto the plaza and keep all enemy units from setting foot on it.

If you are defending a settlement against a siege, you win by either destroying or routing all enemy units or by preventing the enemy from taking the town within the time limit.

Reinforcements

If you've got reinforcements on the way, adopt a defensive posture and wait for them to arrive. The best way to win a battle is with overwhelming force, so don't go off half-cocked. Make your enemy come to you and tire his forces out while he does.

Friendly vs. Allied

Friendly armies are of a different clan, family, or empire but allied with your own. Friendly reinforcements appear on the battlefield en masse and are always under the control of their own General, not you.

Allied troops are of the same clan, family, or empire as your own. If they arrive under the command of a General, that General (not you) issues their orders. If they are under the command of a captain, you control the units as if they were a part of your own army.

TEN TIPS FOR VICTORY

1. **Crush weaker enemy troops first. Destroying or routing them quickly may cause your enemy's elite troops to rout.**

2. **Let your enemy exhaust himself coming to you. You should make the first move only if he has adopted a defensive posture and refuses to march on you.**

3. **Always capitalize on flanking opportunities. Tie up enemy units with frontal assaults by your infantry and hit them from behind or from the side with cavalry.**

4. **Force your enemy to react to your moves, rather than constantly playing catch-up. Not only will this frustrate his attempts to form a battle plan, it will also exhaust his troops.**

5. **Know your units' special abilities, as well as the abilities of your enemy's troops. Examine them in detail and refer to the Factions section of this guide.**

6. **If facing a superior force, leave an avenue of escape open. Discretion is the better part of valor, so retreat if you need to!**

7. **Don't charge toward a distant enemy. March toward them and charge a very short distance to get the advantage of the charge and minimize the fatigue penalty.**

8. **Lure the enemy into position with an obvious undefended flank or isolated unit, and have a trap ready to be sprung when they take the bait.**

9. **Make sure to pay attention to your units' facing, and pivot them to deal with flanking attempts.**

10. **Learn to use woods, hills, and other terrain to your advantage in combat. The element of surprise can quickly turn the tide of battle in your favor.**

IMPERIAL CAMPAIGN

The **Imperial Campaign** is the main single-player mode featured in *Rome: Total War*. In this mode, you assume complete control over one of three powerful Roman families—the **Julii**, **Brutii**, or **Scipii** family. Your objective is simple: conquer foreign lands and subjugate their people for the glory of the Roman Empire!

You can also play the other factions in the game—every time you complete either an Imperial or a short campaign, you'll unlock foreign nations such as Carthage and the Greek Cities.

Campaign games are neatly split into two major elements. The first is the **Campaign Map**, where each faction runs and manages its **settlements**, builds its **armies**, and moves its troops about the world. The second is the **battlefield**, where epic clashes between two or more armies are resolved in glorious, real-time battle.

This chapter focuses on the former—the many actions you may take on the Campaign Map, outside the field of battle. If you're looking for tips on how to command your troops on the battlefield, flip to **Chapter III: Total War**.

CHAPTER GLOSSARY

There are many terms used in this large chapter, and it's tough memorizing the meaning of each one. When you encounter a word or term you're unfamiliar with, check this glossary for a quick description. You can find more details on every one of the following terms by referring to their appropriate sections in this chapter.

ABILITY: This term refers to the four different abilities that **Named Characters** may possess: **Command**, **Management**, **Influence**, and **Subterfuge**. Some abilities are only available to certain types of Named Characters.

AGENT: This term refers to **diplomats**, **spies**, and **assassins**. Note that agents are Named Characters.

ARMY: This term refers to a collection of land-based military **units** that moves and fights together. Armies can either be led by a **General** or a **Captain**.

AUTOMANAGE: This term refers to the act of enabling the computer to Automanage your settlements for you.

BUILDING: This term refers to any item that can be constructed within a settlement. This includes items that are not truly buildings, such as **walls** and **roads**.

CAPTAIN: This term refers to temporary leaders for armies. Captains are only used when there's no suitable General present to lead an army. They have no special abilities, and they can perform neither **field construction** nor **field recruitment**. They are simply taken from the ranks of one of the army's units, and they return to their unit when a General joins the army.

CHARACTER TRAIT: This term refers to the certain Character Traits that Named Characters acquire as they age. These traits can have both positive and negative affects on the Named Character.

CONSTRUCT: This term refers to the act of **construction**. This is used in reference to **buildings** when settlement construction is discussed, and in reference to **forts** and **watchtowers** when field construction is discussed.

CURSOR: This term refers to the **mouse cursor**, also called the **mouse pointer**, which is always present onscreen. The cursor is used to interact with every facet of the Campaign Map. Note that the graphic that represents the mouse cursor is context-sensitive, meaning that it changes as the cursor is moved over different types of objects. This helps to illustrate the function that can be performed by "clicking" on the object.

FACTION: These are the different cultures and peoples that exist in the Imperial Campaign. There are 20 separate factions at the start of the campaign, and every faction is rivaled against every other faction. Some factions choose to become temporary allies, while others choose to make war with one another. A few will rise, and many others will fall.

FAMILY: This term can be used to refer to any one of the three Roman families in the Imperial Campaign—the **Julii** family, the **Brutii** family, and the **Scipii** family. Each family is an individual **faction**. Though all three Roman families begin the campaign as allies, they all secretly rival against each other, seeking to gain enough power to eventually challenge the Roman **Senate** and become the almighty **Imperator** of Rome.

FAMILY MEMBER: These are the members of your faction's **family**. They're unique individuals, and are the most important and valuable units under your command. Male family members that have "come of age" may be used as **Generals** for your armies, or as **Governors** for your settlements. Each family member has special **abilities** that no other type of unit possesses, and their level of skill in these abilities increases over time. Note that family members are Named Characters.

FIELD CONSTRUCTION: This term refers to the act of constructing a fort or a watchtower. These items can only be constructed by an army that is led by a General, and they cannot be constructed within settlements.

FIELD RECRUITMENT: This term refers to the act of recruiting **mercenaries**. Mercenary units can only be recruited by an army that is led by a General, and they cannot be recruited within settlements.

FLEET: This term refers to a collection of naval units that moves and fights together.

GARRISON: This term refers to the military units that are stationed within a settlement. Newly recruited units join a settlement's garrison when they finish their training. A garrison becomes an **army** when it moves out of a settlement.

GENERAL: Your faction's family members become Generals whenever they're not residing in a settlement. For many reasons, Generals are the most important units in any army, and a force led by a General is one to be reckoned with.

GOVERNOR: Your faction's family members become Governors whenever they enter a settlement. Governors take charge and improve the quality of life in a settlement, as they offer a variety of benefits to the settlement.

ICON: This term refers to a variety of items that appear on the Campaign Map. Every item on the map is an icon that represents the actual unit, army, settlement, agent, or fleet.

INCOME: This term refers to the money that is generated by a settlement.

IMPERATOR: This term refers to the Imperator (Emperor) of Rome. Your overall objective is to become the Imperator of Rome during a normal campaign.

LEFT-CLICK: This term refers to the act of "clicking" the **left mouse button**. This is usually done to select items on the Campaign Map, as well as tabs and buttons within **scrolls**.

NAMED CHARACTER: This term refers to every character in the game that has its own unique name. Such characters are either **agents** or family members of your faction. Named characters have unique abilities that they can improve upon over time. They also acquire certain **Character Traits** and **Retinues** as they age.

PORTRAIT: This term refers to the small pictures of the various units, agents, and family members that are shown in the **Review Panel**, and also in certain scrolls.

RECRUIT: This term refers to the act of recruiting new units within a settlement.

REPAIR: This term refers to the act of repairing damaged buildings within a settlement.

RETRAIN: This term refers to the act of retraining existing units within a settlement. This can be done to replace a number of the unit's men who have died in battle, or to **upgrade** the unit when higher-quality weapons and armor are available at the settlement.

RETINUE: This term refers to the friends and various other "hangers-on" that are always found with Named Characters. They can have either a positive or negative effect on Named Characters, who gain a variety of Retinues as they age.

RIGHT-CLICK: This term refers to the act of "clicking" the **right mouse button**. This is often done to issue orders to the currently-selected item, or to call up a scroll that provides more information on an item.

SCROLL: This term refers to the many different menus you review and interact with during the Imperial Campaign. These menus are referred to as scrolls because that's what they look like.

SENATE: This term refers to the group of officials who hold stations within the Senate of Rome. The Senate determines all manner of Roman policy and law, and is based in Rome.

SETTLEMENT: This term refers to the **cities** and **towns** that appear in every territory of the Campaign Map. They provide factions with **income**, and with the ability to **recruit** new units. A faction that controls a settlement also owns its surrounding **territory**.

TERRITORY: This term refers to the lands that make up each island and continent in the game world. Each territory features one **settlement**. The faction that controls the settlement also controls its surrounding territory.

TOOL TIP: This term refers to the small, informative windows that "pop up" when you move the mouse cursor over different objects in the game. They provide helpful, "at-a-glance" details on the object.

UNIT: This term mainly refers to a collection of military soldiers or naval ships. However, it is sometimes used in reference to other things, such as agents.

Beginning an Imperial Campaign

Main Menu

Single Player Menu

Choose **Single Player** from the **Main Menu** to access the **Single Player Menu**. Next, choose **Imperial Campaign** to proceed to the **Campaign Setup Options** menu.

Campaign Setup Options

The **Campaign Setup Options Menu** is the final menu you visit before the Imperial Campaign begins. Here, you may view and adjust several different options for the campaign you're about to start. Once you've set the options to your liking, click the **arrow** in the lower-right corner to begin the Imperial Campaign.

Many of these options cannot be altered once you begin the campaign, so make sure to review them carefully before proceeding.

Choosing a Faction

Select the **faction** you wish to control by clicking on its symbol in the upper-right section of the options menu. You may play through the campaign as one of three different Roman families:

Faction Symbols

the Julii family (red symbol), the Brutii family (green symbol), or the Scipii family (blue symbol).

The faction you choose has an impact on your initial strategies for the campaign. Take the following observations into consideration before you decide which faction you wish to control:

The **JULII** family (red faction symbol) controls northern Italy. At the start of the campaign, it is their job to protect the northern Roman territories, and to eventually conquer foreign lands to the north.

The **BRUTII** family (green faction symbol) controls southern Italy. Their initial priorities are to ensure no attack from the southeast reaches Rome, and to eventually conquer foreign lands overseas to the southeast.

The **SCIPII** family (blue faction symbol) controls central Italy, and the small island of Sicilia Romanus to the southwest. They are the last line of defense should a rival faction break through to strike at the heart of the Rome. This faction's early priorities are to defend the core of Italy, and to eventually conquer lands overseas to the southwest.

Advice Level

Advice Level Window

Rome: Total War features two helpful advisors; one to assist you in becoming familiar with the intricacies of the Campaign Map, and another to provide sound tactics on the battlefield. The **Advice Level** option allows you to establish how often the advisors will appear to offer their advice. This setting can be later adjusted from within the campaign's **Game Options Menu**.

We recommend you keep the Advice Level at its highest setting until you feel completely comfortable with the intricacies of the Imperial Campaign. You can change the level of advice or turn it off at any time, though, in the game options.

Campaign Difficulty

You're able to set the **Campaign Difficulty** to the desired level from this pull-down window. This affects the aggressiveness of the computer-controlled rival factions on the **Campaign Map**, not on the battlefield.

Campaign Difficulty Window

We recommend you play your first campaign with the Campaign Difficulty set at its default—**Medium Difficulty**.

Battle Difficulty

Battle Difficulty Window

This pull-down window allows you to set the **Battle Difficulty** to the desired level. This affects how cunningly the computer controls its armies on the battlefield.

> We recommend you play through your first campaign with the Battle Difficulty set at its default—**Medium Difficulty**.

Arcade Style Battles

Arcade Style Battles let you focus on crushing your enemies with sheer force rather than outwitting them with crafty battlefield tactics. Click the checkbox next to the Arcade Style Battles option if you prefer to fight more action-oriented battles, as opposed to ultra-realistic ones. Selecting this option simplifies the real-time battles that occur in the Imperial Campaign by turning off several realism settings that would otherwise "run in the background."

Short Campaigns

To win the Imperial Campaign, you must become the Imperator (Emperor) of Rome. The road to this end is both long and difficult—you must conquer rival factions, and swell your empire, until you gain enough political sway to challenge the other families of Rome. Though all Roman factions begin the campaign as allies—noble families joined in the cause of strengthening and expanding their beloved empire—your overall objective is to eventually conquer Rome itself.

If this sounds like a daunting task, never fear. You have the option of playing a **Short Campaign** instead. You don't need to worry about becoming the Imperator when playing a short campaign. Instead, the conditions of victory for each Roman family change as follows:

JULII FAMILY: You must conquer the Gauls, a rival faction of barbarians who occupy the lands to the northwest of Rome.

BRUTII FAMILY: You must conquer the Macedonians and the Greeks, two rival factions located overseas to the southeast of Rome.

SCIPII FAMILY: You must conquer the Carthaginians and the Numidians, two rival factions located overseas to the southwest of Rome.

The Campaign Map

The Campaign Map

Once you've finished tweaking the pre-campaign options, the Imperial Campaign begins. The first thing you see is the **Campaign Map**, where your every turn begins and ends. From this map, you manage your **settlements**, construct new **buildings**, recruit new **units**, move and attack with your **armies**, and much more. In short, everything that occurs outside of battle is handled via the Campaign Map.

The Campaign Map has a lot going on, and it can all seem quite confusing at first. Fortunately, we break everything down in the following sections. By the time you've finished reading this chapter, you'll be a pro at managing your chosen faction.

Let's start with the basics of what you see on the Campaign Map.

The Control Panel

The Campaign Map is divided into two parts: the Campaign Map itself, and the **Control Panel**, which runs along the bottom of the screen. The Control Panel can be logically broken down into three sections; from left to right, those sections are called the **Mini-Map**, the **Review Panel**, and we've grouped everything else into what we call the **right side** of the Control Panel.

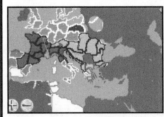

The Control Panel

It's important to become familiar with the Control Panel, as it is used to do just about everything on the Campaign Map. Let's go over each part of the Control Panel.

The Mini-Map

The Mini-Map appears on the far-left side of the Control Panel. It shows a top-down view of the entire game world. The blue lines on the map represent your current "field of vision"—the section of the world map that is currently being shown on the Campaign Map.

Left-clicking on any area of the Mini-Map jumps the camera to that section of the world. This is a quick way to change your point of view.

At the start of the campaign, most of the Mini-Map is shaded out. These shaded areas are parts of the world you haven't yet explored. The Mini-Map updates itself automatically as you send troops and agents out to explore new territories.

IMPERIAL CAMPAIGN

As new territories are discovered, they appear in color on the Mini-Map. A territory's color denotes the faction that owns the territory. Move the mouse pointer to any visible territory on the Mini-Map, and a **tool tip** pops up, which provides information on the territory's name, its capital settlement, and the faction that currently controls it.

NOTE

Tool tips appear when you move the mouse cursor over just about anything on the Campaign Map. They quickly display useful information regarding the area, item, or object that you're currently "mousing over."

You may send a diplomat to a neighboring faction to enter negotiations over map information. If the diplomatic talks go well, then information on nearby territories is revealed to you, and the Mini-Map is automatically updated. This is a quick way to learn more about the world around you. For more information on the use of diplomats, please see their section, which appears later in this chapter.

The **+/- buttons** on the Mini-Map allow you to zoom in-and-out. Use these buttons to get a closer look at the location of a territory's capital settlement, or for a better view of its borderlines.

The Review Panel

The Review Panel takes up the central portion of the Control Panel. It is a context-sensitive tool, meaning that items displayed in the Review Panel  change depending on the item that is currently selected on the Campaign Map. For example, when you have a settlement selected, the Review Panel displays a variety of information pertaining to that settlement. If you then select an army, the Review Panel changes to show information regarding that army.

There are four **tabs** that run along the top of the Review Panel. These are called **Review Panel Tabs**. Left-clicking on a Review Panel Tab allows you to view specific information on the currently-selected item, which is displayed in the main area of the Review Panel. From left to right, the Review Panel Tabs are as follows: the **Army/Navy Tab**, the **Town/City Tab**, the **Agents Tab**, and the **Fleet Tab**.

NOTE

A Review Panel Tab is "grayed-out" when it cannot display any information relevant to the currently-selected item.

ARMY/NAVY TAB: Left-clicking on this tab displays all of the units that make up the currently-selected army, or naval force, in the Review Panel. If you have a settlement selected, then the settlement's **GARRISON** is displayed. If there are no troops to display for the currently-selected item, then this tab will be grayed-out.

TOWN/CITY TAB: Left-clicking on this tab displays all of the buildings that have been constructed within the currently-selected **SETTLEMENT**, in the Review Panel. This tab is grayed-out if a settlement is not currently selected.

AGENTS TAB: Left-clicking on this tab displays information on the **AGENTS** that are visiting the currently-selected settlement, or traveling along with the currently-selected army, or naval vessel, in the Review Panel. This tab is grayed-out if there are no agents present.

FLEET TAB: Left-clicking on this tab displays the **ARMY** that is being transported by a **FLEET** of naval vessels. This tab is only clickable when you've selected a fleet that is transporting military units.

You may also right-click on each of the first three Review Panel Tabs to bring up faction-wide information on your armies/navy, towns/cities, and your agents. You can do this even when the Review Panel Tab is currently grayed-out.

Here's a description of what happens when you right-click on each Review Panel Tab:

Military Forces Scroll

Right-clicking on the Army/Navy Tab calls up the **Military Forces Scroll**. This scroll lists basic information on every military force you currently control, divided into three separate columns. From left to right, those columns appear as follows:

NAME: This column shows the name and portrait of the military force's commanding officer, be it a **GENERAL**, **CAPTAIN**, or **ADMIRAL**.

STATUS: This column tells you where the force is located on the Campaign Map.

SOLDIERS: This column lets you know how many soldiers are present in each military force.

Clicking on any force calls up a second scroll, the **Army/Navy Details Scroll**, which provides detailed information on the selected force's commanding officer. Form more information, please refer to the **Army Details Scroll** section, which appears later in this chapter.

You can sort the list of military forces by clicking on any one of the three column headers at the top of the scroll.

Right-clicking on the Town/City Tab calls up the **Settlements List Scroll**. This scroll lists basic information on every **settlement** you currently control, divided into four separate columns. From left to right, those columns appear as follows:

Settlements List Scroll

NAME: This column shows each settlement's name, size, and icon as it appears on the Campaign Map.

POPULATION: This column tells you how many people currently live in each settlement.

PUBLIC ORDER: This column displays the **PUBLIC ORDER** figure for each settlement.

GOVERNOR: This column shows the portrait of each settlement's **GOVERNOR**, provided one is currently in office.

Clicking on any settlement calls up a second scroll, the **Settlement Scroll**, which provides detailed information on the selected settlement. For more details, please see the Settlement Scroll section, which appears later in this chapter.

You can sort the list of settlements by clicking on any one of the four column headers at the top of the scroll.

Right-clicking on the Agents Tab calls up the **Agents List Scroll**. This scroll lists basic information on every agent you currently control, divided into two separate columns. From left to right, those columns appear as follows:

Agents List Scroll

NAME: This column shows each agent's name, portrait, and a number of tiny icons to indicate the agent's current level of skill in his own unique **ABILITY**.

STATUS: This column tells you the location of each agent, and whether the agent is a **diplomat**, **spy**, or **assassin**.

Clicking on any agent calls up a second scroll, the **Character Details Scroll**, which provides detailed information on the selected agent.

You can sort the list of agents by clicking on either column header at the top of the scroll.

"Right Side" Items

For the purposes of organization, we've grouped everything to the right of the Review Panel into what we call the "right side" of the Control Panel. Let's review these "right side" items.

Construction Button

The **Construction Button** is the button to click when you want to construct any sort of building. The function of this button changes depending on whether you have an army or a settlement selected on the Campaign Map.

- If you have an **ARMY** selected, then the **FIELD CONSTRUCTION SCROLL** appears when you **LEFT-CLICK** the Construction Button. From this scroll, you may choose to build a **FORT**, or a **WATCH-TOWER**. For more information, please see the **FIELD CONSTRUCTION** section that appears later in this chapter.

- If you have a **SETTLEMENT** selected, then the **SETTLEMENT SCROLL** appears, with its **CONSTRUCTION TAB** highlighted. From here, you are able to construct buildings within the settlement. For more information, please see the **CONSTRUCTING BUILDINGS** section that appears later in this chapter.

 NOTE

Only an army led by a General can perform field construction.

Whenever a building is being constructed, the face of the Construction Button changes to show the amount of construction progress on the building, and the type of building that is currently being constructed.

Construction Progress

RECRUITMENT BUTTON

The **Recruitment Button** is the button to click when you want to train agents, or additional units for your armies. The function of this button changes, depending on whether you have an army or a settlement selected on the Campaign Map.

- If you have an **ARMY** selected, the **ARMY DETAILS SCROLL** appears when you **LEFT-CLICK** the Recruitment Button. From this scroll, you may choose to recruit **MERCENARIES** to join the ranks of the currently-selected army. For more information, please see the **FIELD RECRUITMENT** section that appears later in this chapter.

- If you have a **SETTLEMENT** selected on the Campaign Map when you **LEFT-CLICK** the Recruitment Button, then the **SETTLEMENT SCROLL** appears, with its **RECRUITMENT TAB** highlighted. From here, you are able to train new units for your armies, within the settlement. For more information, please see the **RECRUITING UNITS** section that appears later in this chapter.

 NOTE

Only an army led by a General is able to perform field recruitment.

Whenever a unit is being trained, the face of the Recruitment Button changes to show the progress on the unit's training, and the type of unit that is currently being trained.

Recruitment Progress

"NEXT PIECE" TOGGLER

The **"Next Piece" Toggler** is a fast and easy way to cycle through specific types of Campaign Map items; specifically, your **armies**, **agents**, and **settlements**.

"Next Piece" Toggler

For example, if you want to quickly view your settlements to make sure each one is busy constructing a building, start by left-clicking on any one of them. Then use the toggler's arrows to cycle forward and backward through each of your settlements.

To cycle through your agents or armies, select one of them on the Campaign Map. Then use the togger's arrows to skip from one to the next.

Shown beneath the "Next Piece" Toggler is your faction's total **cash reserve** (in the Roman currency, "Denari"), along with the current **campaign date**, and an icon to represent the current **season** (summer or winter).

Using the "Next Piece" Toggler is a great way to double-check that you've taken every necessary action before ending your turn.

Movement Points Indicator

To the right of the "Next Piece" Toggler is the **Movement Points Indicator**—a thin, vertical bar that tells you how many **Movement Points** the selected unit, agent, or army has left for the current turn.

Each movable unit on the Campaign Map has its own supply of Movement Points. When all of its Movement Points have been depleted, the unit can move no further.

At the start of each turn, every unit's Movement Points Indicator appears as a full, blue-colored bar. As you move your units about the Campaign Map, the Movement Points Indicator's blue coloring "drains," and is replaced by black. The Movement Points Indicator is completely black when a unit has used up all of its Movement Points, illustrating that the bar is empty, and that the selected unit has run out of Movement Points for this turn.

Faction Button

Click the **Faction Button** to call up the **Overviews Scroll**. This important scroll allows you to review all vital information regarding your faction, and details on the current campaign.

Four **tabs** run along the top of the Overviews Scroll; from left to right, they appear as follows: the **Senate Tab**, the **Diplomacy Tab**, the **Financial Tab**, and the **Faction Tab**. Clicking on a tab displays information regarding that tab's topic in the Overviews Scroll.

Overviews Scroll: Senate Tab

Clicking the **Senate Tab** displays information pertaining to the **Senate** of Rome in the Overviews Scroll. There are three more tabs you can click here, which allow you to review an assortment of items regarding the Senate:

SENATE POLICY TAB: Click this tab to view the Senate's policies toward every non-Roman faction in the campaign. Click on each faction's **SYMBOL** and read all about the Senate's feelings toward them.

SENATE MISSIONS TAB: Click this tab to review the details of your current **SENATE MISSION**. If you haven't been assigned to a mission by the Senate, then no information is displayed here. For more on Senate Missions, please see the **DEALING WITH THE SENATE** section, which appears later in this chapter.

SENATE FLOOR TAB: Click this tab to see how your faction stacks up against the other Roman families, with regard to the Senate, and the People, of Rome. For more information, please refer to the **DEALING WITH THE SENATE** section, which appears later in this chapter.

Overviews Scroll: Diplomacy Tab

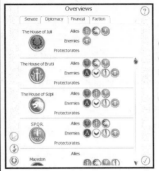

Clicking the **Diplomacy Tab** displays basic diplomatic information regarding the campaign's remaining factions in the Overviews Scroll. This allows you to quickly learn which factions are allies, and which ones are at war with each other.

It's wise to check the Overviews Scroll's Diplomacy Tab before declaring war on a faction. The information provided can help you decide whether or not declaring war against a certain faction is a good idea.

Overviews Scroll: Financial Tab

Clicking the **Financial Tab** displays your faction-wide financial information in the Overviews Scroll. Figures are shown to illustrate your faction's income from **farming**, **mining**, **trade**, **taxes**, and the like. Your faction's expenditures from **wages**, **army upkeep**, **recruitment**, **construction**, and the like, are also shown. The lower portion of the scroll crunches all of the numbers, giving you the total income and expenditures for your faction, and projecting your faction's financial profits (or losses) for the turn.

Overviews Scroll: Faction Tab

Clicking the **Faction Tab** displays overview-type information regarding your faction in the Overviews Scroll. The top portion lists the name of your **capital city**, the name of your **faction leader**, and his number of **heirs**.

The next portion lists your faction's progress through its wars against rival factions. This includes the total number of **regions gained**, **battles won**, and **battles lost** by your faction.

Then, the next portion tells you the **victory condition** for the current campaign. This condition varies, depending on whether or not you opted to play a Short Campaign when you began the campaign.

Below the victory condition, you're able to set global variables for settlement **Automanagement**. There are four options you can tweak here:

AUTOMANAGE EVERYTHING: This sets the AI to manage recruitment and construction across all of your settlements, including those that have a governor.

AUTOMANAGE TAXES ONLY: This sets the AI to manage only taxes across all of your settlements, including those that have a governor.

AI SPEND POLICY SLIDER: This slider gives you the power to limit the amount of funds your Automanaged settlements may devote to unit recruitment and building construction. Lower the setting when you want to build up your cash reserve, and raise it when you want to strengthen your empire through settlement Automanagement.

NOTE

For more information on settlement Automanagement options, please refer to the Settlement Scroll section, which appears later in this chapter.

OVERVIEWS SCROLL: LEFT-SIDE BUTTONS

 Faction Rankings Button

 Family Tree Button

 Senate Offices Button

The lower-left corner of the Overviews Scroll features three small **buttons**: The **Faction Rankings Button**, the **Family Tree Button**, and the **Senate Offices Button**. Clicking on one of these three buttons calls up a separate scroll, which provides information on the topic of the button you clicked.

There are three options you can tweak here:

Clicking the Faction Rankings Button calls up the **Faction Rankings Scroll**. This scroll lets you view your faction's progress through the campaign in a convenient graph, and also allows you to compare your faction's campaign dominance against each of your rival factions' in a variety of ways. This handy tool can help you plan out your campaign strategies with greater wisdom and efficiency.

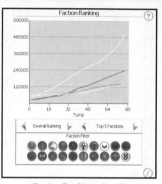

Faction Rankings Scroll

Below the graph, the left set of arrows let you cycle through different aspects of faction power: **Military**, **Production**, **Territorial**, **Financial**, **Population**, and **Overall**.

The right set of arrows let you choose which factions you wish to compare on the graph: your **Own Faction**, **All Factions**, the **Top 5 Factions**, your current **Neighboring Factions**, or you can set up your own **Custom Selection**.

For a custom selection of factions, simply click on each faction's symbol at the bottom of the scroll to add, or remove, the faction's progress line.

It's wise to check the Faction Rankings Scroll before committing to war with another faction. You can compare your relative strengths and decide whether or not declaring war is a sound strategy.

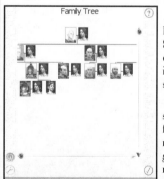

Family Tree Scroll

Clicking the Family Tree Button calls up the **Family Tree Scroll**. This scroll lets you view all of your faction's **family members**, including those you cannot control, such as wives and sisters.

Family member portraits shown in **color** represent your faction's living, breathing family members. Portraits that are grayed-out represent family members that have tragically died during the course of the campaign.

The larger portraits represent your faction's Governors and Generals. Smaller portraits show their wives and sisters. Mousing over any portrait brings up a tool tip description of that family member.

Set Faction Heir Button The **Faction Heir** becomes the **Faction Leader** when the current leader passes on. Left-click on any large, color portrait to select that family member as the Faction Heir. You must then confirm your selection by clicking the small **Set Faction Heir Button**, which is located in the lower-left corner of the scroll.

Clicking the Senate Offices Button calls up the **Senate Officials Scroll**. This scroll lets you view the family members that have been awarded high-ranking **Senate Offices** as a result of their tireless efforts to strengthen and expand the Roman Empire. Family members from each Roman faction are shown here, not just the ones from the faction you control.

Senate Officials Scroll

END TURN BUTTON

 Everything that happens on the Campaign Map is **turn-based**, not real-time. When you've finished managing your settlements, moving your armies, and so on, it's time to end your turn so that you may begin a new one. To do this, simply left-click the **End Turn Button**.

Your turn ends immediately when you click on the End Turn Button. The game then simulates a turn for every other remaining faction in the current campaign. When all other factions have taken their turn, it then becomes your turn again.

Each turn on the Campaign Map is considered to be a six-month period, in terms of game time. This means that six whole months have passed each time you start a new turn. The seasons change to illustrate this—you continually move from summer to winter with each new turn. Make sure you've done everything you need to do before clicking the End Turn Button.

Viewing the Campaign Map

Now that we've gone over the basic operations of the Control Panel, let's talk about the Campaign Map itself.

Camera and Viewpoint Controls

You can change your view of the Campaign Map quite easily just by using the mouse.

Move the mouse pointer to the top or bottom of the screen to scroll your view of the map north or south. Moving the pointer to the left or right of the screen scrolls the map west or east.

 **NOTE**
You may also use the arrow keys on your keyboard to change the view of the map in this manner.

Zoomed in   Zoomed out

The mouse wheel is used to zoom the camera both in and out. This is a handy way to get a closer look at the Campaign Map, or to get a wider view of the surrounding terrain.

Don't forget: You can also click on the Mini-Map to quickly change your view!

Map Items and Icons

Settlements, armies, agents, and fleets all appear on the Campaign Map as **icons**—small figures that represent the actual items on the Campaign Map. Left-clicking on any map icon selects the item. The Review Panel then changes to display information relevant to the item you've just selected for

A Variety of Map Icons

use. To deselect the current item, simply left-click on anything other than a map icon.

NOTE

For a detailed description on settlement, army, agent, and fleet icons, please refer to their individual sections, which appear later in this chapter.

Terrain

The entire Campaign Map is covered by various types of **terrain**. Moving the mouse cursor over certain terrain types, such as roads, causes a handy tool tip to appear, which displays general information about the terrain.

You can also view tool tips for any form of terrain. Begin by left-clicking on a patch of empty ground to **deselect** any currently-

A Variety of Terrain

selected item. Next, move the mouse cursor over the terrain you wish to examine, then right-click and hold the mouse button until the terrain's tool tip pops up.

CAUTION

Be sure to deselect any currently-selected item, or you might accidentally issue an order when you right-click to call up the terrain's tool tip.

Terrain plays a large role in every campaign game. Let's go over some of the different impacts terrain can have.

- **UNIT MOVEMENT:** Armies and agents must travel across terrain whenever they move. Different forms of terrain affect how far your units may move. For example, an army can make good time marching along on a paved road, but its movement radius significantly decreases when it must traverse snow-covered hills and valleys.

- **CHOKE POINTS:** Some forms of terrain, such as mountains, rivers, and dense forests, are completely impassible to your units. Of course, this means that no other faction can send their armies across such terrain, either. For this reason, certain areas on the map, such as narrow mountain passes, and river fords, make for strategic **CHOKE POINTS**—important sections of terrain where a well-placed force can completely block another faction's units from proceeding.

- **AMBUSHES:** While an army can't cross through a thick forest, there are many areas on the map that feature thinner woods. Armies are able to cross through these sparse forests, but they serve a more important purpose: they make for excellent cover, and allow your troops to set up a strategic **AMBUSH!** For more information, please see the ambush section that appears later in this chapter.

- **BATTLEFIELDS:** Whenever you engage an enemy force in combat, no matter who attacks who, the battle is always fought on the type of terrain that the involved armies are currently standing on. This can play a major role in determining the victor of the battle, as some units fare much better in certain climates and environments than others.

Terrain can have dramatic strategic impacts. Always try to make the most out of the terrain you control.

Victoria, the Campaign Advisor

When you play with the **Advice Level** turned on, you receive periodic bits of information from **Victoria**, the Campaign Advisor. She guides you through the many different aspects of playing the Imperial Campaign, providing hints, tips, and details on just about every subject. We strongly recommend that you listen to everything Victoria has to say. Knowledge is power!

Victoria

Asking Victoria for Advice

Victoria usually appears whenever there's something new to tell you. Sometimes she doesn't, but there's always a way to get advice from your trusty advisor.

ADVISOR BUTTON

The Settlement Scroll features a few small buttons on its left side. One of these buttons resembles Victoria—it's called the **Advisor Button**. Click the Advisor Button whenever you'd like to hear **Victoria's** suggestions about which buildings to construct and which units to train in each of your settlements.

Here's how it works:

- **LEFT-CLICK** the Advisor Button after selecting the **CONSTRUCTION TAB** to hear Victoria's advice on which building to construct next.

- **LEFT-CLICK** the Advisor Button after selecting the **RECRUITMENT TAB** to hear Victoria's advice on which type of unit you should recruit next.

THE "?" BUTTON

Every scroll in the game features a **"?" Button** in its upper-right corner. Clicking this button summons the advisor, who then gives details on how the scroll is used. Whenever you're unsure about a scroll's features, click the "?" Button to learn all about them.

Messages and Notifications

At the start of most turns, several **messages** and **notifications** will drop down from the upper-left corner of the screen. These let you know about important bits of news that have occurred since your last turn.

Each message is represented by a categorical picture. Left-click the picture to bring up a scroll that provides further details on the message. Right-click the picture to dismiss the message. A message's picture is grayed-out if it has been read, but not yet dismissed.

Here are some examples of the types of messages and notifications you receive:

CONSTRUCTION REPORTS: These let you know that a building has been fully constructed since your last turn. It's a wise to construct a new building in the settlement now.

RECRUITMENT REPORTS: Each unit that has been fully trained and recruited since your previous turn appears in these reports. Check each of your settlements to make sure they're recruiting new units.

FACTION ANNOUNCEMENTS: These notifications deal with events that occur within your faction. They include births, marriages, deaths in the family, and so on.

SENATE MISSIONS: From time to time, the Senate of Rome will bestow missions upon you. You're notified whenever you receive a new mission. You're also notified if you complete a mission, or if you've failed to do so within the mission's turn limit.

SENATE OFFICE GAINED: When any of your faction's family members complete an action that improves upon the Empire, they are often rewarded by being granted a **SENATE OFFICE**. This gives your entire

faction a higher standing within the eyes of the Senate, and puts you one step closer to becoming the mighty Imperator of Rome.

HAZARDS: There are many different types of hazard notifications. They include earthquakes and uncontrolled fires (which damage your settlements), the capture and subsequent assassination of one of your undercover agents, and so on.

WAR DECLARED: When any faction decides to make war with another faction, you are notified by one of these messages.

FACTION DESTROYED: Each time a faction has been eliminated, you receive a message to let you know that you've got one less potential enemy to deal with.

It's important to read each message at the start of every new turn. This helps keep you up-to-date on all the latest news.

Named Characters

Named Characters are your faction's agents and family members. Each agent, and every member of your faction's noble family, is not a generic unit—they are individual people, each with their own name and unique abilities. A Named Character's level of skill in his abilities regularly increases as he moves through life, meaning that these units become more and more valuable to you as they age.

Agent

Agents can perform a variety of important services for your faction, depending on whether the agent is a **diplomat**, **spy**, or **assassin**.

- **DIPLOMATS** have the **INFLUENCE ABILITY**. Their skill in this ability is represented by a number of green **INFLUENCE WREATH** icons.

- **SPIES** and **ASSASSINS** utilize the **SUBTERFUGE ABILITY**. Their skill in this ability is represented by a number of black **SUBTERFUGE EYE** icons.

NOTE

For more information on the specific types of agents, and the details on their unique abilities, please refer to their individual sections, which appear later in this chapter.

Family Member

Family members have the potential to become great leaders for your faction. For this reason, among many others, family members are the most valuable units under your command. As such, each family member is constantly protected by a number of **bodyguards**, which usually consist of heavy cavalry units.

All of your faction's family members have a rating in three separate abilities: **Command**, **Management**, and **Influence**. The higher their rating, the better they are at utilizing that ability.

At your discretion, you can use your faction's family members as Generals, or as Governors.

Generals

A family member becomes a General whenever he is out in the field, and not currently residing within one of your settlements. If two or more family members are present in a single army, then the one with the highest Command rating is considered to be the army's General.

NOTE

*Generals are able to boost their units' **morale**, and they can **rally** troops on the battlefield. For more information on these topics, please refer to the appropriate section in **Chapter III: Total War**.*

Governors

A family member becomes a Governor whenever he enters one of your settlements. If two or more family members are present in a single settlement, then the one with the highest Management rating becomes the settlement's Governor.

A settlement that has a Governor presiding over it gains a variety of bonuses, depending on the Governor's rating in his **Management Ability**, and on the types of Character Traits and Retinues he has accumulated over the course of his lifetime. For more information on these topics, please refer to the following section, **Character Details Scroll**.

NOTE

Governors become Generals the moment they leave a settlement.

Character Details Scroll

Right-clicking or double left-clicking on any Named Character calls up the **Character Details Scroll**. The top portion of the scroll lists the **Character Details**, which consist of his **occupation**, **name**, and the current ratings in each of his unique **abilities**. Every ability is rated by a number of small icons—the more icons you see, the greater the Named Character's talent for his distinctive abilities.

Here's a rundown on the four different abilities that Named Characters can possess:

COMMAND ABILITY: This indicates the Named Character's overall ability to lead troops effectively on the battlefield. This skill is represented by a number of yellow **COMMAND STAR** icons. Only **FAMILY MEMBERS** have this ability.

MANAGEMENT ABILITY: This indicates the Named Character's overall ability to effectively manage a settlement. This skill is represented by a number of white **MANAGEMENT COLUMN** icons. Only **FAMILY MEMBERS** have this ability.

INFLUENCE ABILITY: This indicates the Name Character's overall ability to sway others with his personal charm and magnetism. This skill is represented by a number of green **INFLUENCE WREATH** icons. Only **FAMILY MEMBERS** and **DIPLOMATS** have this ability.

SUBTERFUGE ABILITY: This indicates the Named Character's overall ability to perform a variety of covert operations. Only **SPIES** and **ASSASSINS** have this ability.

Character Traits

Named Characters earn Character Traits as they move through life. These traits can have either a positive or negative influence on the Named Character's abilities, and they help to define the Named Character's persona.

Character Traits are shown on the right side of the Character Details Scroll. Mouse over each trait for a tool tip description of how they affect the Named Character.

Character Retinues

Along with Character Traits, a Named Character also gathers an assortment of Retinues as they age. Retinues are people who are often found with the Named Character; they're usually his closest friends.

You can tell a lot about a person just by looking at the people they choose to spend their time with. Like Character Traits, Retinues help to define the persona of a Named Character, and they can have either a positive or negative affect on his abilities.

Retinues are shown on the left-hand side of the Character Details Scroll. Mouse over each Retinue for a tool tip description of their affects on the Named Character.

NOTE

When a family member is leading an army, his Character Details, Character Traits, and Retinues are found in the Army Details Scroll. When one is running a settlement, this information is shown in the Settlement Scroll. For more information on these two scrolls, please refer to their individual sections, which appear later in this chapter.

Captains

When a family member is nowhere to be found, a Captain will rise to the task of becoming the leader of an army that has none. Captains are only temporary leaders—they offer none of the benefits of a true General.

A Captain is taken from a unit of troops within an army until a proper General is able to take command. When this occurs, the Captain instantly returns to his appropriate place within his unit.

Captains cannot become Governors, even when they enter a settlement that has none. However, if a settlement with no Governor should fall under attack, a Captain will rise to lead the settlement's garrison against the invaders.

Furthermore, Captains are unable to perform field construction and field recruitment—only Generals are able to perform such acts. For more information on these two items, please refer to their individual sections, which appear later in this chapter.

Dealing with the Senate

The Senate of Rome plays a big role in your quest to become the Imperator. Let's discuss how to get the most out of the Senate.

Senate Missions

Senate Missions Scroll

The Senate regularly bestows **Senate Missions** upon you. These missions can range from simple diplomatic trade agreements with rival factions, to aggressive acts of war against others.

You receive a notification at the start of a turn when the Senate gives you a mission to complete. The notice tells you about the job at hand, the number of turns you've been given to complete it, and the reward you'll get for your efforts. You can review this information again at any time by clicking the Faction Button on the right side of the Control Panel, selecting the Senate Tab at the top of the Overviews Scroll that appears, and finally, by selecting the **Senate Missions Tab**.

It's up to you whether or not you choose to complete a Senate Mission. Sometimes, the risks are not worth the rewards. Be advised that, while the Senate honors you for completing their missions, you lose their favor if you continually choose not to complete them.

NOTE

You're unable to dismiss Senate Missions. If you don't want to complete the current mission, you have to wait until the mission's turn limit expires before you're assigned to another one.

Senate Floor

Senate Floor Scroll

In order for you to become the Imperator of Rome, you eventually need to challenge the Senate. Before you can do that, you must gain enough support within the Senate, and also with the People of Rome. You can check your progress in this, along with the progress of the other Roman families, by clicking the Faction Button on the right side of the Control Panel, selecting the Senate Tab at the top of the Overviews Scroll that appears, and finally, by clicking the **Senate Floor Tab**. Mouse over the faction symbols within the scroll for informative tool tips on each family's standings.

Generally speaking, completing Senate Missions increases your political pull within the Senate, while failing to complete them reduces it. Capturing foreign settlements and lands strengthens your influence over the People of Rome, while losses of battles and settlements, and prolonged periods of inaction, weaken it. These aren't hard-and-fast rules, so do the best you can to maximize your power over both groups. This will eventually earn you the right to challenge the Senate, and to become the grand Imperator of Rome.

Settlements

Settlements are the backbone of your faction. They determine your presence in the world, provide you with income, and allow you to recruit new units for your armies. Proper management of your settlements is critical for campaign domination.

Settlement Icons

Settlement Icon

Cities and **towns** are known as settlements. Each territory on the Campaign Map features a settlement, represented on the map by a **Settlement Icon**. Whichever faction controls the settlement also controls the surrounding territory.

If you have any sort of presence nearby, be it an army or an agent, then the names of foreign settlements are shown beneath their icons on the Campaign Map. Settlements you control also feature small **Info Windows** below their names, which contain important facts about the settlement's current status, illustrated by icons. These icons allow you to quickly see how well your settlements are fairing.

Here's a quick breakdown on settlement Info Windows:

The first line lists the settlement's name. This line may also include an icon to reveal the settlement's current status, but only if the settlement is **under siege**, has contracted the **plague**, or if its citizens are **revolting**.

- If one of your settlements has fallen **UNDER SIEGE**, refer to the **BREAKING A SIEGE** section, which appears later in this chapter.

- If your settlement has contracted the **PLAGUE**, you need to construct buildings that promote **PUBLIC HEALTH** in the settlement, such as **SEWERS**. For more information, please see the following sections of this chapter.

- If your settlement's citizens are **REVOLTING**, you need to solve the problem quickly. One of the first things you can do is lower taxes. You can also increase the settlement's **GARRISON**, place a **GOVERNOR** in charge, and construct buildings that contribute to **PUBLIC ORDER**, such as **TEMPLES** and **AMPHITHEATERS**. For more information, please see the later sections of this chapter.

Income Icon

The first icon appearing in the Info Window is the **Income Icon**. The number next to this icon shows how much revenue the settlement is generating.

Face Icon

The next icon is the **Face Icon**. This lets you know how happy a settlement's citizens are feeling. The icon's color varies to show different levels of happiness.

Green Face: People are very happy living in the settlement. They have all they could ask for, and more. They simply adore you.

Yellow Face: People are content living in the settlement. They lead comfortable lives, but wouldn't mind a few improvements here and there. They're largely indifferent to your rule of law.

Blue Face: People are unhappy living in the settlement. Thoughts of rebellion are brewing in their minds. They're beginning to resent you, and demand a change.

Red Face: People detest living in the settlement. Plans to revolt against you are in the works, and will soon be implemented unless you do something to make them happy immediately.

Population Icon   The **Population Icon** lets you know whether or not a settlement's populace is growing. Like the Face Icon, the Population Icon appears in different colors to illustrate the settlement's current state of **population growth**.

GREEN: The settlement's population is **GROWING.** You're doing something right!

ORANGE: The settlement's population is **STABLE.** Take a closer look and determine how to increase population growth. Your settlements should always be increasing in size.

RED: The settlement's population is **SHRINKING.** Have a closer look, figure out what's gone wrong, and correct the problem before it gets worse.

 NOTE

You can review the contributing factors to a settlement's population growth by calling up the Settlement Details Scroll. For more information, please see the scroll's sidebar, which appears later in this chapter.

 Training Icon   The **Training Icon** appears in a settlement's Info Window when new units are being **recruited** or when existing units are being **retrained** within the settlement.

NOTE

For more information on unit recruitment, please see the Recruiting Units section, which appears later in this chapter.

 Construction Icon   The **Construction Icon** appears in a settlement's Info Window when new buildings are being **constructed** or when damaged buildings are being **repaired** within the settlement.

 NOTE

For more information on building construction, please see the Constructing Buildings section, which appears later in this chapter.

 Gears Icon   The **Gears Icon** appears in a settlement's Info Window to show that the settlement is currently being Automanaged by the computer. You can turn Automanagement on and off by clicking the option in the Settlement Scroll.

 **NOTE**

For more information on settlement Automanagement, please refer to the Settlement Scroll section, which appears later in this chapter.

 **TIP** Pressing the Ⓒ key toggles your settlements' Info Windows on and off.

Selecting a Settlement

To select a settlement, left-click on its icon on the Campaign Map. When you select a settlement, notice that the Review Panel changes to show the current settlement's .

When you want to manage a settlement, you first need to open its Settlement Scroll. There are a variety of ways to access the Settlement Scroll, and any one will work.

- **DOUBLE LEFT-CLICK** on the settlement's icon on the Campaign Map.

- **RIGHT-CLICK** on the portrait of the settlement's **GOVERNOR** within the Review Panel. (A Governor must be present within the settlement, and the settlement must be selected on the Campaign Map.)

- **LEFT-CLICK** the **CONSTRUCTION BUTTON**, located on the right side of the **CONTROL PANEL**. (The settlement must be selected on the Campaign Map.)

- **LEFT-CLICK** the **RECRUITMENT BUTTON**, located on the right side of the **CONTROL PANEL**. (The settlement must be selected on the Campaign Map.)

Managing Your Settlements

Proper management of your settlements allows you to assemble and maintain immense, powerful armies, which in turn allow you to dominate rival factions in battle. Factions that do not bother to manage their settlements with care will eventually be crushed by the ones that do. Fortunately, this section deals with the intricacies of settlement management, giving you the information you need to strengthen your empire and crush your foes.

THE SETTLEMENT SCROLL

The Settlement Scroll lists all information on the currently-selected settlement. From this scroll, you can do anything within a settlement. Tools within the Settlement Scroll allow you to manage the settlement, review its statistical facts and figures, construct new buildings, repair damaged buildings, recruit new units, and to retrain existing units that are present within the settlement's garrison.

The Settlement Scroll can be broken down into five separate sections: the **Governor's Details**, the **Settlement Details**, the **Set Policies** section, the **Orders** section, and the **Orders Queue**.

SETTLEMENT SCROLL: GOVERNOR'S DETAILS

Governor's Details

The settlement's current Governor is shown at the top of the Settlement Scroll, if one is present. The Governor's name and abilities are displayed here, which are collectively known as the **Governor's Details**. His Character Traits and Retinues are displayed below. For more information on these topics, please refer to the Character Details Scroll section, which appears earlier in this chapter.

SETTLEMENT SCROLL: SETTLEMENT DETAILS

Settlement Details

Settlement Details are located beneath the Governor's Details section. Here, a summary of all the most vital statistics regarding the settlement are displayed: the income generated by the settlement, the settlement's public order percentage, the settlement's current population, and the settlement's projected rate of population growth.

INCOME: This is the total amount of money that the settlement will generate over the course of the turn. You can increase a settlement's income by raising its **TAX RATE**, or by constructing buildings that are beneficial to the settlement's economic structure, such as **MARKETS, PORTS, FARMS, MINES, ROADS**, and the like.

PUBLIC ORDER: This is a percentage of how happy the settlement's population is with your leadership. High percentages (100% and above) are ideal for most settlements. You can increase a settlement's public order percentage by placing a proper **GOVERNOR** in office, by constructing buildings that provide public order benefits, such as **TEMPLES** and **SEWERS**, and by increasing the number of military units within the settlement's **GARRISON**. (They help to keep the peace.)

POPULATION: This is the total number of people who currently live in the settlement. Settlements with high populations are considered to be larger and more advanced, and are therefore able to construct more advanced buildings. Such buildings provide greater benefits to the settlement, and to your faction as a whole.

POPULATION GROWTH: This percentage figure represents how quickly the settlement's population is increasing. All things being equal, a settlement's population should always be increasing in size. You can increase this figure by lowering the settlement's **TAX RATE**, which stimulates a growth in population, and by constructing buildings that promote public health and happiness, such as **FARMS, SEWERS, TEMPLES**, and the like.

SETTLEMENT DETAILS SCROLL

Settlement Details Button

Clicking on the small Settlement Details Button, which is located in the lower-left corner of the Settlement Scroll, calls up the Settlement Details Scroll. This scroll provides extensive information on the settlement.

Settlement Details Scroll

The top three fields of the scroll deal with the contributing factors to the settlement's population growth, public order, and income. Each contributing factor is represented by a tiny icon. Positive factors are listed above the negative factors in each of the three fields, and you can move the cursor over each contributing factor's icon for a tool tip description on its impact.

The next line on the scroll tells you how many turns the settlement can withstand a siege. This important piece of information can help you decide how strong the settlement's garrison should be kept. Settlements that cannot withstand a siege for very long should be protected by a large military force—one that can repel a hostile army in the event of a siege.

View Settlement Button Faction Capital Button Trade Details Button

Three small buttons are located on the lower-left side of the Settlement Details Scroll. From top to bottom, they appear as follows: the **View Settlement Button**, the **Faction Capital Button**, and the **Trade Details Button**.

- Click the **VIEW SETTLEMENT BUTTON** to zoom-in and get a "battlefield" view of the settlement. This can help you prepare for an attack by learning the layout of the settlement, and determining which areas would make for the strongest defensive positions.

- Clicking the **FACTION CAPITAL BUTTON** sets the settlement as your faction's **CAPITAL**. New Named Characters and units you earn by completing **SENATE MISSION** always appear at your faction's capital settlement.

- Click the **TRADE DETAILS BUTTON** to call up the **TRADE DETAILS SCROLL** for the settlement. The left-hand column of this scroll lists in-depth information on the goods that the settlement currently exports/ imports to and from its neighboring settlements, via land and sea trade. The income generated through such trade is shown in the scroll's right-hand column.

Trade Details Scroll

The lower portion of the scroll crunches the numbers, giving you the settlement's **total income** through trade, farming, and mining.

SETTLEMENT SCROLL: SET POLICIES

Set Policies

Below the Settlement Details section is the portion of the Settlement Scroll where you're able to **Set Policies**. Here, you're given the option of whether or not you want the computer to Automanage the settlement for you.

When Automanagement is turned on, you're able to set the settlement's **Build Policy**, which gives the computer an idea of how you want it to manage the settlement for you. You have five different Build Policy options:

- **BALANCED:** Order the computer to Automanage the settlement so that it's "well-rounded." Selecting this option strikes a balance between all of the other Build Policies, giving none of them priority.

- **FINANCIAL:** Order the computer to Automanage the settlement so that INCOME-producing buildings such as FARMS and MARKETS are favored in settlement construction.

- **MILITARY:** Order the computer to Automanage the settlement so that unit-producing buildings such as BARRACKS and STABLES are favored in settlement construction.

- **DEFENSIVE:** Order the computer to Automanage the settlement so that WALLS are favored in settlement construction.

- **CULTURAL:** Order the computer to Automanage the settlement so that TEMPLES, ARENAS, and other such buildings that promote PUBLIC ORDER and POPULATION GROWTH are favored in construction.

The computer's ability to construct buildings and recruit units is dependent on whether or not you've enabled it to do so from within the Overviews Scroll. Furthermore, the amount of cash the computer will devote to improving your settlement through the Automanagement Build Policy you've chosen is directly related the AI Spend Policy Slider, a tool that is also located in the Overviews Scroll. For more information, please refer to the Overviews Scroll: Faction Tab section, which appears earlier in this chapter.

When Automanagement is turned off, you're able to manually adjust the settlement's **tax rate**. The tax rate can be set from **low** to **very high**. Experiment with different tax rates, and watch as the figures under the Settlement Details section change to reflect the new tax rate's impact.

Notice that lower tax rates increase population growth and public order figures, while sacrificing some of the income generated by the settlement. Higher tax rates increase income, but reduce the rate of population growth, and the settlement's percentage of public order. Take this into account when deciding on a tax rate for your settlement.

SETTLEMENT SCROLL: ORDERS SECTION

Orders Section

The **Orders** section of the Settlement Scroll is located beneath the Set Policies section. The Orders section features four tabs; from left to right, they appear as follows: the **Construction Tab**, the **Recruitment Tab**, the **Repair Tab**, and the **Retrain Tab**. Clicking on a tab enables you to issue specific orders regarding the tab you selected. Each of these items is covered in its own section, which appear later in this chapter.

IMPERIAL CAMPAIGN

Settlement Scroll: Orders Queue

Orders Queue

When you use the Orders section of the Settlement Scroll to command the construction of a building, the recruitment of a unit, and so on, the items are then "queued-up" in the **Orders Queue**, which is located just below the Orders Section. The Orders Queue shows each building you've ordered the settlement to construct or repair, and any unit you've ordered to be recruited or retrained within the settlement. If you don't like the sequence in which your orders will be carried out, or if you have second thoughts on the orders you've given, you can left-click on any item you've queued-up to remove it from the Orders Queue.

CAUTION

Most buildings require several turns to construct. If you remove a building from the Orders Queue when it's in mid-construction, you'll have to begin all over again.

Settlement Scroll: Left-Side Buttons

Building Browser Button   **Advisor Button**   **Settlement Details Button**   **Locator Button**

There are four small buttons located on the lower-left side of the Settlement Scroll. From top to bottom, they appear as follows: the **Building Browser Button**, the **Advisor Button**, the **Settlement Details Button**, and the **Locator Button**.

Clicking the **BUILDING BROWSER BUTTON** calls up the **BUILDING BROWSER SCROLL**. For more information, please see the following section of this chapter, **CONSTRUCTING BUILDINGS.**

Clicking the **ADVISOR BUTTON** summons **VICTORIA**, the Campaign Advisor. For more information, please see the **VICTORIA, THE CAMPAIGN ADVISOR** section, which appears earlier in this chapter.

Clicking the **SETTLEMENT DETAILS BUTTON** calls up the **SETTLEMENT DETAILS SCROLL**. For more information, please see the **SETTLEMENT DETAILS SCROLL** sidebar, which appears earlier in this chapter.

Clicking the **LOCATOR BUTTON** centers your view of the Campaign Map on the settlement.

Constructing Buildings

Constructing new buildings improves your settlement's capabilities. If possible, each of your settlements should always be busy constructing buildings. There are a wide variety of buildings to construct, and each one offers its own post-construction advantage(s) to the settlement.

Construction Orders/Queue

Constructing buildings is easy. Start by left-clicking on a settlement to select it, then click the **Construction Button** that's located on the right side of the Control Panel. This opens the Settlement Scroll, with its Construction Tab selected.

A variety of buildings are shown in the Orders section, which is located just below the Construction Tab on the scroll. The types of buildings you're able to construct vary depending on the size of the settlement's population, and the settlement's current **Governor's Building**.

Move the mouse cursor over each building for a quick tool tip that displays the building's name, a brief description of its benefits, its construction cost, and the number of turns it will take to complete the construction of the building. A right-click on a building brings up the **Building Details Scroll**, which provides more detailed information.

To begin construction, left-click on any building to add it to the Orders Queue, which is located below the Orders section. Left-click on any building within the Orders Queue to remove it if you have second thoughts. You're free to "queue up" as many buildings as you like—each one will be constructed in sequence.

Advisor Button

If you're unsure which building you should construct next, you can ask Victoria for her advice. Click the small Advisor Button on the left side of the Settlement Scroll to summon Victoria, and listen to her suggestions.

Building Browser Button

Clicking the small **Building Browser Button**, which is located on the left side of the Settlement Scroll, calls up the **Building Browser Scroll**. This scroll shows a table that illustrates the "technology tree" for your faction. This table details the currently-selected settlement's progress through the technology tree, and it therefore can help you decide which buildings you want to construct.

NOTE

Buildings that appear in color on the technology tree have already been constructed in the settlement.

Building Browser Scroll

The scroll's top row lists the five different Governor Buildings that can be constructed. When your settlement's population reaches a certain height, you're able to construct the next Governor Building. Upgrading a settlement's Governor Building in this fashion "opens up" the column of buildings that appears beneath it, enabling you to construct advanced buildings that provide greater benefits to your settlement.

It sounds confusing, but climbing the technology tree is actually quite simple. Start by increasing a settlement's population—this allows you to construct advanced Governor Buildings, which in turn allow you to construct upgraded versions of every other type of building. Simple as that!

Moving the mouse cursor over each building gives you a handy tool tip description, which tells you whether or not you're able to construct the building in the currently-selected settlement.

Right-clicking on any building that appears on the Building Browser Scroll's technology tree—even ones you're currently unable to construct—calls up the **Building Information Scroll**. This scroll displays extensive information on the building you've clicked.

Building Information Scroll

You can access the Building Information Scroll for buildings you've already constructed in a settlement as well. Select the settlement, then click the Review Panel's Town/City Tab to view the settlement's buildings. Right-click on a building in the Review Panel to call up its Building Information Scroll.

Review Panel: Town/City Tab

You have the option to **destroy** a building you've constructed by clicking the **Destroy Building Button**, which is located in the lower-left corner of the Building Information Scroll. This gives you an immediate supply of funds—approximately one-third of the building's original construction cost.

CAUTION

Don't click the **Destroy Building Button** by accident!

Repairing Buildings

Repair Orders/Queue

Buildings can become damaged during an attack on a settlement, after a natural disaster such as an earthquake, or by the covert acts of a rival faction's assassins. No matter the cause, damaged buildings cannot be used, and offer none of their usual benefits, until they've been completely repaired.

Fortunately, repairing buildings is even easier than constructing them. Left-click on a settlement to select it, then click the Construction Button that's located on the right side of the Control Panel. This opens the Settlement Scroll, with its Construction Tab selected. Click on the **Repair Tab** to review the buildings that have sustained damage within the settlement.

To begin repairs on a damaged building, left-click on one to add it to the Orders Queue, which is located below the Orders section. Left-clicking on any building within the Orders Queue removes it. You're free to "queue up" as many buildings for repair as you like—each one will be repaired in sequence.

A settlement's citizens don't enjoy the sight of damaged buildings—it reminds them of how fragile their lives are, and that war is rampant all around them. Repairing damaged buildings quickly restores the settlement's public order percentage.

Recruiting Units

Recruitment Orders/Queue

Recruiting new units is vital to increasing your military dominance in the Imperial Campaign. New units can be added to existing armies to thicken their ranks, and may also be grouped together to form entirely new armies. If possible, each of your settlements should always be busy recruiting new units.

To view the units that can be recruited in a settlement, left-click on the settlement to select it, then click the **Recruitment Button** that's located on the right side of the Control Panel. This opens the Settlement Scroll, with its Recruitment Tab selected.

An assortment of different units is shown in the Orders section of the scroll, which is located just below the Recruitment Tab. The types of units you can recruit vary depending on the buildings you've constructed in the settlement.

Move the mouse cursor over each unit for a quick tool tip that displays the unit's name, a brief description of its military purpose, its recruitment cost, and the number of turns it will take to complete the unit's training.

Unit Information Scroll

You can also right-click on a unit to bring up its **Unit Information Scroll**, which provides more detailed information on the unit. This same scroll can be called up for units you've already recruited by right-clicking on the unit's portrait within the Review Panel. To select a unit for training, left-click on one to add it to the **Recruitment Queue**, which is located below the Orders Section. Left-click on any unit within the Recruitment Queue to remove it if you have second thoughts. You're free to "queue up" as many units as you like—each one will be trained and recruited in turn.

Advisor Button

If you're unsure which unit you should recruit next, you can ask Victoria for her advice. Click the small Advisor Button on the left side of the Settlement Scroll to summon Victoria and listen to her suggestions.

Newly-recruited units are taken from a settlement's populace. Because of this, it may not be wise to recruit new troops in a settlement, depending on the state of its population growth. Weigh your options before committing to unit recruitment.

Retraining Units

Retrain Orders/Queue

When an army enters a settlement, there's a chance that the settlement might be able to **retrain** some of the army's units. This is only possible if the settlement has constructed the proper buildings required for a unit's retraining.

To retrain units, select the settlement and then click the Recruitment Button, which is located on the right side of the Control Panel. This opens the Settlement Scroll for that settlement, with its Recruitment Tab selected. Click the **Retrain Tab** to view all of the units in the settlement's garrison that can be retrained.

Units that can be retrained appear in the Orders section of the Settlement Scroll. Click each unit's **portrait** to add them to the Orders Queue. Unlike recruitment, retraining a full queue of units (up to 10 at a time) takes only one turn.

When you add units to the Orders Queue to retrain them, they are removed from the settlement's garrison, and they offer no benefits to the settlement for the current turn.

There are two important advantages to retraining existing units:

- **Units that have lost some of their men in battle are returned to full numbers when they are retrained.**

- **Units retrained at a settlement that has constructed a BLACKSMITH, ARMORY, or a similar brand of unit-upgrade building, gain permanent bonuses to their attack and defense values due to higher-quality weaponry and armor. This upgrade does not occur if the unit has already received the upgrade elsewhere.**

NOTE

If the army's units are at full numbers, and if the settlement can offer no weapon or armor upgrades, then the Retrain Tab is grayed-out in the Settlement Scroll.

An Upgraded Unit

When a unit has received an upgrade from a blacksmith or an armory its portrait indicates this with a number of colored **sword icons** for attack bonuses, and **shield icons** for armor bonuses. These upgraded values are also shown on the unit's **Unit Information Scroll**. The color of the upgrade icon represents the level of the equipment upgrade:

- **BRONZE-colored sword/shield icons indicate a +1 bonus to a unit's attack/armor values.**

- **SILVER-colored sword/shield icons indicate a +2 bonus to a unit's attack/armor values.**

- **GOLD-colored sword/shield icons indicate a +3 bonus to a unit's attack/armor values.**

An Experienced Unit

Before you retrain your units, you should first take a look at their **Experience Chevrons**, which are shown on each unit's portrait. Units that have gained Experience Chevrons in battle, and that have also lost some of their men, will become "diluted" by the raw recruits that are added to their group through retraining. This lowers a unit's total number of Experience Chevrons, making it less valuable to your General on the battlefield. For more information, please refer to the Unit Experience section that appears later in this chapter.

Of course, even the most experienced unit won't do you much good if only a handful of its soldiers are left. When you don't want to dilute a highly-experienced unit that has taken heavy losses in battle, you can choose to **merge** them with another unit of similar experience instead. This increases the number of men in the unit, without sacrificing their cumulative number of Experience Chevrons. For more information, please see the Merging Units section that appears later in this chapter.

> It's always wise to consider your options before choosing to retrain your units. With care, you can consistently improve upon your units, without sacrificing their value on the battlefield.

Settlement Rally Points

Setting a Rally Point

You're able to set a **rally point** for each of your settlements. When a rally point has been set, units recruited from within the settlement march off to gather at the rally point as soon as they've finished their training. When no rally point is set, newly-recruited units always appear in the settlement's garrison. When the garrison is full, newly-recruited units appear just outside the settlement on the Campaign Map.

To set a rally point, you must first select a settlement by left-clicking on its icon on the Campaign Map. Move the mouse cursor to the area of the map where you want newly-recruited units to gather, then hold the Alt key as you right-click to set the rally point. A blue line appears on the map to illustrate the route that newly-recruited units will take to reach the rally point you've just set.

> You can set the same rally point for several different settlements. When you do this, all units recruited within those settlements gather at the designated rally point. This allows you to amass a large, diverse army at critical points on the Campaign Map.

Armies

Armies are collections of two or more military **units**, up to a maximum of 20 units per army. Any group of units that marches and fights together is considered to be an army.

Powerful armies enable you to attack rival factions, and to protect your own. Proper management of your settlements and resources allows you to develop and maintain massive, powerful armies.

Army Icons

Army Icon

Each army appears as an **Army Icon** on the Campaign Map—a single figure that represents the presence of a much larger force. You can tell a lot about the size and strength of any army by examining its icon.

For starters, every Army Icon features a **banner**. The banner has a specific color and faction symbol to let you know which faction controls the army.

A Weaker Army   **A Stronger Army**

An Army Icon's banner is important for another reason. Look closely, and you see that a percentage of the banner is darker than the rest. This "dark area" of the banner represents the size and strength of the army—the more dark area you see, the mightier the army.

Army w/General   **Army w/Captain**

There's one more thing you can learn by examining an Army Icon. An Army Icon's figure wears a cloak when the army has the advantage of being led by a General. Army Icon figures without cloaks have no true leadership, and are being led by a **Captain** that has been pulled from the ranks of a unit instead.

When a General commands an army, his number of yellow **Command Stars** is shown to the left side of the Army Icon. These represent the General's rating in his Command Ability. If the General has no Command Stars, then none are displayed on the Army Icon. For more information on Generals and their abilities, please see the Named Characters section, which appears earlier in this chapter.

> It's wise to maintain a constant vigil over your rival factions' Army Icons. This allows you to keep tabs on their strength, presence, and to prepare yourself for war if you see their armies amassing to strike.

Selecting an Army

In order to issue orders and commands to your armies, you must first select one of them. To select an army, left-click on its Army Icon on the Campaign Map. The units that make up the selected army are then displayed in the Review Panel. The small number in the upper-left corner of each unit's portrait denotes the number of individual soldiers that together make up the unit.

Managing Your Armies

The next few sections tell you how to interact with, and manage, the individual units of a selected army.

ARMY DETAILS SCROLL

Double left-click on an Army Icon to call up the **Army Details Scroll** for that army. You can also right-click on an Army Icon to view this scroll; just make sure you don't have anything else selected when you do this, or you may issue an order by mistake!

The Army Details Scroll provides information relevant to the currently-selected army's leader, be he a General or a Captain.

If the army is led by a General, then the **General's Details** are shown at the top of scroll. Here, you can review the General's ratings in his Command, Management, and Influence abilities. The General's Character Traits and Retinues are shown below the General's Details. You can right-click on the portrait of the General to bring up the **General's Scroll**, which gives you the details on the General's personal bodyguards. For more information on a General's abilities, Character Traits and Retinues, please refer to the Character Details Scroll section, which appears earlier in this chapter.

NOTE

An army led by a General is able to perform field construction and field recruitment. For more information on these two topics, please refer to their individual sections, which appear later in this chapter.

If the army is led by a Captain, then there's not much to review in the Army Details Scroll. Captains have no special abilities, can earn neither Character Traits nor Retinues, and are unable to perform either field construction or recruitment.

NOTE

For more information on Captains, please see their section, which appears earlier in this chapter.

UNIT DETAILS SCROLL

After selecting an army, right-click on the portrait of any unit in the Review Panel to call up its **Unit Details Scroll**. This scroll provides in-depth information on the soldiers that make up the unit.

The top portion of the scroll lists the unit's **name** and **statistical figures**. The rest of the scroll gives information on the unit's special abilities, and a few paragraphs that describe the unit in greater detail.

You can choose to **disband** a unit by clicking the small **Disband Unit Button** that's located in the lower-left corner of the scroll. Units that are part of a settlement's garrison are added to the settlement's population when they are disbanded.

Disbanding units is a good idea when your armies' upkeep costs are through the roof, and your cash reserve is dwindling. Choose which units you wish to disband wisely.

MERGING UNITS

Review Panel: Army Units

Every army is restricted to a maximum of 20 units in total, regardless of the number of men there are in each individual unit. Because of this limitation, it is often wise to **merge** the units within an army after they've suffered significant losses in battle. This is a great way to consolidate your units, making room in your army for new recruits.

When you want to merge two units, left-click on a unit's portrait in the Review Panel. Hold the mouse button as you drag the unit onto another, then release the button to merge the units together. Note that you can only merge units of the same type, and only when one (or both) of the units is short on men. Any "leftover" men form a separate, smaller unit.

It is possible to "dilute" an experienced unit by merging it with a less-experienced unit. If possible, always try to merge units with the same experience values to prevent this from happening. For more information on Unit Experience, please refer to that section, which appears later in this chapter.

CAUTION

Merging units is one of the few actions in the campaign that cannot be undone. Save your progress often!

Moving Your Armies

Movement Area

In order to branch out and conquer foreign lands, you must first learn how to move your armies about the Campaign Map. Start by selecting the army you wish to move by left-clicking on its Army Icon. Once an army has been selected, its bright-green **Movement Area** appears, surrounding it. An army's Movement Area gives you a visual illustration of the distance the army can travel during the current turn.

Once an army has been selected, there are two ways you can move it:

The easiest way to move an army is to right-click on the area of the Campaign Map where you want the army to move toward. Once you've issued the order, a green-colored **Movement Line** appears, which the army immediately begins marching along until it reaches its destination or runs out of **Movement Points**. You can speed up the army's

Moving an Army

movement animation by clicking and holding either mouse button until the move is complete.

The other way to move an army is to right-click and **hold** the mouse button. With the mouse button depressed, you can move the cursor about the map, and the green-colored Movement Line appears to illustrate the path that the army will take to reach its destination. When you're happy with the route, simply release the mouse button to order the army to move.

The second option is the preferred method, because it allows you to see the exact route your army will take before you give it the order to march. If you don't like the path of travel, and want to cancel the move order, you can **left-click** while still holding the **right mouse button**, and the move order is canceled before it's handed down.

Multiple-Turn Moves

If you order an army to move to any location that's outside of their green-colored Movement Area, the green-colored Movement Line changes, becoming a multi-colored Movement Line. Each color in the Movement Line represents the distance the army will travel over the next few turns. For example, if a Movement Line contains three different colors, then it will take the army three turns to reach its destination.

CAUTION

An army moves as soon as you give the order. You might not be able to undo a "wrong move" if the army has run out of Movement Points. Always make sure you move your forces correctly to avoid wasted turns.

MERGING ARMIES

There may come a time when you wish to merge two armies together to create a stronger military force. This process is as simple as giving a movement command.

Start by selecting one of the two armies you'd like to merge together, then right-click on the other army to move the first one toward it. When the two armies meet, they merge and become a single force.

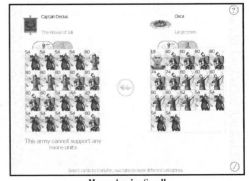

Merge Armies Scroll

If the two armies you're attempting to merge have a combined number of units higher than the 20-unit maximum, the **Merge Armies Scroll** automatically appears. Use this scroll to trade units between the two armies until you're happy with the results.

To trade a unit from one army to the other, left-click on the unit's portrait, and then click the **Transfer Arrow** that's located in the center of the scroll. The unit is moved and joins the ranks of the other army. You can also select multiple units to trade at once by holding the Ctrl key as you left-click each unit's portrait.

Once you're happy with the results of the transfer, click the check box located in the lower-right corner of the scroll to complete the merge.

Splitting Armies

Review Panel: Army Units

You might also wish to split an army into two or more smaller forces. This can be strategically sound when you want to "sandwich" an enemy army between two of yours, for instance.

Start by selecting the army you wish to split apart. Portraits of the army's units appear in the Review Panel. Hold the Ctrl key and left-click on each unit's portrait, selecting the units you wish to separate from the "parent" army. Notice that the green-colored Movement Area appears when you select the first unit.

Once you've finished selecting the units that you want to split from the parent army, choose to move them away from the main force by right-clicking on the Campaign Map. Be advised that this will move the units you've just selected, so make sure you don't order them to march off in the wrong direction.

Merging with Settlements

You may want to bring in extra troops to guard a hot-spot settlement, or to upgrade an army's units at a settlement that can offer improved weapons and armor. To do this, you must merge the army with the settlement's garrison. Select the army on the Campaign Map, then right-click on the settlement you want it to merge with. The army joins (or becomes) the settlement's garrison when it enters the settlement.

If the total number of units between the army and the settlement's garrison exceed the 20-unit maximum, the Merge Armies Scroll appears. Swap units between the army and the settlement's garrison until you're satisfied with the results. For a detailed explanation on how this works, please see the Merging Armies section that appears earlier in this chapter.

Field Construction

Armies led by Generals are able to construct **forts** and **watchtowers**. Select the army, then click the Construction Button that's located on the right side of the Control Panel. This calls up the **Field Construction Scroll**.

Field Construction Scroll

Choose to construct either a fort or a watchtower from this scroll. Both have a construction cost attached, and are erected as soon as you give the order—there's no construction waiting period.

Watchtowers extend your army's field of vision over the surrounding territory. They can only be constructed within territories that your faction controls.

Watchtower

>
> **TIP**
> Construct watchtowers in areas where you have a weak presence. This allows you to monitor those regions, watching for rival factions armies.

Fort

Forts are temporary defensive structures for your armies. It's strategically sound to construct a fort in an area you want your army to defend, such as a narrow mountain pass, for example. This improves your army's ability to hold the pass and drive any invading forces away.

Forts have no nationality. Any faction's army can enter and occupy a fort without having to declare war on the faction that built it, provided the fort is vacant at the time.

Forts require regular attention to maintain. They fall into ruin, and are subsequently removed from the Campaign Map, if no one's around to uphold them after six months have elapsed (one complete turn). A single unit or agent is enough to keep a fort in order, so it's wise to leave at least one person behind should you decide to move the army out of a fort.

> **TIP**
> Forts are cost-efficient and appear instantly on the Campaign Map. They greatly improve your army's ability to defend a region from enemies, and help keep away bandits from your wealthier trade routes. Be sure to take full advantage of forts!

NOTE

Some terrain types and certain areas of the Campaign Map won't allow you to perform field construction. Move your army elsewhere and try again.

Field Recruitment

Army Details Scroll

Armies led by Generals can recruit **mercenaries** to quickly thicken the ranks of the army. Mercenaries are more expensive to hire, but are useful if you need troops in a hurry and are campaigning away from your territory. Also, because there are limited numbers of mercenaries available in each region, hiring them denies their accessibility to your enemies. Select the army, then click the **Recruitment Button** that's located on the right side of the Control Panel. This calls up the **Army Details Scroll**, where a list of mercenaries available for recruitment is shown.

Left-click on a mercenary to add it to the Orders Queue at the bottom of the scroll. Left-click a mercenary in the Orders Queue to remove it. Right-clicking on a mercenary calls up the Unit Details Scroll for that mercenary unit, which provides extensive information.

Hire All Mercenaries Button

When you're happy with your selection of mercenaries, click the **Hire All Mercenaries Button** to add them to the General's army. The mercenary units are instantly added to the army's ranks, and appear in the Review Panel. You may now control them just like any other unit.

NOTE

If no mercenaries are available to recruit in the current territory, then the Recruitment Button is grayed-out when you select your army.

Setting an Ambush

An **ambush** allows you to get the drop on an enemy faction's army. When a hostile army encounters another one that has set up an ambush, they are automatically drawn into battle at a distinct disadvantage.

Ambush Icon

To make an army set up an ambush, simply order it to move onto a patch of terrain that's sparsely populated by trees. These thinly-wooded areas make perfect ambush-points for any army. When the ambush is ready, the Army Icon's figure kneels down to show that the army is hidden, and ready to spring into battle.

Should a hostile army come into close-contact with a ready-to-ambush army, they are forced into battle at a severe disadvantage. The ambushed army is not allowed to deploy its troops at the start of battle, and its units are set up in a straight-line formation, with the army's General (or Captain) at the front—they're in marching formation, and are unprepared for the surprise-attack. The ambushed army must scramble to ready their troops, while the ambusher wastes no time ordering theirs to charge!

The other advantage to setting an ambush is the fact that it makes your army all but invisible to your rival factions. They are not shown on the Campaign Map until they move, or until the ambush is sprung by a passing enemy army.

CAUTION

Don't forget that you can become the victim of an ambush, too. Always watch out for thinly-wooded patches of terrain, and never underestimate the enemy's potential to have a military force present in these areas.

Attacking

In order to defeat your rival factions, you must eventually send out your armies to **attack** them. Your armies can attack other armies, and can also **besiege** enemy settlements. Choosing to attack a rival faction's army or settlement is a declaration of war against that faction, so be prepared to face swift retaliation after the smoke clears.

ATTACKING ARMIES

To order an attack on another army, you must first select your army by left-clicking its icon on the Campaign Map. With your army selected, right-click on the rival army you want them to attack. This orders your force to move toward the enemy and attack them at once.

BATTLE DEPLOYMENT SCROLL

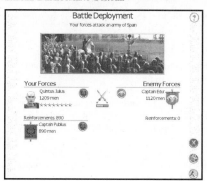

Battle Deployment
Your forces attack an army of Spain

Your Forces
Quintus Julius
1,209 men
****
Reinforcements: 890
Captain Publius
890 men

Enemy Forces
Captain Edur
1,120 men
Reinforcements: 0

The **Battle Deployment Scroll** appears when your army attacks or is attacked by a rival faction's army. This scroll provides information on the upcoming battle, and presents you with a few options for handling the fight.

Strength Comparison

The **Strength Comparison** is located in the center of the Battle Deployment Scroll. This is an "army vs. army" ratio for the upcoming fight, which takes into account any **reinforcements** that may be present. Mousing over the Strength Comparison symbol causes a tool tip to appear, which gives you the odds for the battle at hand.

> **TIP**
> You should *always* check the Strength Comparison ratio before committing to battle.

You have three options for handling most battles:

Fight Battle Button

Clicking the **Fight Battle Button** grants you control of your units, and allows you to engage the enemy forces on the battlefield in epic, real-time mayhem. This lets you implement your own combat tactics and strategies, and also to protect your most valuable units.

Resolve Battle Button

On the other hand, you can click the **Resolve Battle Button** to have the computer quickly resolve the battle for you. This certainly speeds things up, but be forewarned that the computer may not handle the fight in the same manner as you would yourself. Your army may therefore suffer heavier losses as a result, and you might even lose the battle entirely. You're also unable to protect your General(s) and other valuable units from harm when you have the computer automatically resolve the battle for you.

Withdraw Button

Your third option is to **withdraw** from the battle entirely. Should the odds not favor your forces, it may be wise to click the **Withdraw Button**. If you are the defending army, then clicking this button causes your forces to back away from the enemy, potentially allowing them to march further into your territory. Withdrawing from a battle also counts as a loss on your battle record, which can cause you to lose favor with the People of Rome. Still, a hasty retreat can allow you to regroup with your other armies, bringing in a much larger force that's more capable of crushing the enemy's. Weigh your options carefully and choose wisely before you commit to battle.

> **TIP**
> When you know a battle is about to occur, you should *always* save your game before the Battle Deployment Scroll appears. You never know what might happen on the battlefield.

BESIEGING FORTS AND SETTLEMENTS

You can order your army to **besiege** a rival faction's settlement. Besieging settlements is often the best way to conquer new settlements and territories for your faction.

To order your army to besiege a settlement, select the army, then right-click on the settlement you wish to besiege. Your army immediately marches toward the settlement and begins the siege.

> **NOTE**
> *While a settlement is under siege, its icon on the Campaign Map changes to illustrate this status. The settlement's icon becomes surrounded by wooden stakes, indicating that it has fallen under siege.*

Besieging a settlement is different than attacking it. During a siege, the settlement is surrounded by a hostile army, and is cutoff from the outside world. No one may enter or leave a settlement while it's under siege. The faction that owns the settlement must find a way to **break the siege** before its people are starved into submission.

Depending on the size and state of a settlement, it may be able to withstand a siege for several turns, or none at all. You can quickly check to see how many turns remain before the settlement falls to the besieging army by mousing over the besieged settlement—the tool tip that appears shows the number of turns remaining before the settlement is forced to surrender.

You can see how long each of your settlements can withstand a siege by calling up their Settlement Details Scroll. For more information, see the sidebar that appears earlier in this chapter.

Besieging a settlement offers two major advantages over attacking it outright. Firstly, a besieged settlement's garrison dwindles with every turn that passes—its troops are starving to death as a result of the siege. This is a great way to weaken a settlement before you storm its gates and take it by force.

The second advantage of besiegement is that it can grant you the ability to conquer a settlement without putting your army in harm's way. If the siege is not broken by the time the settlement's food reserves run out, then the settlement is lost to the defending faction, and automatically falls under your control. This process may take several turns, but it's often better to lose time instead of men.

SIEGE DETAILS SCROLL

Siege Details Scroll

When your army initiates a siege on a settlement, the **Siege Details Scroll** appears. This scroll provides information regarding the siege. You can access this scroll again at any time by selecting your army, and then right-clicking on the settlement they're besieging.

The upper portions of the Siege Details Scroll provide information on the settlement's defenses, the **siege equipment** you've constructed (if any), and the number of turns the settlement can withstand the siege.

You may want to construct siege equipment to attack the settlement with your army. It's very difficult, and sometimes impossible, to break through a settlement's defensive walls without the proper siege equipment. Settlements that do not have walls can be attacked without siege equipment.

Build Orders/Queue

Construction of siege equipment uses two resources: time and **Build Points**. Your army's Build Points are shown in the line just above the available siege equipment. Left-click on an item of siege equipment to add it to the scroll's **Build Queue**. Left-clicking on an item within the Build Queue removes it.

Here are descriptions on the four different types of siege equipment:

- **RAMS** can bash open a settlement's gates, allowing your army to pour in.

- **LADDERS** are set against a settlement's wall. Your men can climb the ladders to enter the settlement, though they may have to battle defending soldiers atop the wall first.

- **TOWERS** work like ladders; they're positioned against a settlement's wall, allowing your soldiers to scale them and enter the settlement. Towers can also hold extra units, such as archers, so they're recommended over ladders.

- **SAPS** are used to destroy chunks of a settlement's wall from underground. When saps have been constructed, units that have the **SAPPING ABILITY** can be ordered to dig a tunnel under the settlement's wall, sabotage the wall's foundation, and bring a portion of the wall crashing down.

If you've sent a **spy** to infiltrate the settlement, then the agent will open the settlement's gates to your army when you move to attack!

CONQUERING SETTLEMENTS

Conquered Settlement Options

After you've taken control of a rival faction's settlement (through besiegement, or after successfully attacking and securing it with your army), you're presented with the three following options:

- **OCCUPY THE SETTLEMENT:** This option does not change the population of the settlement, and that is its main advantage. The settlement's citizens are permitted to continue going about their daily lives; they simply have new leadership. Your army is not allowed to loot or harm the township in any way, though some minor looting is bound to occur. As such, you gain minimal funds from looting when you choose to occupy a settlement, which is the main drawback to this option. Public unrest may also be a factor in the early stages of the occupation, depending on how radically different your faction is from the one that used to control the settlement.

- **ENSLAVE THE POPULATION:** Choosing this option ships a large percentage of the settlement's population off to other settlements in your empire, where they are put to work as slaves. This strengthens your other settlements by bolstering their populations, while weakening the one you've just conquered. Note that only settlements run by a **GOVERNOR** are able to gain population in this manner. This option helps to ensure that you'll face minimal problems due to public unrest, no matter how different your faction's culture might be from the one that previously controlled the settlement.

- **EXTERMINATE THE POPULATION:** The settlement's entire population is put to death by your army when you choose this brutal option. Grand-scale looting of the settlement is the main attraction here, as it immediately grants you a large chunk of cash. Furthermore, there is no need to worry about civic disorder in the settlement, as none of its former citizens are left in a position to revolt! The main drawback to this option is the settlement's lack of population—it will take time before you see the settlement generate any sort of significant income.

Consider every option before you decide what to do with a newly-conquered settlement.

Breaking a Siege

It is imperative that you defend your settlements from hostile armies. When you lose a settlement, you lose the territory and power that came along with controlling it, while the invading faction gains both. You also lose favor with the Senate, and with the People of Rome, should one of your settlements fall to outside invaders. When one of your settlements falls under siege, your top priority should be to **break the siege** as quickly as possible. There are two ways to do this.

The easiest way to break a siege is to order the settlement's garrison to sally forth and engage the enemy army in battle. This is also dangerous, because you must open the settlement's gates to send out your troops. Should things go horribly wrong on the battlefield, the enemy army will be able to storm your settlement without having to take the walls first!

If you have a capable army nearby, then the safest way to break a siege is to send the army to attack the besiegers. In this case, your army is known as a **relief force**. Even if your relief force is defeated in battle, they will likely have weakened the enemy army considerably, putting your settlement's garrison in a better position to finish the job.

Reinforcements

Using Reinforcements

You don't have to fight a battle with just one army. With proper planning, it's possible to enter the battlefield with **reinforcements**. When fighting with reinforcements, you significantly increase your odds of victory.

Reinforcements can be used in any sort of battle. They can be used during an attack on an enemy army, while defending against an enemy force, during the besiegement of a settlement, and even when you're attempting to break a siege on one of your own settlements. Both attacking and defending armies alike can take advantage of reinforcements.

To utilize reinforcements, two or more of your armies must be adjacent to the enemy settlement or force. When this occurs, the two armies that are directly involved in the battle (the attacking army and the defending army) are considered to be the **main forces** in the battle. All adjacent armies are used as reinforcements.

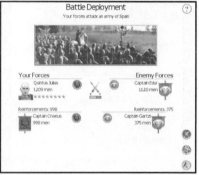

Battle Deployment Scroll: Reinforcements

The amount of control you have over your reinforcing army varies, depending on whether or not the reinforcing army is **friendly** (meaning it belongs to your faction), or the army of an **allied** faction (a rival faction with which you have chosen to ally yourself; all Roman families begin the campaign as allies).

If one of your allies sends a reinforcement army to assist you in battle, then you have no control over its army.

If the reinforcing army is friendly, the amount of control you have over it then depends on whether or not the reinforcing army is led by a General, or a Captain.

- If a **GENERAL** is in command of the reinforcing army, then you have no control over the army, even though it belongs to your faction. The computer controls the army for you, and may not enter the fight until your main force suffers heavy casualties.

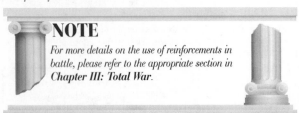

- **If a CAPTAIN is in charge of the reinforcing army, then you are able to control its units, but only after your main force has suffered significant losses.** You are granted control over a unit of the reinforcing army each time an entire unit belonging to your main force falls in battle.

As with any battle, your main force, and your reinforcing army, both enter the battlefield according to their positions on the Campaign Map. For example, if your main force attacks from the north, and your reinforcements are in position nearby to the south, then you begin the battle with both your armies "sandwiching" the enemy force from the north and south sides of the battlefield. Strategic attacks such as this can crush a powerful enemy army in short order.

NOTE

For more details on the use of reinforcements in battle, please refer to the appropriate section in **Chapter III: Total War***.*

UNIT EXPERIENCE

Units gain **experience** as they face and defeat enemies on the battlefield. This makes sense, because such units have seen harsh battles and have managed to survive them, so they naturally become hardened against the many horrors of war.

In general, the more experienced the unit, the better it fares in combat, and the less likely it is to run when faced with overwhelming odds. An army made up of experienced units often decimates an army full of rookies, so be careful not to waste your experienced units on the battlefield.

An Experience Unit

A unit's experience is indicated by the number of colored **Experience Chevrons** that appear in the lower-left corner of its portrait. Experience Chevrons are gained in the following order: **Bronze Chevrons** come first, then **Silver Chevrons**, and then finally **Gold Chevrons** are earned.

There are three chevrons to earn for each color. For example, a unit that has earned three Bronze Experience Chevrons gains their first Silver Experience Chevron after surviving the next battle, provided they take part in the bloodshed. The amount of action a unit sees on the battlefield directly relates to the amount of post-battle experience it gains.

New recruits have no Experience Chevrons, as they've never been exposed to life-or-death combat. Because of this, it pays to think twice before choosing to **retrain** experienced units at a settlement—hardened soldiers can become "diluted" by the number of raw recruits that join their ranks, lowering the unit's overall experience value.

Likewise, you should always try to match experienced units of an army together whenever you choose to **merge** your units. This ensures the units lose none of their experience, as they would if they were merged with rookies.

Agents

Agents are non-military units that can be recruited to serve your faction. Each agent is a Named Character—an individual person with his own unique name and abilities. For more information on Named Characters, please refer to their section, which appears earlier in this chapter.

There are three different types of agents: **diplomats**, **spies**, and **assassins**. Each type of agent has its own unique abilities, and every one is vital to your success in the Imperial Campaign.

Agent Icons

Diplomat Icon	Spy Icon	Assassin Icon

Each type of agent has its own **Agent Icon** to represent the agent's location on the Campaign Map. There are separate icons for diplomats, spies, and assassins. Unlike units and armies, agents are specialists that journey alone, though they can also be made to travel along with an army by **merging** with the army.

Review Panel: Agents Tab

If an agent is **visiting** a settlement, or traveling with an army, its icon does not appear on the Campaign Map. To issue commands to such agents, you first need to left-click the settlement or army that the agent is visiting, and then click on the Review Panel's Agent Tab. This displays every agent that's currently visiting the selected settlement or army in the Review Panel. You may then left-click on an agent's portrait to select it and issue orders.

Recruiting Agents

Recruit Orders/Queue

Like military units, agents are **recruited** at your settlements. The agents available for recruitment in a settlement will vary, depending on the buildings you've constructed in that settlement.

To recruit an agent, you must first select a settlement by left-clicking on its icon on the Campaign Map. Next, click the **Recruitment Button** that's located on the right side of the Control Panel. This calls up the Settlement Scroll for that settlement, with its Recruitment Tab selected.

Left-click on the agent you wish to recruit in the Orders section of the scroll, which is located just beneath the Recruitment Tab. This adds the agent to the **Recruitment Queue**, which is located below the Orders section. The agent has now been selected for training and recruitment. If you have second thoughts, left-click on an agent to remove it from the Recruitment Queue.

To learn more about an agent, right-click on its portrait within the Settlement Scroll. This calls up the agent's Unit Information Scroll, which displays a paragraph-length description on the agent.

Moving Agents

Agents are moved about the Campaign Map just like armies and units. Select an agent by left-clicking its icon, and the agent's green-colored **Movement Area** appears on the map. Order the agent to move by right-clicking anywhere on the Campaign Map. You may also hold the mouse button and drag the pointer about the map to view the **Movement Line** that the agent will follow before releasing the mouse button to order the move.

CAUTION

Movement orders are carried out immediately. Make sure you've considered the move carefully before issuing the order.

Diplomats

Diplomat

Diplomats are used to negotiate a variety of deals and treaties with rival factions. These agents can be trained and recruited at settlements that have constructed a **Governor's Villa**, a **Warlord's Hold** (for barbarian settlements), or a more advanced type of **Governor Building**. Diplomats are valuable agents that are often required for the completion of **Senate Missions**, so having one at every corner of your empire is often advantageous.

To begin negotiations, select one of your diplomats, and then move him into a rival faction's settlement, army, or diplomat. This calls up the **Diplomacy Scroll**, where you're able to pose offers and make various demands. Even factions you are currently warring against will listen to your offers, though they're skeptical and less likely to deal.

The chances of success during any negotiation are dependent on the **Influence Ability** ratings of the involved parties—the party with the higher rating in this ability often comes out ahead of the deal. Each negotiating character's current rating in their Influence Ability is shown near their portraits on the Diplomacy Scroll.

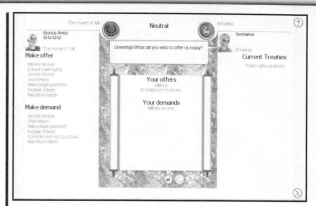

Diplomacy Scroll

The right-hand column of the Diplomacy Scroll sums up your relationship with the faction you're currently negotiating with, listing the all of the treaties you've brokered with them in the past.

The left-hand column of the scroll is where you choose your offers and demands for the treaty at hand. The offers you pose and the demands you make are added to the treaty in the center of the scroll. Left-click on any item to add or remove it from the treaty.

Click the small **Offer Button** after you've finished setting up the treaty. The other party responds by doing one of three things: **accepting** the offer, **refusing** the offer, or by making his own **counteroffer**.

When you're given a counter-offer, you can either accept it, or you can choose to counter back with a different offer. Negotiations can go back and fourth in this fashion for several "rounds." However, the other party will eventually lose his patience if a deal isn't struck soon.

You don't always have to make demands when negotiating a treaty. If you wish, you can simply offer items as a gift to the other faction. This earns you favor with the faction, and can be a wise tactic when you wish to allay their apprehension of a seemingly-imminent attack from yours.

You can also **bribe** characters and troops to disband, withdraw, or even join your forces. It's expensive, but if well-timed, it can swing a campaign in your favor.

Spies

Spy

Spies are the eyes and ears of your faction. These agents can be trained and recruited at settlements that have constructed a **market**, or a more-advanced building of the same type. You can never have too many spies—they are invaluable agents for your cause.

A spy can carry out a wide variety of covert operations. When on an investigation mission, the amount of detail in the information relayed to you by a spy varies, depending on the spy's current rating in his **Subterfuge Ability**.

Be warned that spies who have low Subterfuge ratings might be caught during risky operations. When caught in the act, a spy is either thrown out of the settlement or army he was investigating, or he's immediately put to death.

Spying on Rivals

TIP

Should one of your spies be cast out of a rival faction's settlement or army, you can usually order the spy to reenter and resume his investigation on your next turn.

Here's a list of the different tasks a spy can accomplish for you:

- Moving a spy into an rival faction's **SETTLEMENT** reveals extensive information on the settlement, such as the buildings it has constructed, and the number and types of units that are present in the settlement's **GARRISON**. Should you choose to attack the settlement, the spy will kindly open its gates to your army.

- A spy can gather information on a rival faction's **ARMY** as well. Move the spy into the army, and it will travel along with it, letting you keep tabs on the number of men, and the types of units, that make up the army.

- Spies can be used as counter-agents in your own settlements and armies. They're able to detect a rival faction's spy who has infiltrated one of your settlements or armies. They also act as "secret police" in your settlements, helping to quell public dissent. As such, the settlement's **PUBLIC ORDER** is often increased when a spy is present. If possible, you should always leave a spy to watch over each of your settlements.

- Spies have a large vision radius on the Campaign Map. This is perhaps their most overlooked ability. Sending out a "network" of spies helps to ensure that you're never the victim of a surprise attack by a rival faction.

Assassins

Assassin

Assassins can make matters of war easier on your armies by covertly killing the Named Characters that are present at a rival faction's settlement, or the ones that are traveling along with their armies. Assassins are also capable of wreaking havoc on settlements by secretly **sabotaging** their buildings. These agents can be trained and recruited at settlements that have constructed a **forum**, or a more-advanced building of the same type.

Order an assassin to carry out a **mission** by selecting the assassin and then moving him into a rival faction's settlement or army. This calls up the **Select Mission Target Scroll**.

Select Mission Target Scroll

The Select Mission Target Scroll allows you to view the Named Characters that your agent can **assassinate** within the army or settlement. If your assassin is attempting a mission inside of a settlement, then you're also able to view the buildings that the assassin can try to **sabotage**. The probability of a successful "hit" on a target appears next to each one.

Left-click on a target that's listed in the Select Mission Target Scroll to select it, and then click the small **Accept Mission Button** that's located in the lower-left corner of the scroll. This orders your assassin to attempt the assassination or sabotage mission.

The higher an assassin's rating is in his **Subterfuge Ability**, the better his odds are at completing his covert missions. Still, you're never guaranteed success on any assassination or sabotage mission, and a failing one may very well result in the capture, and subsequent killing, of your assassin. Choose your targets wisely!

Naval Vessels and Fleets

War is waged on both land and sea in the Imperial Campaign. Settlements that have constructed **ports** and the like are able to recruit various types of **naval units**, establishing a militant naval presence. A collection of ships form a naval unit, and a collection of naval units is known as a **fleet**.

Fleet Icons

Fleet Icon

Like armies, your fleets are shown as **icons** on the Campaign Map—a single nautical vessel that represents a vast fleet of ships. These icons are called **Fleet Icons**.

IMPERIAL CAMPAIGN

Selecting a Fleet

Selecting a fleet works the same as selecting anything else on the Campaign Map—simply left-click on a Fleet Icon to select the fleet it represents. You may issue commands to a fleet once it has been selected.

Moving a Fleet

Moving a fleet works the same as moving an army or an agent. Select the fleet you wish to move by left-clicking on its icon, and the fleet's green-colored **Movement Area** then appears. Right-click on any nearby body of water to order the fleet to set sail.

Fleet Movement Area

Merging Ships

Like an army, a fleet may contain no more than 20 units of ships, in total. A fleet that has taken significant losses in combat may need to be strengthened by adding new units.

When dealing with a fleet's 20-unit maximum, a unit of two ships takes up the same amount of space as a unit of 40. Because of this, it is often wise to **merge** a fleet's units together in order to make room for fresh, new vessels.

Review Panel: Naval Units

Merging naval units within a fleet works the same as merging units of soldiers within an army. First, select the fleet by left-clicking its icon on the Campaign Map. The units of ships that make up the fleet are then displayed in the Review Panel. Left-click on a unit of ships, hold the mouse button, drag the unit on top of the one you want it to merge with, then release the button to order the merge. Note that you can only merge units of the same type, and only if one (or both) of the units is short on ships. Any "leftover" ships are placed into a separate, smaller unit.

Merging Fleets

Like armies, you can merge two fleets together to form a much larger naval force. Select a fleet, then right-click on another one to order the merge.

If there are more than 20 units of ships to divide amongst the two fleets, then the **Merge Fleets Scroll** appears. This scroll works just the same as the **Merge Armies Scroll**. Select and transfer units between the two fleets until you're satisfied with the results of the merge. For a detailed description on how this works, please see the Merging Armies section, which appears earlier in this chapter.

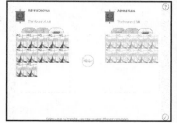

Merge Fleets Scroll

Splitting Fleets

Splitting a fleet allows you to create two or more smaller naval forces. This can be useful when you wish to blockade an enemy port, while at the same time leaving a fleet behind to guard your own, for instance. Splitting up a fleet works the same as splitting army.

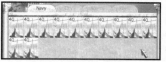

Review Panel: Naval Units

Start by left-clicking on the fleet you wish to split apart, which selects it. The units of ships that make up the selected fleet are then displayed in the Review Panel. Hold the Ctrl key as you left-click on each unit you want to separate from the "parent" fleet. When you're satisfied with your selection, right-click on nearby waters to order the selected ships to split from the main fleet, and form a secondary one. Be advised that this moves the selected ships to the area you click, so make sure you don't send them sailing off in the wrong direction.

Attacking with a Fleet

There may come a time when you need to engage a rival faction in naval combat. The following sections deal with the two different types of combat situations that can erupt on the sea.

ATTACKING A FLEET

Attacking an enemy fleet works the same as attacking an enemy army. Select your fleet, then right-click on the one you wish to battle. Be advised that such an attack is always considered an act of war.

The difference between combating the enemy on land and fighting at sea is the fact that *Rome: Total War* has no system for handling naval combat on a battlefield. Because of this, all sea battles are quickly and automatically resolved by the computer—you're unable to control your units during nautical combat. All things being equal, the larger fleet often comes out on top in a naval battle, but not without losing some of its ships.

BLOCKADING A PORT

The other aggressive move you can make with a fleet is to **blockade** a rival faction's **port**. When you blockade a port, the settlement connected to the port no longer gains income from **sea trade**. This weakens the settlement, along with the faction that controls it.

To blockade a port, start by selecting one of your fleets, and then right-click on the port to issue the blockade command. The fleet sets sail to the port, sets up a blockade, and prevents all incoming trade vessels from docking. Be warned that blockading a rival faction's port is a declaration of war against that faction.

Should a rival faction choose to blockade one of your ports, you need to send a fleet to attack and break through the enemy's blockade. The longer a blockade lasts, the more harmful are its effects on your settlement's income from sea trade.

Troop Transportation

Fleets are valuable for many reasons, but the most important one might be their ability to **transport** land units overseas. Agents and armies alike can be transported in this fashion.

To order an agent or army to **board** a fleet, first select the agent or army, then right-click on the fleet you want them to board. You may then select the fleet and order it to set sail with its passengers. Note that the **Movement Points** used by passengers before they board a fleet will limit the movement of the fleet for the turn.

You can order a fleet's crew of passengers to **disembark** by selecting the fleet and then right-clicking on a nearby port or shore. You may also choose to unload specific units by selecting each one in the Review Panel before you issue the order to disembark.

Changing Game Options

Return to Game
Game Options
Audio Options
Video Options
Load Game
Save Game
Quit Game

Game Options Scroll

You can alter a few **game options** through the **Game Options Scroll**. Press the [Esc] key to call up the Game Options Scroll at any point during your turn.

Here is a description of the different choices you can make from this menu:

RETURN TO GAME: Closes the Game Options Menu and returns you to the Campaign Map.

GAME OPTIONS: Check the boxes to toggle the various **CAMPAIGN** and **REALISM** settings on and off. You can also adjust the **ADVICE LEVEL** to the desired setting from within its pull-down window.

AUDIO OPTIONS: Manipulate the sliders to set the in-game **VOLUMES** to the desired level. You can also turn **SUBTITLES** on and off.

VIDEO OPTIONS: Manipulate the sliders and check the boxes to alter **VIDEO OPTIONS**. You can improve the look of the game or increase performance.

LOAD GAME: Load a previously saved or autosaved game from within this menu.

SAVE GAME: Save the current campaign game after giving it a filename from within this menu.

QUIT GAME: Quits out of the campaign and returns you to the **MAIN MENU**.

HISTORIC BATTLES—
THE BATTLE OF LAKE TRASIMENE

The Battle of Lake Trasimene—217 BC

The rise of Rome was far from inevitable. As the Romans moved to secure their control over the Italian peninsula, another people, the Carthaginians, were busily establishing their own empire in Spain and North Africa. It was inevitable, however, that the two rising powers in the region would clash violently at some point: there simply wasn't room around the shores of the Western Mediterranean for the two empires to co-exist.

If Rome's power lay in its legions, then Carthage's maritime power was based solidly on the wealth that trade brought to the city. The Romans, however, had managed to defeat their local rivals in Italy, successfully challenge Carthaginian supremacy at sea during the 1st Punic War, and then develop a taste for further territorial gains by taking Sardinia and Corsica. Such behavior could not go unchallenged by the Carthaginians. They could not allow power to slip away into the hands of some northern upstarts from Italy.

Fortunately, the Carthaginians were blessed with a great general in Hannibal, who can only be described as a military genius. In 218 BC he led a force from Spain, over the Alps and into Northern Italy to directly challenge Roman power. He defeated the Romans at Trebia in 217 BC and forced them onto the strategic defensive, partly thanks to the Gauls joining the Carthaginians after the battle. Hannibal was unable to profit further from his success, though, as the people of Italy—other than the Gauls—remained largely loyal to the Roman Republic.

But Hannibal pushed hard, and again caught a Roman army at Lake Trasimene. Now he would have another chance to prove his worth, this time against the full might of a Roman consular army under C. Flaminius. He had already demonstrated tactical finesse in commanding many different types of soldiers against the relatively brute force approach of the Roman commander at Trebia. Now Hannibal intended to teach the Romans another hard lesson. It was not to be the last lesson in generalship he would hand out.

Battle Overview

In this battle, you control an ambushed Roman army whose numbers are depleted by a Carthaginian sneak attack. You must quickly react to the Carthaginian advance and repel it before you are overwhelmed and surrounded.

Roman Julii Family (Playable)

As the commander of the Roman army, you have the usual Roman units at your disposal: Hastati, Triarii, Velites, Roman Cavalry, and Principes. However, although it seems like you have more than enough military might to carry the day, nearly a third of your troops are killed by Carthage's sneak attack before the battle even begins, requiring you to quickly repel the Carthaginian charge or face swift and humiliating defeat.

- Roman General (Cavalry) x15
- Roman Cavalry (Cavalry) x45
- Roman Cavalry (Cavalry) x45
- Hastati (Infantry) x60
- Hastati (Infantry) x60
- Hastati (Infantry) x60
- Hastati (Infantry) x60
- Principes (Infantry) x76
- Principes (Infantry) x76
- Principes (Infantry) x61
- Principes (Infantry) x61
- Triarii (Spearmen) x62
- Triarii (Spearmen) x62
- Triarii (Spearmen) x62
- Triarii (Spearmen) x62
- Velites (Missile) x45
- Velites (Missile) x45
- Velites (Missile) x45
- Velites (Missile) x45

Carthaginians (Non-Playable)

Composed of swift cavalry and deadly long-range attackers, the Carthaginians are a formidable force. With the twin advantages of surprise and the military skill of Hannibal, the greatest Carthaginian General of all time, they are not to be underestimated.

- General's Bodyguard (Cavalry) x15
- Round Shield Cavalry (Cavalry) x60
- Round Shield Cavalry (Cavalry) x60
- Round Shield Cavalry (Cavalry) x60
- Long Shield Cavalry (Cavalry) x60
- Libyan Spearmen (Spearmen) x61
- Libyan Spearmen (Spearmen) x61
- Iberian Infantry (Infantry) x60
- Iberian Infantry (Infantry) x60
- Iberian Infantry (Infantry) x60
- Iberian Infantry (Infantry) x60
- Poeni Infantry (Infantry) x61
- Poeni Infantry (Infantry) x61
- Poeni Infantry (Infantry) x31
- Skirmishers (Missile) x45
- Skirmishers (Missile) x45
- Skirmishers (Missile) x45
- Skirmishers (Missile) x30
- Skirmishers (Missile) x30

Strategy

Take Out the Cavalry

The Carthaginians swoop down toward your unprepared army at the start of the battle. However, because they are not marching in formation and need to hit you as quickly as possible, their cavalry reaches you first. Use the Triarii on your left flank and the two units of Triarii on your right flank to charge the three approaching units of Round Shield Cavalry.

Do not send your Roman Cavalry or Roman General into combat against the Round Shield Cavalry, as the Carthaginian cavalry is reinforced by spearmen who will make short work of your horse-mounted units. Instead, have them charge the Long Shield Cavalry that try to make a run right through the center of your forces. When they start getting bogged down by additional Carthaginian units, pull them back so that they don't rout.

As soon as the units on your left flank repel the cavalry charge, send them to reinforce the troops on the front line. The Carthaginian General's Bodyguard rides straight up through the middle of your line, so if you've got spearmen waiting for him, you can deal the Carthaginian morale a deadly blow.

Scatter the Enemy

After shattering the Carthaginian cavalry (and hopefully their General) on your spears, take a good look at the battlefield, which should be littered with several smaller skirmishes. If one of your units is being ganged up on by several Carthaginian units and is clearly in trouble, you're better off using that unit to lead off the Carthaginians while you commit your forces to taking a decisive advantage in more evenly-matched battles.

Run off enemy Skirmishers with your remaining Roman Cavalry and Roman General. You don't have to kill the Skirmishers; just drive them far enough from battle so that it will take them a while to return to it.

Heavy infantry is best used to smash the Carthaginian forces. If you can flank their spearmen with heavy infantry, you'll quickly obliterate them.

If you survive the first two minutes of the battle and it at least seems as if it could go either way, you're in good shape. Achieving a clear victory in a battle where you're utterly outnumbered and outmaneuvered is almost too much to ask for—be happy with any victory, no matter how close.

HISTORIC BATTLES— THE BATTLE OF RAPHIA

Raphia—217 BC

More than a century after the death of Alexander the Great, his successors were still struggling for dominance over his fragmented empire, including that of the Middle East, one of the most fought-over corners of the world. Antiochus III of the Seleucids had designs on regaining control of Coele-Syria (approximately what is now modern Lebanon, Israel and Jordan), which had been annexed earlier by Egypt. Antiochus could do little about the situation immediately, but his opportunity came when the new king of Egypt, Ptolemy IV, came to the throne. As he was not an attractive character, there were defections to the Seleucids among Egyptian generals and governors, and war loomed.

By spring 217 BC, both sides had completed their preparations. Egyptian diplomacy had delayed the fighting for long enough. The Egyptians had gathered a mercenary army, but Antiochus had managed to take much of Coele-Syria during the previous year's campaign. The two armies advanced, and clashed near the small town of Raphia, in what is now Gaza, with the sea protecting one flank of each army. Both kings chose to make this flank their strongest, and lead the battle from there.

Although Ptolemy won the battle (Antiochus got carried away in the heat of a cavalry charge and pursuit, and became cut off from his army), he did little to secure any concrete gains from his victory. Antiochus campaigned elsewhere along his borders and did well, eventually returning to Coele-Syria in 200 BC to avenge his defeat and secure the area for the Seleucid throne.

Battle Overview

You only have the option of controlling the Seleucids in this battle, which makes your task a challenging one, as the Seleucids actually lost this battle in 217 BC. At the start of the battle, your general is cut off from the rest of his army, and the Egyptians are massed into a line of deadly archers and lightning-fast cavalry.

Seleucids (Playable)

The Seleucids are slightly outnumbered in this battle and suffer from a lack of missile troops. However, their War Elephants and Silver Shield Pikemen make them a very effective melee fighting force.

- General's Bodyguard (Cavalry) x20
- Companion Cavalry (Cavalry) x40
- Companion Cavalry (Cavalry) x40
- Companion Cavalry (Cavalry) x30
- Companion Cavalry (Cavalry) x30
- Greek Cavalry (Cavalry) x30
- Greek Cavalry (Cavalry) x30
- Armoured Elephants (Cavalry) x18
- War Elephants (Cavalry) x18
- Silver Shield Pikemen (Spearmen) x41
- Silver Shield Pikemen (Spearmen) x41
- Silver Shield Pikemen (Spearmen) x41
- Silver Shield Pikemen (Spearmen) x41
- Silver Shield Pikemen (Spearmen) x41
- Silver Shield Pikemen (Spearmen) x41
- Silver Shield Pikemen (Spearmen) x41
- Silver Shield Pikemen (Spearmen) x41
- Peltasts (Missile) x30
- Peltasts (Missile) x30
- Peltasts (Missile) x30

Egyptians (Non-Playable)

The Egyptian army relies heavily on its archers to pick off your forces from a distance. They're also equipped with some formidable cavalry, but they suffer from a lack of infantry and spearmen. They can't endure hand-to-hand combat for long, unless they pick your troops off from a distance before you reach them.

- Egyptian General (Cavalry) x20
- Nile Cavalry (Cavalry) x40
- Nile Cavalry (Cavalry) x40
- Nile Cavalry (Cavalry) x30
- Nubian Cavalry (Cavalry) x40
- Nubian Cavalry (Cavalry) x30
- Egyptian Chariot Archers (Cavalry) x36
- Camel Archers (Cavalry) x40

- Pharaoh's Bowmen (Missile) x41
- Pharaoh's Bowmen (Missile) x41
- Pharaoh's Bowmen (Missile) x41
- Pharaoh's Bowmen (Missile) x41
- Pharaoh's Guards (Spearmen) x41
- Pharaoh's Guards (Spearmen) x41
- Pharaoh's Guards (Spearmen) x41
- Pharaoh's Guards (Spearmen) x41
- Desert Axemen (Infantry) x31
- Desert Axemen (Infantry) x31
- Desert Axemen (Infantry) x31
- Desert Axemen (Infantry) x31

Strategy

Regroup

The first thing that you absolutely must do at the start of this battle is order your General's Bodyguard back to the center of your troops as fast as they can ride. If you don't do this immediately, your general will quickly be isolated from the rest of his army and killed, dealing a severe blow to your morale.

Order your Silver Shield Pikemen into standard (not phalanx) formation. Select all of your troops and order them into loose formation to lessen the effectiveness of the Egyptian archers. March all of your troops at a walk toward the Egyptians to avoid fatigue.

Keep your cursor over the furthest Egyptian unit from your troops (should be the Egyptian General). When the tool tip information for this unit appears, you're nearly within range of the Pharaoh's Bowmen, so be ready.

As soon as the first Egyptian arrows are fired, it's time to charge! Send your War and Armoured Elephants against the nearest units of Desert Axemen. Your Peltasts should target the Pharaoh's Bowmen, your Silver Shield Pikemen should attack the Pharaoh's Guards and Desert Axemen, and your cavalry should be employed against the Egyptian cavalry, particularly the missile cavalry (Camel Archers and Egyptian Chariot Archers).

The Heat of Battle

This is one of the least predictable Historical Battles in the game, so be ready to think on your feet and react to events as they unfold. Just before your Silver Shield Pikemen reach the Egyptians, order them into phalanx formation to deal much greater damage.

The Egyptians will focus heavily on routing your War Elephants. Let them—while they're attacking that single unit with their cavalry, you can be whittling down their undefended forces (and remember, you've still got a second elephant unit). If an elephant unit starts running amok, however, be sure to use the "kill rampaging elephants" command if the unit is near your own troops.

When you get an opportunity, dedicate your heavy cavalry (elephants and Companion Cavalry) to killing the Egyptian General, which greatly demoralizes the Egyptian forces. Use your elephants to rout the enemy's cavalry.

Once you have scattered the Egyptian forces, watch the southwest corner of the map, where many routed Egyptians may regroup and attempt a second attack. Be ready for them with Silver Shield Pikemen in phalanx formation.

Chase down individual enemy units with your remaining cavalry. Should you be pursued by a larger force, lure the Egyptians into your pikemen and infantry troops. By this point, the Egyptians should be nearly out of ammunition, giving you the upper hand. Hunt down the rest of the shattered Egyptian forces, and victory is yours!

HISTORIC BATTLES—
THE BATTLE OF TELAMON

The Battle of Telamon— 225 BC

After the end of the 1st Punic War and the Pyrrhic War, the Romans had every right to feel pleased with their results. There had been unrest in northern Italy, but the mere appearance of an army had quashed any opposition. The Romans had even decided to close the Temple of Janus in the Forum, something that only occurred when there was peace throughout Roman lands. This was very uncommon indeed.

However, peace never seemed to last. In 225 BC an alliance of Gallic tribes and mercenaries from Transalpine Gaul moved into Etruria through an unguarded pass in the Apennines. To meet this invasion, the Romans called on the resources and manpower of all of middle and southern Italy, who rapidly mobilized defensive forces. As a result, they succeeded in outmaneuvering the Gauls, and forced the invaders towards the coast of Tuscany, while another army made an unopposed landing at Pisae and prevented them from a line of retreat.

The Gauls were surrounded, trapped. At Telamon, on the coast of Etruria, the Gauls stood back to back and waited for the Romans to approach. The Romans, however, had learned from previous wars with the Gauls, and did not let the headlong rush of Gallic warriors dishearten them....

After Telamon the Romans decided that enough was enough. Northern Italy would have to be secured and the Gauls defeated, a task that would virtually double the area under Rome's direct control. By 220 BC nearly all the Gallic tribes had submitted and Carthage was severely weakened by the loss of one of its main sources of mercenaries. The peace won would not be long lasting.

Battle Overview

As warlord of a trapped Gaelic army, you must defeat the two Roman armies closing in on you, no easy feat considering that each of them is the size of your own band of warriors. You must quickly destroy or rout the Romans directly in front of you, preserving enough of your army to deal with the Romans marching up from behind.

Gauls (Playable)

Your Gaelic army is short on cavalry and spearmen, but your Chosen Swordsmen are nearly fearless in battle, and your Warhounds are the bane of Roman horsemen.

- Barbarian Warlord (Cavalry) x30
- Barbarian Noble Cavalry (Cavalry) x55
- Barbarian Noble Cavalry (Cavalry) x55
- Skirmisher Warband (Missile) x55
- Skirmisher Warband (Missile) x55
- Chosen Swordsmen (Infantry) x56
- Chosen Swordsmen (Infantry) x56
- Chosen Swordsmen (Infantry) x56
- Chosen Swordsmen (Infantry) x56
- Chosen Swordsmen (Infantry) x56
- Chosen Swordsmen (Infantry) x56
- Warhounds x55
- Warhounds x55

Roman Julii Family (Non-Playable)

Individually, neither Roman Julii army would be a match for the Gauls. However, as allies, they outnumber the Gauls 2-to-1. Their Triarii are deadly against the Gaul's already limited cavalry, and their Roman Cavalry are fierce attackers that can assume a wedge formation and plow through the Gaelic lines.

Roman Army #1

- Roman General (Cavalry) x15
- Roman Cavalry (Cavalry) x55
- Roman Cavalry (Cavalry) x55
- Velites (Missile) x55
- Velites (Missile) x55
- Velites (Missile) x55
- Hastati (Infantry) x55
- Hastati (Infantry) x55
- Hastati (Infantry) x55
- Triarii (Spearmen) x57
- Triarii (Spearmen) x57
- Triarii (Spearmen) x57

Roman Army #2

- Roman General (Cavalry) x15
- Roman Cavalry (Cavalry) x55
- Roman Cavalry (Cavalry) x55
- Roman Archers (Missile) x55
- Roman Archers (Missile) x55
- Hastati (Infantry) x55
- Hastati (Infantry) x55
- Hastati (Infantry) x55
- Principes (Infantry) x56
- Principes (Infantry) x56
- Triarii (Spearmen) x57
- Triarii (Spearmen) x57
- Triarii (Spearmen) x57

Strategy

Defeat the Army Ahead of You

To have any hope of victory, you must crush the Roman army in front of you quickly, suffering as few casualties as possible. From the start of the battle, take out the first two rows of the Roman army.

Target the two units of Roman Cavalry with your Skirmisher Warbands. Send your Warhounds after them as well. Charge each of the three units of Velites and each of the three units of Hastati with your six units of Chosen Swordsmen. Hold back your Barbarian Noble Cavalry and Barbarian Warlord for the moment.

Attack any enemy units that break through the line with your Barbarian Warlord and Barbarian Noble Cavalry. As soon as a Roman unit routs, immediately reassign any attacking Gaelic units to nearby enemies. Your Warhounds should send the Roman Cavalry fleeing in record time.

Watch out for enemy spearmen! The Romans will take any opportunity to lure your few cavalry into the waiting pikes of the Triarii.

Repel the Army Behind You

Don't become so preoccupied with the Romans ahead of you that you forget the ones advancing from behind. Meet their cavalry charge with your Warhounds and Skirmisher Warbands, just as you did with the first army. Target enemy spearmen with your Chosen Swordsmen, and have them perform their Warcry special ability prior to attacking in order to improve their odds in combat.

Beware of routed Romans rediscovering their courage behind you as well. Although their morale will be shaky at best, and their numbers will probably be too depleted to be much of a hassle, you've got better things to do than be attacked from behind while you're trying to destroy the main line of the second Roman army.

Don't hesitate to use the nearby woods to your advantage, either. Hide units in them and lure in smaller groups of Romans that you can quickly overwhelm.

Once you break the back of each Roman army, you should have little trouble hunting down the small bands of resistance that stand between you and total victory.

HISTORIC BATTLES— THE SIEGE OF GERGOVIA

Gergovia—53 BC

Julius Caesar was appointed proconsul for the combined provinces of Illyricum, Cisalpine, and Transalpine Gaul—a vast territory for him to rule, but still not quite enough. Fortunately, he commanded one of the best armies of the day, tough veteran legionaries with good military engineering skills. Even so this wasn't big enough for his purposes, and he eventually raised legions from among the native people who weren't Roman citizens by birth, something of a first for a Roman general.

In a series of rapid campaigns, he defeated an array of Gallic tribes across modern France from the Rhine to the English Channel. Caesar had an eye on political power in Rome, not just on simply conquering a bunch of barbarians. He even found time to bridge the Rhine to fight the Germans, and cross into Britannia to teach the natives there a lesson in Roman warfare. All throughout these campaigns, he still had to have an eye on the political maneuverings of his fellow Romans, Crassus and Pompey, and how his own victories would look to the Senate. Fortunately, Crassus was to be dead quite soon, urged into foolish military adventurism by Caesar himself.

All was going well until 54 BC when a revolt broke out, led by Vercingetorix, an Avernian aristocrat. Thrown temporarily onto the back foot, Caesar was forced to react to the Gaul and his attacks, rather than the other way around. The Gauls annihilated one of his legions in the winter of 54–53 BC, and disaster never seemed far away. The rebellious Gauls were proving to be a huge problem.

In 53 BC, the Gauls and Romans met at Gergovia. After the fighting, Caesar's talent for positive propaganda on his own behalf was put to a severe test. This battle was one of his few setbacks (not a defeat, no—or if it was, it was someone else's fault). Vercingetorix and the Gauls got the better of the Romans, but Caesar was to have his revenge and ultimate victory, one year later at Alesia.

Vercingetorix paid the price for his defiance of Roman authority. After his surrender, he was paraded through Rome and publicly beheaded.

Battle Overview

As Julius Caesar, Roman General of the Julii family, you have to fight your way out of one of the few ambushes Caesar ever fell into. From the start of the battle, you are surrounded on three sides by Gauls. To the west is the unguarded Gaelic settlement, barred by a solid oaken gate. Your mission is twofold: Drive off or kill the Gauls, and keep your Battering Ram intact so that you can smash down the Gaelic settlement's gate.

Roman Julii Family (Playable)

Although outnumbered, the Julii force is made up of some of Rome's finest warriors, all of whom are commanded by Rome's most legendary general, Julius Caesar. Keeping your forces together and not allowing them to be flanked by the Gauls is essential for victory.

- Roman General (Cavalry) x10
- Legionary Cohort (Infantry) x41
- Legionary Cohort (Infantry) x41
- Legionary Cohort (Infantry) x41
- Legionary Cohort (Infantry) x41
- Legionary Cohort (Infantry) x41
- Legionary Cohort (Infantry) x41
- Legionary Cohort (Infantry) x41
- Legionary Cohort (Infantry) x41
- Legionary Cohort (Infantry) x41
- Legionary Cohort (Infantry) x41
- Legionary Cohort (Infantry) x41
- Legionary Cohort (Infantry) x41
- Archer Auxilia (Missile) x31
- Archer Auxilia (Missile) x31
- Legionary Cavalry (Cavalry) x30
- Legionary Cavalry (Cavalry) x30

Gauls (Non-Playable)

The Gauls may have the numerical advantage in this battle, but they have two things working against them. First, they start off spread out, encircling the tightly-packed Roman soldiers; this virtually guarantees that they are unable to flank the Julii. Second, they are up against Julius Caesar, the most decorated Roman general in history.

- Barbarian Warlord (Cavalry) x20
- Naked Fanatics (Infantry) x30
- Naked Fanatics (Infantry) x30
- Chosen Swordsmen (Infantry) x41
- Chosen Swordsmen (Infantry) x41
- Chosen Swordsmen (Infantry) x41

- Druids (Infantry) x30
- Warband (Infantry) x41
- Warband (Infantry) x41
- Swordsmen (Infantry) x41
- Swordsmen (Infantry) x41
- Swordsmen (Infantry) x41
- Swordsmen (Infantry) x41
- Warhounds x20
- Barbarian Noble Cavalry (Cavalry) x30
- Barbarian Noble Cavalry (Cavalry) x30
- Barbarian Noble Cavalry (Cavalry) x30
- Barbarian Noble Cavalry (Cavalry) x40
- Barbarian Noble Cavalry (Cavalry) x40
- Skirmisher Warband (Missile) x30
- Skirmisher Warband (Missile) x30

Strategy

Wait For the Northern Charge

From the start of the battle, prepare your forces to resist the Gaelic advance by halting all of your units and ordering your Legionary Cohorts into testudo formation. Send your Legionary Cavalry and Roman General to the east, to reinforce the Legionary Cavalry defending the Battering Ram. Remember, if the Battering Ram is destroyed, you lose the battle.

Order your Archers Auxilia to fire Flaming Arrows at the Gauls' Barbarian Noble Cavalry in an effort to drop their morale. (Remember, horses hate fire!) Defend the archers from the northern Gaelic charge with a couple of units of Legionary Cohorts, but leave the vast majority of your infantry where it is.

Having met the northern charge, don't forget about the Gauls to the south, who advance shortly. If you can turn or destroy most of the northern Gauls before their southern reinforcements arrive, you've just made your job a lot easier.

The best way to demoralize the northern Gauls is to kill or rout their Druids, which provide a morale boost to nearby Gaelic units. The Gauls' Warbands also suffer from a lack of courage, so driving them from the battlefield can help to rout other Gaelic units.

Repel the Southern Charge

The southern Gaelic forces charge in shortly after the northern Gauls attack, led by the Barbarian Warlord. It goes without saying that the Barbarian Warlord is a high-value target. Killing or routing him greatly demoralizes the Gauls.

Fire Flaming Arrows at remaining units of Gaelic cavalry and the Warhounds (if they're still in the fight) to drive them off.

If you defend yourself with ruthless efficiency and eradicate the Gaelic forces as they attack, you should find this a very manageable battle. Victory is achieved when you kill or rout all Gaelic forces, or when you use the Battering Ram to open the settlement gates and move your troops into the town square to occupy it.

HISTORIC BATTLES—
THE BATTLE OF THE RIVER TREBIA

Battle of the Trebia— 218 BC

As Rome secured control of the Italian peninsula, Carthage was establishing an empire in Spain and North Africa. It was inevitable that these two rising powers would clash violently for control of the Western Mediterranean. Carthage needed space for its trade and maritime empire, and the Romans simply saw Carthage as another threat. War was bound to come, sooner or later.

Fortunately for the Carthaginians, they had the services of Hannibal Barca, one of the greatest generals of all time. Marching from Spain, he slipped past one Roman army and into northern Italy over the Alps, even managing to bring a contingent of elephants with the army. His bold strategy was to march on Rome and break Roman power at its heart. He also hoped to gain allies as he advanced, among peoples disenchanted with the domination of Rome.

After two months of campaigning he was met by a Roman force at the River Trebia. Hannibal used a feigned cavalry retreat to lure the Romans across the freezing river. True to form, and despite the winter floods, the Romans crossed the river and made straight for Hannibal's army. Hannibal was ready and crushed the Roman army. The few Romans who escaped were the ones who broke through the Carthaginian line as it closed around them and then kept running!

Battle Overview

As Hannibal, general of the Carthaginian army, you must lure the Roman Julii into a carefully laid trap and eradicate their superior numbers with cunning strategy. Fortunately, the game begins with your trap in place, so all you have to do is know when and how to strike the Julii.

Carthaginians (Playable)

A combination of fast cavalry, deadly ranged attackers and powerful War Elephants is all that remains of the force that Hannibal led across the frigid Alps. Although outnumbered by the Roman Julii soldiers, the Carthaginians have all the power they need to win the battle and suffer relatively few losses.

- General's Bodyguard (Cavalry) x1
- Round Shield Cavalry (Cavalry) x60
- War Elephants (Cavalry) x30
- Armoured Elephants (Cavalry) x30
- Numidian Mercenaries (Cavalry) x30
- Sacred Band Cavalry (Cavalry) x40
- Long Shield Cavalry (Cavalry) x40
- Barbarian Cavalry Mercenaries (Cavalry) x40
- Poeni Infantry (Spearmen) x61
- Poeni Infantry (Spearmen) x61
- Sacred Band (Spearmen) x41
- Skirmishers (Missile) x100
- Skirmishers (Missile) x100
- Cretan Archers (Missile) x60
- Iberian Infantry (Infantry) x80
- Barbarian Mercenaries (Infantry) x80

Roman Julii Family (Non-Playable)

The Julii are trained to face their foes on an open battlefield and overwhelm them with superior numbers. Unfortunately for them, Hannibal and the Carthaginians have no desire to stand out in the open and wait for the Romans to attack. Although the Carthaginians should prove to have superior tactics, the Julii's superior numbers make them a threat not to be taken lightly.

- Roman General (Cavalry) x10
- Equites (Cavalry) x40
- Equites (Cavalry) x40
- Triarii (Spearmen) x102
- Triarii (Spearmen) x102
- Triarii (Spearmen) x102
- Triarii (Spearmen) x102
- Velites (Missile) x60
- Velites (Missile) x60

- Velites (Missile) x60
- Velites (Missile) x60
- Hastati (Infantry) x100
- Hastati (Infantry) x100
- Hastati (Infantry) x100
- Principes (Infantry) x101
- Principes (Infantry) x101
- Principes (Infantry) x101
- Principes (Infantry) x101

Strategy

Bait the Trap

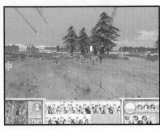

From the start of the battle, the Carthaginian trap is set. Your Sacred Band Cavalry and Long Shield Cavalry lie in wait behind a tree line to the south. Your Numidian Mercenaries and Barbarian Cavalry Mercenaries are hidden behind another grove to the north. The Julii army marches east toward you, oblivious to the fact that they are heading past the four hidden cavalry units.

At the start of the battle, direct your Skirmishers and Cretan Archers to attack the Julii Velites that make up the front line of the Roman army. This will likely cause them to rout, especially if your Cretan Archers are using Flaming Arrows.

When the Velites turn and run, order your Skirmishers and Cretan Archers to fire at the next wave of Julii soldiers, the Hastati. When your Skirmishers start to back away from the battle, send in your Poeni Infantry and Sacred Band (in phalanx formation) to keep the Julii from advancing too far too quickly.

As soon as the rear of the Julii army clears the tree line, send your hidden cavalry units to attack them from the rear, targeting heavy infantry units and the Roman General. Once the battle is underway, charge the enemy lines with your elephants and send the Julii running in all directions (especially if you've killed the Roman General).

CAUTION

Fleeing units may recover their morale and end up near the hidden cavalry units before you can charge. If this happens, follow the same strategy as outlined above, but beware that you have lost the element of surprise.

Crush the Julii

Between the destruction being wreaked by your War Elephants, Armoured Elephants, and the death of the Roman General, the Julii forces should be close to routing. Tear through the ranks of their heavy infantry with your cavalry (especially the elephants) to break the spine of the Julii army.

Once you've sent the Julii scattering, simply chase down any remaining Julii and destroy them or send them fleeing. Your elephants are particularly useful for achieving the latter objective. When the battle is over, you can chase down and destroy any remaining Julii with your cavalry, or just choose to enjoy the victory.

HISTORIC BATTLES—
THE BATTLE OF ASCULUM

Battle of Asculum— 279 BC

Pyrrhus, the King of Epirus, had a long career as a soldier, pretty much starting at the age of 12. He was related to Alexander the Great through his mother, and was drawn into the Wars of the Successors after Alexander's death. In the process, he managed to get himself deposed and reinstated as King of Epirus and proclaimed the King of Macedonia, and then promptly dethroned in Macedonia. Pyrrhus consciously modeled himself on Alexander and even claimed that Alexander talked to him in dreams. Even after losing the Macedonian throne, he kept looking for something to conquer, like his hero.

It was at this point that ambassadors from Tarentum arrived to ask for help against some western "barbarians" who called themselves "Romans." Pyrrhus needed little further encouragement and, in 280 BC, landed in Italy. His first overtures to the Romans offering mediation between them and the citizens of Tarentum were rejected. His victory at Heraclea was not enough to win the war, however, even when he marched on Rome. Incidentally, his opponent at Heraclea, Appius Claudius, was responsible for giving the Roman army its first taste of new punishment: decimation. Pyrrhus had hoped to win over Rome's allies and client cities to his banner, but every one of them shut the gates against him, and he was forced to winter in Campania, even though he had been close enough to Rome to see the smoke of the city on the horizon.

In 279, Pyrrhus advanced again. This time he moved up the Adriatic coast, methodically reducing the Roman colonies there. Perhaps he hoped that the locals would rise and follow him, but the Romans moved too and sent an army to confront him under the command of P. Sulpicius Saverrio and P. Decimus Mus. The two armies confronted each other near the River Aufidus, upstream from the spot were the equally bloody Battle of Cannae would be fought some 63 years later.

Asculum was to give the world the concept of the pyrrhic victory: a victory won at so great a cost that it was almost a defeat. As Pyrrhus himself remarked "If we are victorious in one more battle with the Romans, we shall be utterly ruined."

Battle Overview

The SPQR army has the unenviable task of repelling the incursion of Pyrrhus' Seleucids into Roman territory. Although the SPQR has a slight numerical superiority, the Seleucids have a clear edge when it comes to power, with several units of Phalanx Pikemen and a unit of War Elephants, the heaviest of all cavalry units.

SPQR Forces

You command a division of troops who fight under the banner of the SPQR (Senate and People of Rome). With limited cavalry and a strong reliance on infantry troops, your strength lies in the discipline of your soldiers.

- **Roman General (Cavalry) x15**
- **Velites (Missile) x80**
- **Velites (Missile) x80**
- **Velites (Missile) x80**
- **Hastati (Infantry) x60**
- **Hastati (Infantry) x60**
- **Hastati (Infantry) x60**
- **Hastati (Infantry) x60**
- **Hastati (Infantry) x60**
- **Principes (Infantry) x61**
- **Principes (Infantry) x61**
- **Principes (Infantry) x61**
- **Principes (Infantry) x61**
- **Principes (Infantry) x61**
- **Triarii (Spearmen) x42**
- **Triarii (Spearmen) x42**
- **Triarii (Spearmen) x42**
- **Triarii (Spearmen) x42**
- **Triarii (Spearmen) x42**
- **Equites (Cavalry) x30**

Seleucids (Non-Playable)

The Seleucids are the latest in a long line of brash challengers seeking to break the vaunted Roman army and conquer their lands. But few enemies of Rome have ever struck with such force as the Seleucids, who arrive at the battle with hundreds of pikemen and a unit of War Elephants.

- General's Bodyguard (Cavalry) x30
- War Elephants (Cavalry) x15
- Phalanx Pikemen (Spearmen) x60
- Phalanx Pikemen (Spearmen) x60
- Phalanx Pikemen (Spearmen) x60
- Phalanx Pikemen (Spearmen) x60
- Phalanx Pikemen (Spearmen) x60
- Companion Cavalry (Cavalry) x30
- Barbarian Mercenaries (Infantry) x60
- Archers (Missile) x60
- Peltasts (Missile) x60
- Peltasts (Missile) x60
- Levy Pikemen (Spearmen) x60
- Levy Pikemen (Spearmen) x60
- Levy Pikemen (Spearmen) x60
- Samnite Mercenaries (Infantry) x60
- Militia Hoplites (Spearmen) x60
- Rhodian Slingers (Missile) x60

SPQR Strategy

Hold the Line

Let the Seleucids make the first move by waiting for them to charge you. This guarantees that their soldiers will already be slightly fatigued by the time they reach you, while your troops are fresh as daisies.

While you're waiting for the Seleucids to reach you, select all of your troops that are capable of missile attacks (Velites, Hastati and Principes). Enable fire-at-will mode for all of them, and keep them selected.

As the Seleucids draw near, you might come under light missile attack. Don't worry about that right now; hold the line. As soon as the Companion Cavalry and War Elephants come within range of your Velites, Hastati, and Principes, attack them with ranged weapons. You should break their wills almost instantly and rout them.

Next, turn your attention to the General's Bodyguard unit, composed of heavy cavalry. Use some of your missile-firing troops to inflict punishment from a distance, and support them with Triarii and Equites. Killing the enemy general will drastically affect the Seleucids' morale.

Breaking the Seleucids

Once you have driven off or killed the Seleucids' cavalry and general, it's time to focus on their spearmen. Send light infantry around to the side of the Seleucids' spearmen units and pepper them from a distance with missiles.

By sending two or three units of infantry against a single unit of Seleucid Pikemen, you can break their morale with amazing speed and send them fleeing from the battlefield. As always, keep your soldiers from pursuing fleeing troops, assigning them to fight other nearby Seleucids instead.

Once you've routed all nearby infantry and spearmen units, re-form your battle line and wait for the Seleucids to re-form their shattered ranks. Don't get fooled into pursuing units to the southwest, as several units of Levy Pikemen, Phalanx Pikemen, and Barbarian Mercenaries may regroup there and pick off your units.

From this point, send out groups of three or four units to hunt down and destroy individual Seleucid units. You should have no trouble breaking the morale of an enemy unit and moving on to the next one—just be sure not to send your soldiers into situations where they might be overwhelmed by reinforcements. Continue in this manner until you have defeated or destroyed the Seleucids.

Historic Battles— The Battle of Carrhae

The Battle of Carrhae— 55 BC

Carrhae was a battle that need not have happened.

It was the success of Julius Caesar in Gaul that led Licinius Crassus, a rival for power, to move against the Parthians: Caesar was doing rather too well. Crassus had been a member of the First Triumvirate with Caesar and Pompey, and then a consul with Pompey. His achievements were in danger of being overshadowed.

In 55 BC Crassus went to Syria—a province he had been given when the spoils of the Empire were divided up—with war on his mind. The Parthian Empire to the east was an opportunity for glory and even greater wealth, although his desire for a war was completely unnecessary and probably beyond his skills to manage. To be fair to Crassus, he was an adequate general, rather than a great commander like Caesar or Pompey. He probably knew that he owed his place in the Triumvirate to his enormous wealth. There also have to be some doubts as to Julius Caesar's true motives in writing to Crassus urging him to go to war.

In 53, he got his war but foolishly rejected local advice and marched directly towards the Parthian heartland; he had been advised to attack through the mountains of Armenia. The legions crossed the Euphrates at Zeugma, pressed eastwards but, on hearing that the Parthians were near, Crassus reformed the army into a massive marching square. An army of horse archers and cavalry under the inspiring commander Surenas then confronted him. As the Roman infantry stood firm, the Parthians began the battle with a cacophony of beating drums to dishearten their enemies. Then the arrow storm started…

Although it's not usual to tell you about the aftermath of a battle you're about to refight, the fate of Crassus is worth knowing. The Parthians captured and executed him. Crassus was probably the wealthiest man in the Roman world, and the Parthians poured molten gold down his throat. They also slaughtered the Roman wounded and took the survivors into captivity. The final insult was that they captured many standards, including legionary eagles.

Battle Overview

This is another battle in which the side that you command did not win, according to the history books. Before the battle even begins, you lose more than half of your cavalry to the Parthian ambush, leaving you extremely vulnerable to their surrounding Persian Cavalry. You must not only defeat the surrounding mounted archers but also crush the Cataphracts that charge through your lines.

Roman Brutii Family

Your outnumbered and outmaneuvered forces have only one thing going for them: they are all trained to the highest Roman standards. Their stamina and morale are high, and they can assume several defensive postures that cut down on the effectiveness of the Parthian archers.

- **Roman General (Cavalry) x25**
- **Roman Cavalry (Cavalry) x30**
- **Roman Cavalry (Cavalry) x30**
- **Roman Cavalry (Cavalry) x30**
- **Roman Cavalry (Cavalry) x30**
- **Early Legionary First Cohort (Infantry) x62**
- **Early Legionary First Cohort (Infantry) x62**
- **Early Legionary First Cohort (Infantry) x62**
- **Early Legionary First Cohort (Infantry) x62**
- **Early Legionary First Cohort (Infantry) x62**
- **Early Legionary First Cohort (Infantry) x62**
- **Early Legionary First Cohort (Infantry) x62**
- **Early Legionary First Cohort (Infantry) x62**
- **Early Legionary First Cohort (Infantry) x62**

Parthian Armies (Non-Playable)

The Parthians attack in two devastating waves. The first is their initial ambush, which leaves your troops surrounded by Persian Cavalry archers, huddling under their shields for defense. The second is a crushing charge from their heavy Cataphract cavalry. All of the Parthian units are cavalry, giving them a decisive edge when it comes to maneuverability and changing tactics on the fly.

Parthian Army #1

- Eastern General (Cavalry) x25
- Cataphracts (Cavalry) x30
- Cataphracts (Cavalry) x30
- Cataphracts (Cavalry) x30
- Cataphracts (Cavalry) x30

Parthian Army #2

- Eastern General (Cavalry) x25
- Persian Cavalry (Cavalry) x50
- Persian Cavalry (Cavalry) x50
- Persian Cavalry (Cavalry) x50
- Persian Cavalry (Cavalry) x50
- Persian Cavalry (Cavalry) x50
- Persian Cavalry (Cavalry) x50

Strategy

Counterattack

When you start the battle, all of your Early Legionary First Cohorts are in testudo formation, with their shields overhead to block the rain of arrows from the six surrounding Persian Cavalry units. While testudo increases your defense against missile attack, it also limits your Cohorts' effectiveness in hand-to-hand combat and removes their ability to throw spears altogether.

If you stay in testudo, you'll be crushed by the oncoming Cataphracts. You'll also never be able to catch the surrounding Persian Cavalry, leaving you at the mercy of their arrows. At the start of the battle, take your Cohorts out of testudo formation and set their formation to "loose," in order to limit casualties from the Persian Cavalry and to better withstand the eventual Cataphract charge. Set them to "fire at will" mode so that they can return the Persian Cavalry's lethal barrage.

Use your Roman General and Roman Cavalry to chase off nearby Persian Cavalry units. Before the battle begins, three of your four units of Roman Cavalry are destroyed, so you've got to make the most of what's left. Don't let them stray too far from your Legionary Cohorts; it's great if you can kill or rout some Persian Cavalry units before the Cataphracts reach you, but don't let them get caught by the Cataphracts either.

Attacking the Persian Cavalry head-on will just cause them to run from you until you stop chasing them—you'll never actually catch them. To catch them, run past them, make a U-turn and hit them from behind.

When the Cataphracts approach, assign two or three spear-throwing Cohorts to attack each Cataphract unit. Continue using your cavalry to drive off the Persian Cavalry, occasionally attacking a weakened or demoralized Cataphract unit if you get the opportunity.

Be aware of the first Eastern General who charges toward you from the southeast. Use your Roman Cavalry and Roman General to kill or rout him. With any luck, this will send the Cataphracts into a panic before much longer.

Cavalry Hunt

Now that you've taken out the bulk of the Persian hand-to-hand combatants, you must deal with the Persian Cavalry. The easy way to do this is to put your troops back into testudo formation and march them slowly toward the Persian Cavalry. The Persian Cavalry will expend their arrows in a largely ineffective ranged attack and charge when they're out of ammunition. That's when your Legionary Cohorts have the best chance of striking them down.

You can also flank Persian Cavalry units and drive them toward your Legionary Cohorts, catching them in a pincer movement and crushing them between you.

Beware of the remaining Eastern General, however. He doesn't show up until late in the battle, and he comes down from the north. His presence can not only reinforce the wavering morale of Parthian units you've demoralized, it can also send your troops fleeing. When the second Eastern General shows up, commit overwhelming numbers of troops, including any remaining cavalry, to destroying or routing him ASAP. Doing so should mark the beginning of the end of the Parthian ambush and a dramatic reversal of historical fact!

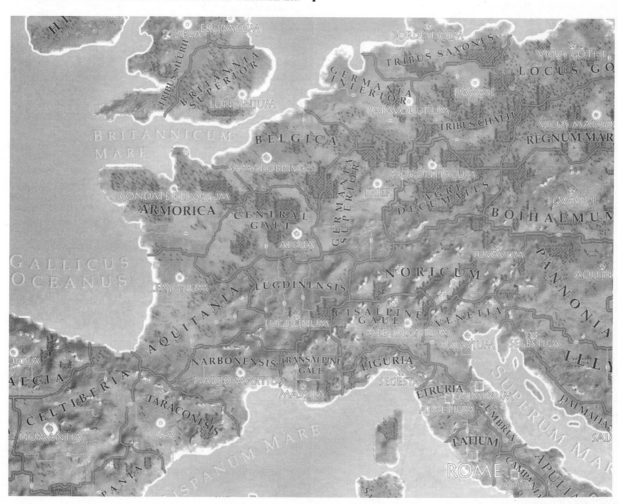

HISTORIC BATTLES—
THE BATTLE OF CYNOSCEPHALAE

The Battle of Cynoscephalae—197 BC

With Carthage defeated at Zama and the Second Punic War brought to a successful conclusion, Rome turned its attention to other matters.

In Greece, the former ally of Carthage, Philip of Macedon provoked Roman hostility just by his continued existence. Romans never forgive or forget those who oppose them, even when this is done unintentionally. It didn't take a lot of effort for Titus Quinctius Flamininus to persuade the Senate that a settling of accounts with Philip was now needed.

In 200 BC a Roman army landed in Thessaly. After some tentative maneuvering by both sides, they camped on either side of a series of ridges and hillocks called "The Dogs' Heads" (for their shapes) and prepared for battle. The fight that followed was characterized by changing fortunes for each side but it was the Romans who eventually gained the upper hand.

Philip's influence in Greece was broken, and a series of small campaigns by Flamininus resulted in the Greek cities being largely independent of Macedonian power by 196. By carefully not taking control for Rome, Flaminius was hailed as a liberator, but in practical terms none of the Greek cities were powerful enough to oppose Rome's will.

Battle Overview

Although the battle begins with your troops being ambushed, you have a number of factors that stack the odds in your favor, not the least of which is the bad planning of the Macedonian assault. Their left flank mistimed the ambush, leaving them isolated and vulnerable. If you can break this flank, you can easily defeat the rest of the Macedonian army.

Roman Scipii Family (Playable)

Despite the fact that the Macedonians kill your lone Roman Cavalry unit before the battle begins, leaving you with a force of mostly foot soldiers, the Macedonian army is heavy with Phalanx Pikemen, who must march in a slow phalanx formation to maximize their attack potential. You also command a unit of Mercenary War Elephants, which are lethal to the health and morale of your enemy and can also fire arrows from a distance.

- Roman General (Cavalry) x60
- Mercenary War Elephants (Cavalry) x10
- Roman Cavalry (Cavalry) x20
- Hastati (Infantry) x80
- Hastati (Infantry) x80
- Hastati (Infantry) x80
- Hastati (Infantry) x80
- Principes (Infantry) x81
- Triarii (Spearmen) x82
- Triarii (Spearmen) x82
- Triarii (Spearmen) x82
- Mercenary Hoplites (Spearmen) x80
- Mercenary Hoplites (Spearmen) x80
- Mercenary Peltasts (Missile) x80
- Velites (Missile) x40

Macedonians (Non-Playable)

The chief strength of the Macedonian army is its abundance of Phalanx Pikemen, which can assume the deadly phalanx formation and utterly obliterate any unit foolish enough to attack them from the front. However, units in phalanx formation are nearly helpless against an attack from the rear or side. If you can avoid the lethal pikes of the Phalanx Pikemen, the rest of the Macedonian army isn't very tough.

- General's Bodyguard (Cavalry) x50
- Macedonian Cavalry (Cavalry) x20
- Light Lancers (Cavalry) x20
- Phalanx Pikemen (Spearmen) x80
- Phalanx Pikemen (Spearmen) x80
- Phalanx Pikemen (Spearmen) x80
- Phalanx Pikemen (Spearmen) x80
- Phalanx Pikemen (Spearmen) x80
- Phalanx Pikemen (Spearmen) x80
- Phalanx Pikemen (Spearmen) x80
- Phalanx Pikemen (Spearmen) x80

- Peltasts (Missile) x80
- Peltasts (Missile) x80
- Peltasts (Missile) x80
- Illyrian Mercenaries (Missile) x80
- Thracian Mercenaries (Infantry) x80

Strategy

Destroy the Left Flank

At the start of the battle, take a look at the Macedonian's misplaced left flank, which is composed of Thracian Mercenaries, two units of Phalanx Pikemen, and some Macedonian Cavalry. These are your first targets. Move your nearby Roman General, Mercenary War Elephants, Hastati, two units of Triarii, and two units of Mercenary Hoplites up to confront them.

Put your Mercenary Hoplites into phalanx formation and march them straight up the hill at the Phalanx Pikemen. Send your Roman General and Mercenary War Elephants toward the Macedonian Cavalry, which should rout almost instantly. Send your Triarii and Hastati against the Thracian Mercenaries.

CAUTION

Don't let your Roman General or Mercenary War Elephants get anywhere near the Phalanx Pikemen's front line, or they'll be destroyed!

Once your Mercenary Hoplites engage and occupy the Phalanx Pikemen, send your Roman General and any other unoccupied units around behind the Phalanx Pikemen and destroy or rout them.

Your Mercenary War Elephants can fire arrows at enemy units, rather than risking their health or morale in melee combat. Simply hold down [Alt] and left-click on an enemy unit to fire arrows at it instead of charging it.

Regroup

After humbling the left flank of the Macedonian army, regroup the units that you used to attack them and hold the nearby wooded hill. This causes the advancing Macedonian army to break its line, undermining the power of its wall of Phalanx Pikemen.

Enable "fire at will" mode on your Mercenary War Elephants, Hastati, and Principes. Let them harass the Macedonians for a bit while you march your Mercenary Hoplites (in phalanx formation) toward the Macedonian missile troops. They should scatter, resulting in a head-to-head collision with the Macedonian Phalanx Pikemen.

From this point, you must send your other units around the Phalanx Pikemen and attack them from behind or from the sides. Your Roman General is the fastest unit you have, and is thus best suited for the job, but you want to be very careful not to let him get surrounded by Phalanx Pikemen, as they'll make short work of him. Hit and run and repeat.

Keep an eye out for the Macedonian General's Bodyguard as well. This heavy cavalry unit charges in with the main Macedonian force and will

probably attack your weaker units on the hillside.

There are only two things you need to do to win this battle—maneuver your troops effectively to flank enemy spearmen, and take the advantage early on by routing the Macedonian left flank and keeping them off balance. If you manage to do both, the battle will end in a sea of white flags running from your troops.

HISTORIC BATTLES—THE BATTLE OF TEUTOBURG FOREST

Teutoburg Forest—9 AD

By 9 AD the frontier of the Roman world lay along the natural moat of the Rhine. To the north, the barbarians lurked in their dark forests (according to the Romans) and plotted the destruction of all things civilized.

The Emperor Augustus was, however, absolutely convinced that the comforts of civilized living could be brought to the German tribes, and pushed for full provincial development of the German interior. However, there seemed to be faint prospect of ever bringing civilization and its comforts to the awkward Germans. This may have been behind the decision to appoint Quinctilius Varus as governor of the province. The man was an able administrator, but not a very good soldier. He was a civilian, with a civilian's mission of collecting taxes, conscripting soldiers, and establishing Roman law. Perhaps Roman efficiency would win over the Germans.

The German tribes, on the other hand, were equally convinced that the comforts of Rome were probably very nice, but not the Roman government and taxes that seemed to go with them. There was little money to pay taxes (barter economies don't need money), free warriors saw conscription as slavery, and Roman law was completely barbaric—why was it right to go around imprisoning people and flogging them when a blood feud settled a dispute properly? Varus established his main camp somewhere on the Weser (best guesses place it somewhere near modern Minden), but as winter approached, Varus, his army and the camp followers pulled back toward winter quarters to the south. This was the opportunity that the Germans had been waiting for. Arminius, their hidden leader, had spent time in Varus' camp but once the Romans were on the march and the route they were to take was established, he disappeared—and the attacks by the wild men of the German forests began....

Battle Overview

The Scipii mission is to lead at least 100 of their soldiers along the road that runs through Teutoburg Forest and get them safely through the town gates at the end of it before nightfall. The mission of the two armies of Germans is to kill most or all of the Romans to keep this from happening.

Roman Scipii Family (Playable)

Your army is large and powerful, but thanks to the lack of cavalry, it's also a slow-moving force. Fortunately, the majority of your troops are trained for the kinds of close-quarters, hand-to-hand combat that you'll be fighting.

- Roman General (Cavalry) x30
- Early Legionary Cohort (Infantry) x81
- Early Legionary Cohort (Infantry) x81
- Early Legionary Cohort (Infantry) x81
- Roman Archers (Missile) x60
- Roman Archers (Missile) x60
- Praetorian Cohort (Infantry) x81
- Praetorian Cohort (Infantry) x81
- Legionary Cohort (Infantry) x81
- Legionary Cohort (Infantry) x81
- Legionary Cavalry (Cavalry) x80
- Urban Cohort (Infantry) x82

German Army (Playable)

Both armies of German soldiers are uncouth barbarians who fight like (and with) animals. They prefer to ambush their foes from a darkened tree line, rather than face them in honorable combat. Where you see one unit of Germans, you can be assured that there are several more lurking nearby.

- Barbarian Warlord (Cavalry) x8
- Barbarian Cavalry (Cavalry) x20
- Chosen Archer Warband (Missile) x41
- Chosen Archer Warband (Missile) x41
- Chosen Axemen (Infantry) x61
- Chosen Axemen (Infantry) x61
- Axemen (Infantry) x61
- Axemen (Infantry) x61
- Axemen (Infantry) x61
- Axemen (Infantry) x61
- Berserkers (Infantry) x80
- Berserkers (Infantry) x60
- Spear Warband (Spearmen) x61
- Warhounds x24
- Warhounds x40

German Army (Non-Playable)

This second horde of German barbarians reinforces the first. If you are playing as the Germans, you do not control these units, but they are considered allies and will attempt to kill the Roman Scipii army.

- Barbarian Warlord (Cavalry) x8
- Barbarian Noble Cavalry (Cavalry) x60
- Chosen Archer Warband (Missile) x41
- Chosen Archer Warband (Missile) x41
- Skirmisher Warband (Missile) x50
- Chosen Axemen (Infantry) x61
- Chosen Axemen (Infantry) x61
- Warhounds x50
- Axemen (Infantry) x61
- Axemen (Infantry) x61

Roman Scipii Family Strategy

First Wave

At the start of the battle, you are already being attacked by a Chosen Archer Warband, two units of Warhounds, two units of Berserkers, two units of Chosen Axemen, and two units of Axemen. Starting at the rear of your army, assign your units to the following targets:

- Early Legionary Cohort to Chosen Archer Warband
- Roman Archers to Chosen Archer Warband
- Legionary Cavalry to Axemen
- Praetorian Cohort to Berserkers
- Roman General to Axemen
- Early Legionary Cohort to Chosen Axemen
- Legionary Cohort to Berserkers
- Legionary Cohort to Chosen Axemen
- Early Legionary Cohort to Warhounds
- Urban Cohort to Warhounds
- Move Praetorian Cohort to middle of troops, use where needed

Watch your units' numbers during the battle and reinforce units that appear to be taking heavy losses. As soon as you destroy or rout a German unit, reassign the Roman units that were fighting them. You don't have any time to waste!

Second Wave

As soon as you kill or drive off the first wave of Germans, gather your forces together on the road and start moving southwest along it. You'll pass a couple of German units hiding in the tree line, but ignore them for now. Remember, you have to reach the town at the end of the road before nightfall.

You'll see a Spear Warband just up ahead. What you won't see until you draw closer are two units of Axemen and a Chosen Archer Warband hiding in the woods near them. Make sure to keep your units close together as you approach, and attack each German unit with overwhelming numbers to destroy or rout them quickly.

Barbarian Cavalry and a Barbarian Warlord charge toward you from the south. Be ready for their attack by fortifying your position with some heavy infantry. Again, as soon as the German units are routed or destroyed, regroup and move as fast as you can down the road.

Third Wave

Don't worry about straggling bands of German soldiers who routed and then regained their nerve. You don't have time to chase them down and kill them. It's worth losing a couple of soldiers to their guerrilla tactics than to lose the whole battle by not making it to town.

Near the end of the road, you can see Warhounds, two units of Axemen, and a Chosen Archer Warband. If you've learned anything by now, you know to expect more units to pop out of the woodwork as you approach, so don't charge blindly at the Chosen Archer Warband. Instead, suffer their slings and arrows and destroy the Axemen unit closest to you.

Watch out for the Skirmisher Warband behind the trees near the Warhounds. A unit of Barbarian Noble Cavalry charges at you from out of the woods beyond them as well.

Don't get tied up fighting the German hordes as they come out of the forest. Instead, punch a hole through their line and make a break for the town gate to the southwest. Remember, you don't need to defeat the Germans to win; you just need to get 100 or more troops inside the town and into the town square to win.

German Strategy

Hit Hard, Hit Fast

At the start of the battle, your following units are attacking: two units of Axemen, two units of Berserkers, a Chosen Archer Warband, and two units of Chosen Axemen. You also have two units of Warhounds hiding in the nearby forest.

Use your units to attack the first several Roman Scipii family units in the line (Legionary Cavalry, Roman General, Praetorian Cohort, Early Legionary Cohort and Legionary Cohort). Hit them from both sides to guarantee an attack on their flanks.

Move from one Scipii unit to the next, killing rather than routing them. Remember, routing units may recover, and if 100 Scipii units make it into the center of the settlement, you lose. If you get a chance to kill the Roman General, take it!

As the Romans advance along the road, use the element of surprise to shoot them from the woods and force them to chase you, preferably into ambushes set by you and your allied German army.

Speaking of the allied army, make sure they do some of the work too! There's no sense putting only your troops into battle, especially since you'll lose if all of your troops are killed or routed.

Victory!

If all else fails, fall back to the town gates for a last stand. Remember, all you have to do to win is prevent 100 Scipii soldiers from entering the gates and reaching the center of town before nightfall. You don't need to kill a single Scipii warrior—just keep them from getting in.

The Siege of Sparta— 272 BC

King Pyrrhus of Epirus liked to believe he was the last of a long line of kings, a great warrior in the tradition of Alexander the Great and worthy enough to be from the heroic age of Greece.

The truth was different.

After his early successes against his Greek and Macedonian neighbors, his luck changed when matched against the Romans at Asculum in 329 BC. Although he won the battle, the cost was so high in men that "pyrrhic victory" is still used to describe a triumph bought at terrible cost.

Bloodied by his campaigns in Italy and Sicily, Pyrrhus returned to Epirus and raised a new army to conquer Greece and Macedonia. He managed quick victories against the Macedonian king, Antigonus, and then turned his attention south to Greece itself, and a great prize beckoned him on: Sparta.

The city-state was only a shadow of what it once had been. The great days of Spartan warriors were long gone, but the lands of Sparta were still well worth conquering. More importantly, Sparta had always relied on its elite Hoplites for defense, men trained from infancy to do nothing but fight. As a result, the city had no walls—it had never needed them!

With most of the Spartan army away on campaign with King Areus, the city looked terribly vulnerable….

Battle Overview

The objective of this battle is simple: defeat the defending Greek armies and capture the city of Sparta. This is an easier task than most sieges, as Sparta is an unwalled city. Destroy or rout all Greek troops and/or occupy Sparta's town center for three minutes to win the battle.

Seleucids (Playable)

Your Seleucid army has a wide range of powerful infantry, cavalry, and siege units. You should have little trouble laying waste to Sparta and the foolish Greeks who defend her.

- General's Bodyguard (Cavalry) x15
- Companion Cavalry (Cavalry) x30
- Elephants (Cavalry) x8
- Armoured Elephants (Cavalry) x30
- Onagers (Siege) x34
- Onagers (Siege) x34
- Phalanx Pikemen (Spearmen) x80
- Phalanx Pikemen (Spearmen) x80
- Phalanx Pikemen (Spearmen) x80
- Phalanx Pikemen (Spearmen) x80
- Levy Pikemen (Spearmen) x80
- Levy Pikemen (Spearmen) x80
- Levy Pikemen (Spearmen) x80
- Levy Pikemen (Spearmen) x80
- Peltasts (Missile) x80
- Archers (Missile) x60
- Rhodian Slingers (Missile) x80
- Rhodian Slingers (Missile) x80
- Militia Hoplites (Infantry) x80

Greeks (Non-Playable)

Although the two combined Greek armies give them a slight numerical advantage, you have the luxury of remaining outside of Sparta and assailing it with your Onagers, requiring the Greeks to come out and face you. Although fierce, the Greeks are hopelessly outmatched if you use solid strategy.

Greek Army #1

- General's Bodyguard (Cavalry) x20
- Militia Hoplites (Infantry) x60
- Spartan Hoplites (Infantry) x60
- Spartan Hoplites (Infantry) x60
- Spartan Hoplites (Infantry) x60
- Spartan Hoplites (Infantry) x60
- Spartan Hoplites (Infantry) x60
- Spartan Hoplites (Infantry) x60
- Peasants (Infantry) x80
- Heavy Peltasts (Missile) x80
- Heavy Peltasts (Missile) x80
- Peltasts (Missile) x80
- Peltasts (Missile) x80
- Peltasts (Missile) x80

Greek Army #2

- General's Bodyguard (Cavalry) x10
- Spartan Hoplites (Infantry) x60
- Spartan Hoplites (Infantry) x60
- Spartan Hoplites (Infantry) x60
- Spartan Hoplites (Infantry) x80
- Militia Hoplites (Infantry) x80
- Militia Hoplites (Infantry) x80

Strategy

Burn It Down

Although you do have to win this battle within a time limit, it's a pretty generous one, so don't rush directly into Sparta and commence street fighting. Your troops can't match the Spartans in urban combat. Instead, select your Onagers, target a concentration of Greek units and fire flaming ammunition at them. The Onagers aren't terribly accurate weapons and are best used against stationary targets, but they do tremendous amounts of damage to units and buildings alike when they do hit.

Make sure to guard your Onagers with at least two units of Phalanx or Levy Pikemen, as well as a couple of missile units. You can expect that the Greeks will come out to try and destroy the siege machines that are setting their town afire, so be ready for them.

Street Fighting

When your Onagers run out of ammunition, it's time to take the fight to the streets. Create small urban warfare units with two units of spearmen (in phalanx formation) at the head, followed by a cavalry unit and a missile unit. Since Sparta has no walls, you can enter the city from any angle, but the easiest way to take it is to enter through the main entrance to the east.

Much of the fighting will actually take place before you even enter the city. As Greek spearmen start coming out of Sparta to attack you, meet them with your own spearmen and missile troops. It's a good plan to send cavalry in for quick charges, especially at their unprotected flanks, but don't let your cavalry face them head-on, or the Phalanx Pikemen will destroy your cavalry.

By the time you enter the city, the majority of the Greek army should be destroyed or routed. Regroup your forces in the city and press on, spearmen in front, followed by cavalry and then missile troops.

One of the Greek General's Bodyguard units defends the center of Sparta. By the time you get to it, it should be one of the last remaining Greek units. Commit the majority of your troops to destroying it, and the day should be yours. To achieve victory, you must either defeat every Greek unit or prevent any of them from setting foot on the town square for three minutes.